W9-DJN-905

WORLD ENCYCLOPEDIA OF PEACE

(SECOND EDITION)

EDITORIAL BOARD

Chairman

YOUNG SEEK CHOUE

GIANLUCA BOCCHI
Casa della Cultura, Milan, Italy

EGBERT BOEKER
Vrije Universiteit, Amsterdam,
The Netherlands

GORAN VON BONSDORFF
Peace Union of Finland, Helsinki,
Finland

RODRIGO CARAZO ODIO
University for Peace, Costa Rica

MAURO CERUTI
University of Bergamo, Bergamo, Italy

EUGENE I. CAHZOV
Russia Cardiology Research Centre,
Moscow, Russia

C. WEST CHURCHMAN
The George Washington University
Washington DC, USA

MICHEL DOO-KINGUE
United Nations, New York, USA

PETER DUIGNAN
Hoover Institution on War,
Revolution and Peace, Stanford, USA

WILLIAM M. EVAN
University of Pennsylvania, Philadelphia,
USA

MICHAEL HAAS
University of Hawaii at Manoa, Honolulu,
USA

ALEXANDER KING
Club of Rome, Paris, France

THOMAS H. LEE
International Institute of Applied Systems
Analysis (IIASA), Laxenburg, Austria

MIRCEA MALITZA
Association of International Law and
International Relations, Bucharest, Romania

PAUL VAN DE MEERSSCHE
Katholieke Universiteit Leuven, Leuven,
Belgium

ROBERT MULLER
United Nations, New York, USA

JAMES O'CONNELL
School of Peace Studies,
University of Bradford, Bradford, UK

PETER J. OPITZ
Universität München, Munich,
Germany

JOZEF PAJESTKA
Institute of Economic Science, Warsaw,
Poland

INDAR JIT RIKHYE
International Peace Academy, New York,
USA

MIHALY SIMAI
Institute for World Economics, Budapest,
Hungary

PAUL SMOKER
Antioch College, Ohio, USA

JAE-SHIK SOHN
Director, Institute of International Peace Studies
Rector, The Graduate Institute of Peace Studies
Kyung Hee University, Seoul, Korea

WORLD ENCYCLOPEDIA OF PEACE

(SECOND EDITION)

VOLUME VIII

Honorary Editor-in-Chief

Javier Perez De Cuellar

Editor-in-Chief

Young Seek Choue

CABRINI COLLEGE LIBRARY
610 KING OF PRUSSIA RD.
RADNOR PA 19087-3699

 **OCEANA PUBLICATIONS, INC.®**
NEW YORK

•

 **SEOUL PRESS**

REF
JZ
5533
.W67
1999
v. 8

World Encyclopedia of Peace (Second Edition)

Published in the United States of America in 1999 and distributed
exclusively throughout the world, except in Korea, by
Oceana Publications Inc.
75 Main Street
Dobbs Ferry, New York 10522
Phone: (914) 693-8100
Fax: (914) 693-0402

ISBN: 0-379-21406-7 (Volume VIII)
ISBN: 0-379-21398-2 (Set)

Library of Congress Cataloging-in-Publication Data

World encyclopedia of peace / honorary editor-in-chief, Javier
Perez de Cuellar, editor-in-chief, Young Seek Choue. -- 2nd ed.
    p. cm.
  Includes bibliographical references and indexes.
  ISBN 0-379-21398-2 (clothbound set : alk. paper)
  1. Peace Encyclopedias. I. Perez de Cuellar, Javier, 1920-
II. Young Seek Choue, 1921-
JZ5533 .W67 1999
327.1'03--dc21   99-34811
                                                                    CIP

Published simultaneously in the Republic of Korea in 1999 by
Seoul Press
Jin Wang Kim, Publisher
Room 303, Jeodong Bldg., 7-2, Jeodong, Chung-ku
Seoul 100-032, Korea
Phone: (02) 2275-6566
Fax: (02) 2278-2551

ISBN: 89-7225-104-6   94330 (Volume VIII)
ISBN: 89-7225-096-1 (Set)

Copyright © 1999 by Institute of International Peace Studies
Kyung Hee University

*All rights reserved. No part of this book may be reproduced or trans-
mitted in any form or by any means, electronic or mechanical,
including photo copying, recording, or by any information on storage
and retrieval system, without permission in writing from the copyright owner and/or the publisher except in the case of brief quota-
tions embodied in critical article, and reviews.*

Printed in the Republic of Korea by Seoul Press

CONTENTS

BIBLIOGRAPHY

This section comprises an alphabetical listing of references in the literature of peace studies and peace research. It is designed to complement the shorter and more focused article bibliographies in Volumes I, II, III, IV and V.

A truly comprehensive peace bibliography would be a vast undertaking; indeed the references listed in Part 1 (Peace—General, including Peace Bibliographies) indicate clearly the scale and the range of the work already completed in this area. In compiling this bibliography we have tried to provide a basic reference guide for the reader. Inevitably, however, the selection is to a degree idiosyncratic, reflecting the interests of those who have assisted us in its compilation.

In order to ensure that it is accessible, the Bibliography has been divided into the following parts:

Part 1:   Peace—General, including Peace Bibliographies
Part 2:   Peace Classics/Peace Plans
Part 3:   Peace Movement
          3.1 History
          3.2 Contemporary
Part 4:   Disarmament and Arms Control
Part 5:   Peace Advocates—Autobiographies and Biographies
Part 6:   Pacifism
Part 7:   Nonviolence
Part 8:   World Order and Internationalism
Part 9:   Peace and ...
          9.1 Economics
          9.2 Politics
          9.3 History
          9.4 Religion
          9.5 Psychology
Part 10:   Peace Research
Part 11:   Peace Education
Part 12:   Local/Regional Conflict and Peace

There are many points at which these subject areas overlap; to avoid excessive duplication of titles, cross-references have been inserted at appropriate points.

Some of the titles reproduced here are no longer available in their original editions. In such cases, the original publication date is given in parentheses followed by full details of a more recent reprinting, wherever this has occurred. Updating was made through generous usage of Internet sources.

Bibliography

Part 1

Peace—General, including Peace Bibliographies

ABRAMS I 1997 *Nobel Lectures Peace*. World Scientific, Singapore & River Edge, NJ

ABU-SHARIF B 1995 *Tried by Fire*. Little, Brown

ADLER M J 1995 *How to Think about War and Peace*. Fordham UP

AGGARWAL L K 1974 *Peace Science: A Bibliography*. University of Pennsylvania, Department of Peace Science, Philadelphia, Pennsylvania

AKARLI E D 1993 *The Long Peace*. I B Tauris

AKSAN V H 1995 *An Ottoman Statesman in War and Peace*. E J Brill

ALBERTI J 1989 *Beyond Suffrage*. Macmillan Press

ALCANTARA H 1996 *Social Futures, Global Visions*. Blackwell Pub.

ALGER C F 1972 *Peaceful Change Procedures Population Raw Materials, Colonies: Proceedings of the Tenth International Studies Conference*, Paris, June 28-July 3 1937. Garland Pub., New York

ALLAN P 1995 *The End of the Cold War*. Martinus Nijhoff

ALMON N E, LUTZ R H 1935 *An Introduction to a Bibliography of the Paris Peace Conference: Collections of Sources, Archive Publications and Source Books*. Stanford University/Oxford University Press, Stanford/London

ALONSO H H 1993 *Peace as a Women's Issue*. Syracuse University

AMERICAN FRIENDS SERVICE COMMITTEE 1965 *Books for Friendship: A List of Books Recommended for Children*. American Friends Service Committee, Philadelphia, Pennsylvania
See also *Part 11: Peace Education*

AMOS S 1982 *Political and Legal Remedies for War*. F. B. Rothman, Littleton Colo

ANDERSON M (ed.) 1976 *Conscription: A Select and Annotated Bibliography*. Hoover Institution Press, Stanford, California

ANGELL N, WOOLF L, STEARNS S J 1973 *The Intelligent Man's Way to Prevent War*. Garland Pub., New York

ANSTEE M J 1996 *Orphan of the Cold War*. Macmillan Press

APOLLINAIRE G 1991 *Calligrammes: Poems of Peace and War (1913-1916)*. Univ. of California Press

APPLEYARD B 1990 *The Pleasures of Peace*. Faber Paperbacks

AREND A C 1988 *Pursuing a Just and Durable Peace*. Greenwood Press

ARIAN A 1996 *Security Threatened*. Cambridge UP

ARNOLD G 1993 *The End of the Third World*. Macmillan Press

ASHRAWI H 1995 *This Side of Peace*. Simon & Schuster

ATHERTON A L 1976 *International Organizations: A Guide to Information Sources*. Gale Research,

Detroit, Michigan
See also *Part 8: World Order and Internationalism*

AUFRICHT H 1943 *War, Peace and Reconstruction: A Classified Bibliography.* Commission to Study the Organization of Peace, New York

AUFRICHT H 1945 *World Organization: An Annotated Bibliography.* Woodrow Wilson Foundation, New York
See also *Part 8: World Order and Internationalism*

AUFRICHT H 1951 *Guide to League of Nations Publications: A Bibliographical Survey of the Work of the League, 1920-1947.* Columbia University, New York
See also *Part 8: World Order and Internationalism*

AYOOB M 1995 *The Third World Security Predicament.* Lynne Rienner

BADEN A L 1933 *Selected List of Recent Writings on Internationalism (Superstate).* Library of Congress, Washington, DC
See also *Part 8: World Order and Internationalism*

BARASH D 1990 *Introduction to Peace Studies.* Wadsworth

BARNABY F 1980 *Prospects for Peace.* Pergamon, Oxford, New York

BARTLETT C J 1996 *Peace, War and the European Great Powers, 1814-1914.* Macmillan Press

BASKERVILLE S 1993 *Not Peace but a Sword.* Routledge

BAUWENS W 1994 *The Art of Conflict Prevention.* Brassey's UK

BEATON L 1966 *The Struggle for Peace.* F. A. Praeger, New York

BECKWITH G C 1972 *The Book of Peace: a Collection of Essays on War and Peace.* J. S. Ozer, New York

BEER F A 1981 *Peace Against War: the Ecology of International Violence.* W. H. Freeman, San Francisco

BEININ J 1991 *Was the Red Flag Flying There?* I B Tauris

BEITZ C R, HERMAN T, GEYER A (ed.) 1973 *Peace and War.* W. H. Freeman, San Francisco

BELLON B P 1992 *Mercedes in Peace and War.* Columbia UP

BENTHAM G VAN 1992 *The Nuclear Revolution and the End of the Cold War.* Macmillan Press

BERCOVITCH J 1991 *International Mediation.* Sage, London

BERCOVITCH J 1992 *Mediation in International Relations.* Macmillan Press

BERGFELDT L 1979 *Nonviolent Action: State of the Literature.* Department of Peace and Conflict Research, Uppsala University, Uppsala

BERNHARDT R 1982 *Use of Force, War and Neutrality. Peace Treaties (A-M).* North-Holland

BETTS R K 1993 *Conflict after the Cold War.* Macmillan, USA

BIGELOW J 1916 *World Peace: How War Cannot be Abolished: How it May be Abolished.* Mitchell Kennerley, New York

BLACK J 1997 *America or Europe? War or Peace?* UCL Press, Los Angeles

BLAINEY G 1988 *The Cause of War.* Macmillan Press

BLUMBERG H H 1991 *Peace.* American Psych Ass

BOOTH K 1991 *New Thinking about Strategy and International Security.* Routledge

BOULDING E 1991 *Peace Culture and Society.* Westview Press

BOULDING E, PASSMORE J R, GASSLER R S 1979 *Bibliography on World Conflict and Peace.* Westview Press, Boulder, Colorado

BOULDING E, PASSMORE J R, SCOTE R, GASSLER 1979 *Bibliography on World Conflict and Peace.* Westview Press, Boulder

BOULDING K E 1978 *Stable Peace.* University of Texas Press, Austin

BOUTROS-GHALI B 1994 *Building Peace and Development.* United Nations

BOUTROS-GHALI B 1995 *An Agenda for Peace.* United Nations

BOWKER R 1996 *Beyond Peace.* Lynne Rienner

BRADLEY J 1989 *War and Peace Since 1945.* East Eur Monographs

BREDIN E 1993 *Disturbing the Peace.* Columbia Press

BRESSLER M 1976 *Peace or War.* Prentice Hall US

BREYCHA-VAUTHIER A C DE 1939 *Sources of Information: A Handbook on the Publications of the League of Nations.* Allen and Unwin/Columbia University, London/New York
See also *Part 8: World Order and Internationalism*

BRIGHT J, JONATHAN D 1973 *War: and Essay with Introductory Words.* Garland Pub., New York

BROCK P 1971 *The Essays of Philanthropos on Peace and War.* Garland Pub., New York

BRODIE F M 1942 *Peace Aims and Post-War Planning: A Bibliography Selected and Annotated.* World Peace Foundation, Boston, Massachusetts

BROOKS E 1994 *Making Peace.* St Martin's Press

BRUNE P 1992 *Those Ragged Bloody Heroes.* Allen & Unwin

BRYANT H B 1990 *A Separate Peace.* Macmillan USA

BRYANT H B 1990 *A Separate Peace—the War Within.* Macmillan USA

BURNER D 1996 *Making Peace with the 60s.* Princeton UP

BURNS R D 1977 *Arms Control and Disarmament: A Bibliography.* ABC-CLIO, Santa Barbara, California/Oxford

BURTON J 1990 *Conflict: Resolution and Prevention.* Macmillan Press

BURTON J 1990 *Conflict: Readings in Management and Resolution.* Macmillan Press

BUTOW R 1974 *John does Associates Backdoor Diplomacy for Peace.* Stanford UP (CUP)

CAHILL K M 1993 *A Framework for Survival.* Basic Books

CALDWELL W E 1967 *Hellenic Conceptions of Peace.* AMS Press, New York

CANCIAN F M 1989 *Making War/Making Peace.* Wadsworth

CAPLOW T 1995 *Systems of War and Peace.* University Press America

CARROLL B A, FINK C F, MOHRAZ J E 1983 *Peace and War: A Guide to Bibliographies.* ABC-CLIO, Santa Barbara, California/Oxford

CARTER A, HOGGETT D, ROBERTS A 1970 *Nonviolent Action: A Selected Bibliography.* Housmans, London

CARTER S 1992 *War and Peace Through Women's Eyes.* Greenwood Press

CASHMAN G 1993 *What Causes War?* Lexington Books

CECIL E A R (Viscount) 1928 *The Way of Peace.* Allan, London

CHACE J 1993 *The Consequences of the Peace.* Oxford UP

CHAMBERS II J W 1991 *The Eagle and the Dove.* Syracuse University

CHANTEUR J 1992 *From War to Peace.* Westview Press

CHARY M S 1995 *The Eagle and the Peacock.* Greenwood Press

CHATFIELD C 1971 *New Wars for Old.* Garland Pub., New York

CHATFIELD C 1972 *The Fight for Peace.* Garland Pub., New York

CHATFIELD C 1994 *Peace/Mir.* Syracuse University

CHOUE Y S 1986 *Proposal for Peace: the Last Option*

for Humankind. Kyung Hee University Press, Seoul, Korea

CHOUE Y S 1986 *World Encyclopedia of Peace*. Pergamon Press, Oxford, New York

CHOUE Y S 1991 *White Paper on World Peace*. Kyung Hee University Press, Seoul

CHRISTIE M G A 1990 *Breach of the Peace*. Butterworth Law Scot

CLARK J 1990 *Waging War*. Clarendon Press

CLARK S R L 1989 *Civil Peace and Sacred Order*. Clarendon Press

CLEMENS W C JR 1965 *Soviet Disarmament Policy 1917-1963: An Annotated Bibliography of Soviet and Western Sources*. Stanford University, Stanford, California

COKER C 1994 *War and the 20th Century*. Brassey's UK

COLLART Y 1958 *Disarmament: A Study Guide and Bibliography on the Efforts of The United Nations*. Nijhoff, The Hague

COOK B W 1976 *Toward the Great Change: Crystal and Max Eastman Feminism, Antimilitarism and Revolution*. Garland Pub., New York

COOKE M, WOOL A 1993 *Gendering War Talk*. Princeton University Press, Princeton NJ

COOKSON 1982 *Friends of Peace*. Cambridge UP

COOK B W 1969 *Bibliography on Peace Research in History*. ABC-CLIO, Santa Barbara, California
See also *Part 10: Peace Research*

COOK B W, CHATFIELD C, COOPER S (eds.) 1971 *The Garland Library of War and Peace, (Catalogue)*. Garland, New York

COOTER R 1993 *Surgery and Society in Peace and War*. Macmillan Press

CORDESMAN A H 1996 *Perilous Prospects*. Westview Press

CORMACK M 1951 *Selected Pamphlets on the United Nations and International Relations: An Annotat-*

ed Guide. Carnegie Endowment for International Peace, New York
See also *Part 8: World Order and Internationalism*

CORTWRIGHT D 1993 *Peace Works*. Westview Press

COWPER H 1994 *World War I and Its Consequences*. Open UP

CREIGHTON C 1987 *The Sociology of War and Peace*. Macmillan Press

CRENSHAW M 1996 *Encyclopedia of World Terrorism*. M E Sharpe

CROZIER B 1988 *This War Called Peace*. Shepheard-Walwyn

CURRENT THOUGHT INC. 1987 *Current thought on Peace and War*. New York

DAS P K 1987 *The Troubled Region*. Sage, London

DAVIES C B 1995 *Moving Beyond Boundaries*. Pluto Press

DEIGHTON A 1993 *The Impossible Peace*. Clarendon Press

DENNEN J VD 1990 *Sociobiology and Conflict*. Chapman & Hall

DICKINSON G L 1924 *War: Its Nature, Cause and Cure*. Macmillan, New York

DICKINSON G L, BUXTON C R, COOK B W (eds.) 1971 *Towards a Lasting Settlement*. Garland Pub., New York

DINSTEIN Y 1994 *War, Aggression and Self-Defence*. Cambridge UP

DONALD C F DANIEL 1995 *Beyond Traditional Peacekeeping*. Macmillan Press

DOOB L W 1981 *The Pursuit of Peace*. Greenwood Press, Westport Conn

DOTY H 1954 *Bibliography of Conscientious Objection to War: A Selected List of 173 Titles, Annotated with a Logical Index and with Notes on Additional Sources*. Central Committee for Conscientious Objectors, Philadelphia, Pennsylvania

DOUMS J 1965 *Bibliography of the International Court of Justice, 1918-1964.* Sijthoff, Leiden

DOWER J 1995 *Japan in War and Peace.* Harper Collins

DOYLE JOHNSTONE ORR 1997 *Keeping the Peace.* Cambridge UP

DOYLE M 1996 *The Ways of War & Peace.* W W Norton

DOYLE M 1997 *Ways of War & Peace.* W W Norton

DUDLEY G 1994 *A Workshop for Peace.* The MIT Press

DUNAY P 1995 *New Forms of Security.* Dartmouth

DUNN T 1963 *Alternatives to War and Violence: A Search.* James Clarke, London

DUNNE J S 1990 *The Peace of the Present.* Univ. of Notre Dame Press

ECKERT E K 1990 *In War and Peace.* Wadsworth, NY

EISENHOWER D 1960 *Peace with Justice.* Columbia UP

EISENHOWER D 1961 *Peace with Justice.* Columbia UP, New York

EISS H 1990 *Literature for Young People on War and Peace.* Greenwood Press

ELIAS R, TURPIN J (eds.) 1994 *Rethinking Peace.* Lynne Rienner Pub., Boulder, Colo

ELLER V 1981 *War and Peace Genesis to Revelation: King Jesus' Manual of Arms for the Armless.* Herald Press, Scottdale

ELLERY W, MEAD E D 1972 *Discourses on War.* J. S. Ozer, New York

EMMONS V 1969 *The Roots of Peace: a Study of Human Potential in Relation to Peace.* Theosophical Pub., House, Wheaton III

EMSLEY C 1989 *War, Peace and Social Change in Twentieth-Century Europe.* Open UP

EMSLEY C 1990 *World War II and Its Consequences.* Open UP

ENGEL T 1964 *Bibliography on Peace Research in History.* Committee on Peace Research in History, Washington, DC
See also *Part 10: Peace Research*

ESDAILE C J 1995 *The Wars of Napoleon.* Longman

EVANS G 1994 *Cooperating for Peace.* Allen & Unwin

FAGEN R 1987 *Forging Peace.* Blackwell Pub.

FALNES O J 1967 *Norway and the Nobel Peace Prize.* AMS Press, New York

FAST H 1992 *War and Peace.* M E Sharpe

FAWAZ L T 1995 *An Occasion for War.* I B Tauris

FERENCZ B B 1991 *World Security for the 21st Century.* Adamantine Press

FERRELL R H 1969 *Peace in their Time.* Norton

FESTE K A 1992 *Plans for Peace.* Greenwood Press

FINK C 1984 *The Genoa Conference.* Syracuse University

FINN R B 1995 *Winners in Peace.* Univ. of California Press

FISCHER D 1989 *Winning Peace.* Taylor & Francis

FISCHER D 1993 *Nonmilitary Aspects of Security.* Dartmouth

FLOTO I 1992 *Colonel House in Paris.* Princeton UP

FLYNN A H (comp./ed.) 1965 *World Understanding: A Selected Bibliography.* Oceana, Dobbs Ferry, New York
See also *Part 8: World Order and Internationalism*

FORCEY L R 1989 *Peace.* Praeger Pub.

FOSTER C 1995 *The Women and the Warriors.* Syracuse University

GADDIS J L 1989 *The Long Peace.* Oxford UP

GALTUNG J 1976 *Peace War and Defense.* Ejlers, Copenhagen

GALTUNG J 1978 *Peace and Social Structure*. Ejlers, Copenhagen

GALTUNG J 1980 *Peace Problems: Some Case Studies*. Ejlers, Copenhagen

GALTUNG J 1995 *Choose Peace*. Pluto Press

GALTUNG J 1996 *Peace by Peaceful Means*. Sage London

GALTUNG J, RUGE M H (comps. and eds.) 1966 *International Repertory of Institutions Specialising in Research on Peace and Disarmament*. UNESCO, Paris
See also *Part 10: Peace Research*

GANDHI A 1996 *World Without Violence*. New Age/ Drake Int.

GARDNER H 1994 *Surviving the Millennium*. Praeger Pub.

GARDNER J F 1976 *The Secret of Peace & The Environmental Crisis*. Myrin Institute, Inc for Adult Education, New York

GARLANDED, CURTI ME 1971 *Bryan and World Peace*. Garland Pub., New York

GEISSLER E 1994 *Control of Dual-threat Agents*. Oxford UP

GILIOMEE H 1991 *The Elusive Search for Peace*. OUP South Africa

GINAT J 1994 *From War to Peace*. Drake Int, Sussex Aca

GLASGOW UNIVERSITY MEDIA GROUP 1985 *War and Peace News*. Open UP

GLEDITSCH N P 1994 *The Wages of Peace*. Sage London

GOEBEL K 1995 *Science after the Cold War*. World Scientific

GOLBY J 1990 *Between Two Wars*. Open UP

GOLDSTEIN E 1991 *Winning the Peace*. Clarendon Press

GOLDSTEIN E 1992 *Wars and Peace Treaties*. Routledge

GOODMAN A E 1992 *Making Peace*. Westview Press

GOUGH B M 1992 *British Mercantile Interests in the Making of the Peace of Paris, 1763*. Edwin Mellen Press

GOW J 1996 *Triumph of the Lack of Will*. C Hurst & Co.

GRAY C, GRAY L, GREGORY G 1968 *A Bibliography of Peace Research, Indexed by Key Words: General Research Analysis Methods*. Eugene, Oregon
See also *Part 10: Peace Research*

GREEN M 1995 *War and Peace with China*. Univ. Press America

GREGORY W H 1992 *The Price of Peace*. Lexington Books

GROUP A S 1994 *Securing Peace in the New Era: Politics in the Former Soviet Union and the Challenge to American Security*. Brookings Inst.

HAAS M 1974 *International Organization: An Interdisciplinary Bibliography*. Hoover Institution, Stanford, California
See also *Part 8: World Order and Internationalism*

HAAS M 1992 *Genocide by Proxy*. Praeger Pub.

HABERMAN F W 1972 *Peace*. Elsevier Pub. Co., Amsterdam, New York

HAMISHLON A 1996 *Elite Military Formations in War and Peace*. Praeger Pub.

HAMPSON F O 1995 *Multilateral Negotiations*. Johns Hopkins UP

HANCOCK 1960 *Studies of War and Peace*. Cambridge UP

HANLON J 1996 *Peace without Profit*. James Currey Pub.

HARDING J 1994 *Small Wars, Small Mercies*. Penguin

HARLE V 1987 *Essays in Peace Studies*. Dartmouth

HARLEY I 1961 *Towards a Science of Peace: Turning Point in Human Destiny.* Bookman Associates, New York

HARRELSON M 1989 *Fires all Around the Horizon.* Praeger Pub.

HASSNER P 1996 *Violence and Peace.* Central European UP

HAWES M K 1990 *Studies in World Peace.* Edwin Mellen, Press

HAYES 1996 *The Peace Ring.* CUP Educational

HEADRICK D R 1992 *The Invisible Weapon.* Oxford UP

HEITLER S M 1994 *From Conflict to Resolution.* W W Norton

HELLWIG M K *A Case for Peace in Reason and Faith.* Michael Glazier

HERBERT F 1989 *Making Weapons, Talking Peace.* Basic Books

HERMAN M 1996 *Intelligence Power in Peace and War.* Cambridge UP, Mass

HERRUP C B 1989 *The Common Peace.* Cambridge UP

HEWLETT R G 1992 *Atoms for Peace and War, 1953-1961.* Univ. of California Press

HINDE R A 1994 *War: a Cruel Necessity?* British Academic

HIRSCH R 1943 *Plans for the Organization of International Peace, 1306-1789: A List of Thirty-Six Peace Proposals.* New York Public Library, New York

HODGKIN A 1994 Chance and Design. Cambridge UP

HOGAN M J 1992 *The End of the Cold War.* Cambridge UP

HOGGETT D 1963 *Nonviolence and Peacemaking: A Bibliography.* Commonweal Trust, Cheltenham

HOGGETT D 1969 *Crisis and Solutions: An Annotated Bibliography for Students.* National Peace Council, London

HOIG S 1990 *The Peace Chiefs of the Cheyennes.* Univ. of Oklahoma Press

HOLCOMBE A N 1967 *A Strategy of Peace in a Changing World.* Harvard University Press, Cambridge, Mass.

HOLSTI K J 1991 *Peace and War: Armed Conflicts and International Order 1948-1989.* Cambridge UP

HOLSTI K J 1996 *The State, War, and the State of War.* Cambridge UP

HOLT J 1992 *The Prize of Peace.* Save the Children

HOWARD M 1978 *War and Liberal Conscience.* Temple Smith, London

HOWE J O 1984 *Armed Peace.* Macmillan Press

HOWELL S 1989 *Societies at Peace.* Routledge

HOWELL S, WILLIS R 1989 *Societies at Peace: Anthropological Perspectives.* Routledge London, New York

HUGGON J 1971 *Bibliography on Peace, Freedom and Nonviolence for Use in Schools.* Kropotkin's Lighthouse Publications, London
See also *Part 11: Peace Education*

HUNTER 1990 *Art of Faith, Art of Peace.* Brookings Inst.

HUXFORD M, SCHELLING S 1975 *Perspectives on War and Peace in a Changing World: A Select Bibliography.* St. Louis University, St. Louis, Missouri

HYATT J 1972 *Pacifism: A Selected Bibliography.* Housmans, London

IKEDA D 1996 *A New Humanism.* Weatherhill

INGLIS F 1993 *The Cruel Peace.* Basic Books

INTERNATIONAL COMMISSION ON PEACE AND FOOD 1994 *Uncommon Opportunities.* Zed Books

INTERNATIONAL PEACE ACADEMY 1980 *Bibliography on Multilateral Negotiations and Third-Party Roles.* International Peace Academy, New York
See also *Part 8: World Order and Internationalism*

ISARD W 1992 *Understanding Conflict and the Science of Peace*. Blackwell Pub.

ISARD W, SMITH C 1982 *Conflict Analysis and Practical Conflict Management Procedures: an Introduction to Peace Science*. Ballinger Pub., Cambridge, Mass.

JACOBSON J R 1990 *Studies in World Peace*. Edwin Mellen, Press

JANDT F E 1987 *Win-win Negotiating*. John Wiley Inc.

JANES R W 1995 *Scholars' Guide to Washington, DC, for Peace and International Security Studies*. Woodrow Wilson Cntr.

JOHNSON H S, SINGH B 1969 *International Organization: A Classified Bibliography*. Michigan State University, East Lansing, Michigan
See also *Part 8: World Order and Internationalism*

JOHNSON J T 1992 *The Quest for Peace*. Princeton UP

JOHNSTONE I 1994 *Aftermath of the Gulf War*. Lynne Rienner

JONES D V 1989 *Code of Peace*. Univ. of Chicago Press

JONSON L 1995 *Peacekeeping and the Role of Russia in Eurasia*. Westview Press

JORDAN J 1989 *Peace Songs*. Kahn & Averill

KAGAN D 1995 *On the Origins of War and the Preservation of Peace*. Hutchinson

KAINZ H D 1987 *Philosophical Perspectives on Peace: an Anthology of Classical and Modern Sources*. Macmillan Press, London

KAKONEN J 1994 *Green Security or Militarized Environment*. Dartmouth

KALLY E 1993 *Water and Peace*. Praeger Pub.

KEGLEY C W 1991 *The Long Postwar Peace*. Longman

KEGLEY C W 1994 *A Multipolar Peace?* Macmillan Press

KELLY W 1994 *Violence to Non-violence*. Harwood Academic

KEMP A (ed.) 1980 *Peace and Violence: Quantitative Studies in International and Civil Conflict*. Human Relations Area Files, New Haven Conn

KENNEDY P M 1992 *Grand Strategies in War and Peace*. Yale UP

KIM Y J 1989 *Studies in World Peace*. Edwin Mellen, Press

KING G E N 1935 *World Friendship: A Bibliography: Sources of Educational Material*. Chapman and Grimes, Boston, Massachusetts
See also *Part 11: Peace Education*

KIRBY S 1991 *The Cost of Peace*. Harwood Academic

KLARE M T 1993 *World Security: Trends and Challenges at Century's End*. Saint Martin's Press

KLEIDMAN R 1993 *Organizing for Peace*. Syracuse University

KNUDSON A C 1947 *The Philosophy of War and Peace*. Abingdon-Cokesbury Press, New York/Nashville, Tennessee

KOHN S M 1987 *Jailed for Peace*. Praeger Pub.

KOLODZIEJ E A 1996 *Coping with Conflict after the Cold War*. Johns Hopkins UP

KORZENNY F 1990 *Communicating for Peace: Diplomacy and Negotiation*. Sage, London

KREITMANN J 1995 *Bread, Peace and Liberty*. Univ Press America

KRIESBERG L 1991 *Timing the De-escalation of International Conflicts*. Syracuse University

KUEHL W F 1975 *Internationalism: A Selected List of Research-Study Materials to Provide Students with Information on the Historical Evolution of an Idea and an Ideal*. Center for the Study of Armament and Disarmament, California State University, Los Angeles, California
See also *Part 8: World Order and Internationalism*

LA BARR D F, SINGER J D 1976 *The Study of Interna-*

tional Politics: A Guide to the Sources for the Student, Teacher and Researcher. ABC-CLIO Books, Santa Barbara, California/Oxford
See also *Part 8: World Order and Internationalism*

LAFFIN J 1994 *The World in Conflict.* Brassey's UK

LA FONTAINE H 1904 *Bibliographie de la paix et de l'arbitrage internationale, Tome Premier: Mouvement pacifique* [Bibliography of Peace and International Arbitration, Vol. 1: Peace Movement]. Institut de la Paix, Monaco

LANGDOM L 1982 *Creating Peace: a Positive Handbook.* Larry Langdon Pub., Cottage Grove

LAVIK N J 1994 *Pain and Survival.* Scandinavian UP

LEAGUE OF NATIONS 1929 *Publications Issued by the League of Nations.* World Peace Foundation, Boston, Massachusetts
See also *Part 8: World Order and Internationalism*

LEAGUE OF NATIONS LIBRARY 1931 *Annotated Bibliography on Disarmament and Military Questions.* League of Nations Publications Department, Geneva

LEBOW R N 1981 *Between Peace and War.* Johns Hopkins UP

LEBOW R N 1991 *Hegemonic Rivalry.* Westview Press

LEDERACH J P 1996 *Preparing for Peace.* Syracuse University

LEGAULT A 1967 *Peace-Keeping Operations: A Bibliography.* World Veterans Federation, Paris

LENTIN 1995 *Peace.* Arnold

LIEBMAN J L 1946 *Peace of Mind.* Simon and Schuster, New York

LLOYD L, SIMS N A 1979 *British Writing on Disarmament from 1914-1978: A Bibliography.* Frances Pinter, London

LOFLAND J 1994 *Polite Protesters.* Syracuse University

LONG, JR. E L R 1983 *Peace Thinking in a Warring World.* Westminster Press, Philadelphia

LONSDALE K 1957 *Is Peace Possible?* Penguin, Harmondsworth

LUTTWAK E 1990 *Strategy.* Belknap

LYONS J G 1940 *Union Now: A Bibliography on the Federal Union of Nations.* Washington Association for Union Now, Washington, DC
See also *Part 8: World Order and Internationalism*

MACEWEN M 1990 *The Greening of a Red.* Pluto Press

MACMILLAN J 1996 *On Liberal Peace.* Tauris Acad Studies

MACQUARRIE J 1973 *The Concept of Peace.* SCM Press, London

M'BOW A M 1980 *Consensus and Peace.* Unesco, Paris

MCGUIGAN D G (ed.) 1977 *The Role of Women in Conflict and Peace.* University of Michigan, Ann Arbor, Michigan

MCKITTRICK D 1996 *The Nervous Peace.* Blackstaff Press

MCLEAN D 1994 *War, Diplomacy and Informal Empire.* Tauris Acad Studies

MACFARLANE 1997 *The Savage Wars of Peace.* Blackwell Pub.

MACIEJEWSKI C 1912 *La Guerre: Ses Causes et les Moyens de la Prévenir* [War: Its Causes and the Means of Preventing It]. Giard and Brière, Paris

MAHMOOD R 1991 *Peace in the Making.* Kegan Paul

MAKOVSKY D 1995 *Making Peace with the PLO.* Westview Press

MALIK H 1996 *The Roles of the United States, Russia and China in the New World Order.* Macmillan Press

MANNO J 1984 *Arming the Heavens: the Hidden Military Agenda for Space, 1945~1995.* Dodd, Mead & Co., New York

MARKOWITZ G E, SHOTWELL J T 1972 *On the Rim of the Abyss.* Garland Pub., New York

MARTIN D, LANDSBURY G 1972 *My Pilgrimage for Peace, and Peace through Economic Cooperation.* Garland Pub., New York

MARULLO S, LOFLAND J (ed.) 1990 *Peace Action in the Eighties: Social Science Perspectives.* Rutgers University Press, New Brunswick NJ

MARWICK A 1990 *War and Change in Twentieth-Century Europe.* Open UP

MATTHEWS M A 1931 *History Teaching and School Text-Books in Relation to International Understanding: Select List of Books, Pamphlets and Periodical Articles.* Carnegie Endowment for International Peace, Washington, DC
See also *Part 11: Peace Education*

MATTHEWS M A 1936 *Peace Projects: Select List of References on Plans for the Preservation of Peace from Medieval Times to the Present Day.* Carnegie Endownment for International Peace, Washington, DC

MATTHEWS M A 1936 *Education for World Peace: The Study and Teaching of International Relations; Select List of Books, Pamphlets and Periodical Articles, with Annotations.* Carnegie Endowment for International Peace, Washington, DC
See also *Part 8: World Order and Internationalism*

MATTHEWS M A 1937 *Women in Peacework.* Carnegie Endowment for International Peace, Washington DC

MATTHEWS M A 1939 *Third Hague Peace Conference: List of References on Proposals and Programs for a Third Conference as Recommended by the Second International Peace Conference 1907.* Carnegie Endowment for International Peace, Washington, DC

MAULEY R H 1981 *Building Positive Peace: Actors and Factors.* Published for International Public Policy Institute by University Press of America, Washington, DC

MCLNTYRE W J 1994 *Children of Peace.* McGill Q UP (UCL)

MELASUO T 1990 *National Movements and World Peace.* Avebury

MELASUO T, ABDEL-MALEK A 1990 *National Move-ments and World Peace.* Avebury, Aldershot, Brookfield

MENON P K 1991 *Studies in World Peace.* Edwin Mellen, Press

MESQUITA B B DE 1992 *War and Reason.* Yale UP

MILLER W R 1961 *Bibliography of Books on War, Pacifism, Nonviolence and Related Studies.* Fellowship of Reconciliation, New York

MILNE A A 1934 *Peace with Honour.* Methuen, London

MITCHELL C 1996 *Handbook of Conflict Resolution.* Pinter

MITCHELL S 1995 *Cremnain Pisidia.* Class Press of Wales

MOLLER B 1992 *Common Security and Non-offensive Defence.* UCL Press

MOLLER B 1996 *Defence Doctrines and Conversion.* Dartmouth

MOORE C W 1996 *The Mediation Process.* Jossey Bass

MOORE S 1994 *Peace without Victory for the Allies.* Berg

MORGAN K 1992 *The People's Peace.* Oxford Paperbacks

MORGAN K O 1990 *The People's Peace: British History 1945-1989.* Oxford UP

MORGENTHAU H J 1948 *Politics Among Nations: The Struggle for Power and Peace.* Knopf, New York
See also *Part 9.2: Peace and Politics*

MORRIS A R 1995 *Charts and Surveys in Peace and War.* HMSO

MUNCASTER Z 1997 *Developing Models of International Conflict.* Cambridge UP, Mass.

MUSHKAT M 1982 *The Third World and Peace: Some Aspects of the Interrelationship of Underdevelopment and International Security.* St. Martin's Press, Hampshire Gower, New York

NAGEL S S 1991 *Systematic Analysis in Dispute Resolution*. Quorum Books

NATHANSON S 1993 *Patriotism, Morality and Peace*. Rowman & Littlefield

NATIONAL PEACE COUNCIL 1911-57 *Peace Year Books*. National Peace Council, London

NEWTON S 1996 *Profits of Peace*. Clarendon Press

NIEZING J 1978 *Strategy and Structure: Studies in Peace Research, 2*. Swets & Zeiflinger, Amsterdam

NOAM 1985 *Turning the Tide*. Pluto Press

NORMAN A 1972 *War and the Workers*. Galand Pub., New York

NORTH R C 1990 *War, Peace, Survival*. Westview Press

NORWEGIAN NOBEL INSTITUTE 1912 *Bibliographie du mouvement de la paix: Littérature pacifiste dans la Bibliothèque de l'Institut Nobel Norvégien* [Bibliography of the Peace Movement: Pacifist Literature in the Library of the Norwegian Nobel Institute]. Williams and Norgate, London

O'CONNELL J 1985 *Peace with Work to Do*. Berg

O'DONOVAN O 1989 *Peace and Certainty*. Clarendon Press

O'HANLON M 1992 *The Art of War in the Age of Peace*. Praeger Pub.

OKERSTROM D 1993 *Peace and War*. Prentice Hall US

OLESHCHUK F 1958 *Is War Invitable?* Foreign Languages Publishing House, Moscow

OSTERUD O 1986 *Studies of War and Peace*. Scandinavian UP

PACIFIST RESEARCH BUREAU 1942 *Five Foot Shelf of Pacifist Literature*. Pacifist Research Bureau, Philadelphia, Pennsylvania

PARSONS A 1995 *From Cold War to Hot Peace*. Michael Joseph

PAUW J D 1992 *Winning the Peace*. Praeger Pub.

PAX CHRISTI INTERNATIONAL 1979 *Books on Nonviolence: Bibliography of the Peace Documentation Centre*. Pax Christi International, Antwerp

PAX CHRISTI INTERNATIONAL 1979 *Books on Security: Bibliography of the Peace Documentation Centre*. Pax Christi International, Antwerp

PEALE N V 1952 *The Power of Positive Thinking*. Prentice-Hall, New York

PERES S 1995 *Battling for Peace*. Weidenfeld & Nicholson

PERRIS G H 1911 *A Short History of War and Peace*. Thornton Butterworth, London
See also *Part 9.3: History*

PICK D 1993 *War Machine*. Yale UP

PILLAR P R 1983 *Negotiating Peace*. Princeton UP

PILLAR P R 1983 *Negotiating Peace: War Termination as a Bargaining Process*. Princeton University Press, Princeton NJ

PIRE D 1967 *Building Peace*. Corgi, London

PITT D 1988 *The Anthropology of War and Peace*. Bergin & Garvey

PLATER C (ed.) 1915 *A Primer of Peace and War: The Principles of International Morality*. P. J. Kennedy and Sons/P. S. King and Son, New York/London

PRINS G 1993 *Threats without Enemies*. Earthscan

PUGH M 1994 *Maritime Security and Peacekeeping*. Manchester UP

RABIE P D 1994 *Conflict, Resolution and Ethnicity*. Praeger Pub.

RABOW G 1990 *Peace through Agreement*. Praeger Pub.

RANDLE R F 1973 *The Origins of Peace: A Study of Peacemaking and the Structure of Peace Settlements*. Free Press/Collier-Macmillan, New York/London

RATNER S R 1995 *The New UN Peacekeeping*. Macmillan Press

RATNER S R 1995 *The New UN Peacekeeping: Building Peace in Lands of Conflict after the Cold War.* Macmillan Press, Hampshire

RAVENAL E 1971 *Peace with China?* Liveright Books

RAY D L 1994 *Environmental Overkill.* Harper Perennial

REVES E 1969 *The Anatomy of Peace.* Smith, Gloycester, Mass.

REVES E 1945 *The Anatomy of Peace.* Harper, New York

REYNA S P 1993 *Studying War.* Gordon & Breach

RICH J 1993 *War and Society in the Roman World.* Routledge

RICHARDOT J 1994 *Journeys for a Better World.* Univ. Press America

RICHARDS H 1994 *Letters from Quebec: a Philosophy for Peace and Justice.* Int Scholars Pub.

RICHARDSON E C, LAWRENCE R H, KENT R E 1920 *The Literature of International Cooperation. The American Library Institute Papers and Proceedings 1919.* ALA, Chicago, Illinois
See also *Part 8: World Order and Internationalism*

ROBERTS N L 1991 *American Peace Writers, Editors, and Periodicals.* Greenwood Press, New York

ROCHON T R 1990 *Mobilizing for Peace.* Adamantine Press

ROGERS P 1992 *A Violent Peace.* Brassey's UK

ROMAN A 1983 *Between War and Peace.* Vantage Press, New York

ROMSICS I 1993 *Wartime American Plans for a New Hungary.* East Eur Monographs

ROPER J 1994 *Keeping the Peace in the Post-Cold War Era: Strengthening Multilateral Peacekeeping.* Brookings Inst.

ROSTOW E V 1995 *Toward Managed Peace.* Yale UP

ROTBLAT J 1993 *Striving for Peace, Security and Development in the World.* World Scientific

ROTH H 1966 *Pacifism in New Zealand: A Bibliography.* University of Auckland, Auckland

ROUNER L S 1990 *Celebrating Peace.* Univ. of Notre Dame Press

RUGGIE J G 1996 *Winning the Peace.* Columbia UP

RUSI A M 1996 *A Dangerous Peace.* Westview Press

RUSSELL B 1968 *Common Sense and Nuclear Warfare.* AMS Press, New York

RUTHERFORD A 1995 *War.* Allen & Unwin

SAGE M M 1996 *Warfare in Ancient Greece.* Routledge

SAINSBURY K 1994 *Churchill and Roosevelt at War.* Macmillan Press

SANTORO C M 1992 *Diffidence and Ambition.* Westview Press

SAUNDERS H H 1991 *The Other Walls.* Princeton UP

SCANLON H L 1940 *The New World Order: Select List of References on Regional and World Federation.* Carnegie Endowment for International Peace, Washington, DC
See also *Part 8: World Order and Internationalism*

SCANLON H L 1946 *The United Nations: A Selected List of Materials on the Organization and Functions of the United Nations....* Carnegie Endowment for International Peace, Washington, DC
See also *Part 8: World Order and Internationalism*

SCHAEFFNER C 1995 *Language and Peace.* Dartmouth

SCHARFFENORTH G, HUBER W, et al. (eds.) 1973 *Neue Bibliographie zur Friedensforschung* [New Bibliography of Peace Research]. Ernst Klett/Kosel, Stuttgart/Munich
See also *Part 10: Peace Research*

SCHELLENBERY J A 1982 *The Science of Conflict.* Oxford University Press, New York

SCHINDLER C, LAPID G 1989 *The Great Turning: Personal Peace Global Victory.* Bear & Co., Santa Fe

SCHULZE H 1996 *States, Nations and Nationalism.* Blackwell Pub.

SCOTTPECK M 1987 *The Different Drum: Community.* Simon and Schuster, New York

SEABURY P 1990 *War.* Basic Book

SEELEY B 1979 *To Study War No More: A Bibliography on War, Peace and Conscience.* Central Committee for Conscientious Objectors, Philadelphia, Pennsylvania

SEGAL G 1988 *Nuclear War and Nuclear Peace.* Macmillan Press

SHANNON T A (Thomas Anthony) 1993 *What are they Saying about Peace and War?* Paulist Press, New York

SHAPLAND G 1996 *Rivers of Discord.* C Hurst & Co.

SHARKANSKY I 1996 *The Ritual of Conflict.* Lynne Rienner

SHEEN F J 1949 *Peace of Soul.* Mc Graw-Hill, New York

SHEPARD C 1995 *Discovering the Past: Peace and War.* John Murray Educ.

SHEPHERD G W 1987 *The Trampled Grass.* Praeger Pub.

SHERE W 1980 *In Search of Peace.* Exposition Press, NY

SHERWOOD D F 1971 *War and the Minds of Men.* Archon Books, Hamden, Conn

SHOGHI E 1984 *Waging Peace: Selections from Bahai Writings on Universal Peace.* Kalimat Press, Los Angeles

SHOWALTER D E 1995 *The Wars of Frederick the Great.* Longman

SILBAJORIS R 1995 *War and Peace.* Twayne

SILVA K M 1992 *Peace Accords and Ethnic Conflict.* Pinter

SILVA K M, SAMARASINGHE S W R (ed.) 1993 *Peace Accords and Ethnic Conflict.* London, New York, Pinter, New York

SMITH G S 1966 *A Selected Bibliography on Peacekeeping.* Canada, Department of National Defence, Ottawa, Ontario

SMITH H W 1995 *Ten Natural Laws of Successful Time and Life Management.* Allen & Unwin

SMITH J D D 1995 *Stopping Wars.* Westview Press

SMOKER P 1990 *A Reader in Peace Studies.* Butterworth Heineman

SOCIETE DES NATIONS BIBLIOTHEQUE/LEAGUE OF NATIONS LIBRARY 1928 *Ouvrages sur l'activité de la Société des Nations catalogués à la Bibliothèque du Secrétariat* [Books on The Work of the League of Nations Catalogued in the Library of the Secretariat]. League of Nations, Geneva
See also *Part 8: World Order and Internationalism*

SOMERVILLE J 1975 *The Peace Revolution: Ethos and Social Process.* Greenwood Press, Westport, Conn

SPANGER H J 1995 *Bridges to the Future.* Westview Press

SPEECKAERT G P 1965 *Bibliographie selective sur l'organisation internationale 1885-1964* [Select Bibliography on International Organisation 1885-1964]. Union des Associations Internationales, Brussels
See also *Part 8: World Order and Internationalism*

START J D 1972 *War and Waste: a Series of Discussions on War and War Accessories.* Garland Pub., New York

STEARUS S J 1971 *The Framework of a Lasting Peace.* Garland Pub., New York

STEBBING J 1991 *The Structure of Peace.* Sussex Aca/ Drake Int.

STEIN W (ed.) 1966 *Peace on Earth: The Way Ahead.* Sheed and Ward, London

STORDEUR R A 1989 *One Road to Peace.* Sage London

SUMMER C 1972 *Addresses on War.* Garland Pub., New York

Swanwick H M 1917 *The War in its Effect upon Women*. Women's International League, London Reprinted 1971 Garland, New York

Swanwick H M 1936 *The Roots of Peace*. Cape, London

Swerdlow A 1993 *Women Strike for Peace*. Univ Chicago Press

Swinne A H 1977 *Bibliographia Irenica, 1500-1970: Internationale Bibliographie zur Friedenswissenschaft; Kirchliche und Politische Einigungs- und Friedensbestrebunge, Öekumene und Volkerverständigung* [International Bibliography of Peace Studies; Religious and Political Efforts for Unity and Peace, Ecumenism and International Understanding]. Gerstenberg, Hildesheim
See also *Part 9.4: Peace and Religion*

Sypher E 1993 *Wisps of Violence*. Verso

Taylor T 1994 *Future Sources of Global Conflict*. Brookings Inst.

Ter Meulen J 1934 *Bibliography of the Peace Movement Before 1899 (Provisional Lists): Period 1776-1898*. Library of the Palace of Peace, The Hague

Ter Meulen J 1936 *Bibliography of the Peace Movement Before 1899 (Provisional Lists): Period 1480-1776*. Library of the Palace of Peace, The Hague

Ter Meulen J, Lysen A 1930 *Deuxième Supplement (1929) au catalogue (1916) de la Bibliothèque du Palais de la Paix* [Second Supplement to the Catalogue of the Library of the Palace of Peace]. Sijthoff, Leiden

Thee M 1996 *Peace*. UNESCO

Thomas N 1959 *The Prerequisites for Peace*. W. W. Norton Company, New York

Thomson D E M, Briggs A 1945 *Patterns of Peacemaking*. Oxford University Press, New York

Thompson W S, Jensen K M, Smith R N, Schranb K M 1991 *Approaches to Peace: an Intellectual Map* (ed.) United States Institute of Peace, Washington, DC

Tillett G 1992 *Resolving Conflict*. Sydney UP (OUP)

Tompkins E B 1971 *Peaceful Change in Modern Society*. Hoover Insitution Press Stanford University, Stanford Calif

Townshend C 1993 *Making the Peace*. Oxford UP

True M 1992 *To Construct Peace*. Twenty-Third Pub.

Turner A 1973 *A Bibliography of Quaker Literature, 1893-1967*. University of Michigan, Ann Arbor, Michigan
See also *Part 9.4: Peace and Religion*

Turner R K, Alexander P S 1947-50 *Documents of International Organizations: A Selected Bibliography*, Vols. 1-3. World Peace Foundation, Boston, Massachusetts
See also *Part 8: World Order and Internationalism*

Unamuno M D 1992 *Peace in War, a Novel*. Princeton UP

United Nations Secretariat 1968 *Disarmament: A Select Bibliography, 1962-1967*. United Nations, New York

United States Library of Congress 1916 *List of References on a League to Enforce Peace*. Library of Congress, Washington, DC
See also *Part 8: World Order and Internationalism*

United States Library of Congress, Division of Bibliography 1921 *Brief Select List of References on Disarmament*. Library of Congress, Washington, DC
See also *Part 8: World Order and Internationalism*

United States Library of Congress 1942 *Post-War Planning and Reconstruction (April 1941-March 1942): Selected and Annotated Bibliography on Post-War Plans and Problems*. Library of Congress, Washington, DC
See also *Part 8: World Order and Internationalism*

United States Department of State 1961 *A Basic Bibliography: Disarmament, Arms Control and National Security*. US Department of State, Washington, DC

Vasquez J A 1992 *The Scientific Study of Peace and War*. Lexington Books

Vasquez J A 1993 *The War Puzzle*. Cambridge UP

VAYRYNEN R 1987 *The Quest for Peace.* Sage, London

VUCINICH W S 1983 *At the Brink of War and Peace.* Columbia UP

WADE 1969 *Russian Search for Peace.* Stanford UP (CUP)

WALLIS J 1993 *Mother of World Peace.* Drake Int., Hearthston

WARNER D 1995 *New Dimensions of Peacekeeping.* Martinus Nijhoff

WEBSTER C K, MANNING C A W (eds.) 1972 *Peaceful Change: an International Problem.* Garland Pub., New York

WEHR P 1994 *Justice Without Violence.* Lynne Rienner

WEIGEL G S 1989 *Tranquillitas Ordinis.* Oxford UP

WELLS D A 1996 *An Encyclopedia of War and Ethics.* Greenwood Press

WHITE N D 1993 *Keeping the Peace.* Manchester UP

WILDMAN A K 1987 *The End of the Russian Imperial Army.* Princeton UP

WILKINS B T 1992 *Terrorism and Collective Responsibility.* Routledge

WILLIAMS S P 1964 *Toward a Genuine World Security System: An Annotated Bibliography For Layman and Scholar.* United World Federalists, Washington, DC
See also *Part 8: World Order and Internationalism*

WINHAM G R 1988 *New Issues in International Crisis Management.* Westview Press

WITHERS G 1991 *Defence Human Resources.* Har-
WOITO R S 1982 *To End War: A New Approach to International Conflict.* Pilgrim Press, New York

WITTNER L S 1993 *The Struggle Against the Bomb.* Stanford UP (CUP)

WOITO R 1982 *To End War: a New Approach to International Conflict.* Pilgrim Press, New York

WOLFF C 1994 *Anguish of Hell and Peace of Soul.* Harvard UP, Mass

WOLFSON M 1992 *Essays on the Cold War.* Macmillan Press

WOLPIN M 1994 *Alternative Security and Military Dissent.* Austin and Winfield

WOODHOUSE T 1991 *Peacemaking in a Troubled World.* Berg, St. Martin's Press, New York

WRIGHT J 1993 *Worth It All.* Brassey's US

YOSHITSU M 1983 *Japan and the San Francisco Peace Settlement.* Columbia UP

ZAGARE F C 1990 *Modeling International Conflict.* Gordon & Breach

ZARTMAN I W 1995 *Cooperative Security.* Syracuse University

ZARTMAN I W 1995 *Elusive Peace.* Brookings Inst

Part 2

Peace Classics/Peace Plans

ANGELL N 1911 *The Great Illusion.* Heinemann, London
Reprinted 1972 Garland, New York

ANGELL N 1921 *The Fruits of Victory.* Collins, London
Reprinted 1972 Garland, New York

ARISTOPHANES 1993 *Aristophanes Plays.* Methuen Drama

BALLOU A (1846) 1910 *Christian Non-Resistance in All its Important Bearings Illustrated and Defended.* Universal Peace Union, Philadelphia, Pennsylvania
Reprinted 1972 Garland, New York

BARA L 1872 *La Science de la paix.* Muquardt, Brussels
Reprinted 1972 Garland, New York

BEAUMONT G 1808 *The Warrior's Looking-Glass.* Crome, Sheffield
Reprinted 1971 Garland, New York

BECKWITH G C 1847 *The Peace Manual: On War and its Remedies.* American Peace Society, Boston, Massachusetts
Reprinted 1971 Garland, New York

BECKWITH G C (ed.) (1845) 1972 *The Book of Peace: A Collection of Essays on War and Peace.* J. S. Ozer, Englewood, New Jersey

BENTHAM J (1786-89) 1939 *Plan for an Universal and Perpetual Peace.* Peace Book Co., London
Reprinted in Cooper S (ed.) 1974 *Peace Projects of the Eighteenth Century.* Garland, New York

BLOCH J DE 1898-1900 *La Guerre [War],* 6 Vols. Guillaumin, Paris
Reprinted 1973 Garland, New York

BLOCH J DE 1899 *The Future of War in its Technical, Economic, and Political Relations: Is War Now Impossible?* Doubleday and McClure, New York
Reprinted 1971 Garland, New York

BOLLES J A 1839 *Essay on a Congress of Nations.* American Peace Society, Boston, Massachusetts
See also *Part 8: World Order and Internationalism*

Boston American Peace Society 1847 by George Cone Beckwith 1972 *The Peace Manual: or, War and its Remedies.* J. S. Ozer, New York

BRYCE J (Viscount) 1917 *Proposals for the Prevention of Future Wars.* Allen, London

BURRITT E (no date) *The Works of Elihu Burritt.* C. Gilpin, London

BUXTON C R (ed.) 1915 *Towards a Lasting Settlement.* Allen and Unwin, London
Reprinted 1971 Garland, New York

CAMUS A 1960 *Neither Victims nor Executioners.* World Without War Council, Berkeley, California

CEADEL M 1996 *The Origins of War Prevention.* Clarendon Press

CHANNING W E 1903 *Discourses on War.* Ginn, Boston, Massachusetts
Reprinted 1972 Garland, New York

CLARK G 1950 *A Plan for Peace.* Harper, New York

CLOOTS A 1792 *La République universelle.* Paris
Reprinted 1973 Garland, New York
See also *Part 8: World Order and Internationalism*

COBDEN R (1867) 1903 *The Political Writings of Richard Cobden,* 2 vols. Fisher, Unwin, London
Reprinted 1973 Garland, New York

Conference to Plan a Strategy for Peace: [report]. *Conference to Plan a Strategy for Peace.* Stanley Foundation, N.Y.: The Conference 1961-1968 V.: ill, New York

CONSIDERANT V 1850 *La Dernière Guerre et la paix définitive en Europe.* Librairie Phalansterienne, Paris
Reprinted in Cooper S (ed.) 1972 *Five Views on European Peace.* Garland, New York

CRUCE E (1623) 1972 *The New Cineas.* Garland, New York

DE LA BOETIE E 1942 *Anti-Dictator: Les Discours sur la servitude volontaire [The Discourse of Voluntary Servitude].* Columbia University Press, New York

DE LIGT B 1931-33 *Vrede Als Daad: Beginselen, Geschiedenis en Strijdmethoden van de Direkte Aktie Tegen Oorlog* [Peace as Deed: Principles, History and Means of Struggle of Direct Action Against War], 2 Vols. Van Loghum Slaterus, Arnhem

DE LIGT B 1937 *The Conquest of Violence: An Essay on War and Revolution.* Routledge, London
Reprinted 1972 Garland, New York

DESIDERIUS E 1974 *The Complaint of Peace.* Translated from the Querela Pacis (A.D. 1521) La Salle, Ill., Open Court

DODGE D L (1812) 1905 *War Inconsistent with the Religion of Jesus Christ.* Cinn, Boston, Massachusetts
Reprinted in Brock P (ed.) 1972 *The First American Peace Movement.* Garland, New York
See also *Part 9.4: Peace and Religion*

DUM R 1973 *The Idea of Peace in Antiquity Translated.* Unversity of Notre Dame Press, Notre Dame [Ind]

DUNCAN P B 1844 *The Motives of War.* Author Publ., London

DYMOND J 1843 *An Enquiry into the Accordancy of War with the Principles of Christianity.* C. Gilpin, London
Reprinted 1973 Garland, New York
See also *Part 9.4: Peace and Religion*

ERASMUS D The instruction of a Christian prince. In: *Three Peace Classics.* Peace Book Club, London

ERASMUS D (1517) 1917 *The Complaint of Peace.* Headley Bros., London

FAGLEY R M 1935 *Proposed Roads to Peace.* Pilgrim, Boston, Massachusetts

FELDER D A 1991 *How to Work for Peace.* Univ. Florida Press

FIELD D D 1872 *Draft Outlines of an International Code.* New York
See also *Part 8: World Order and Internationalism*

GARGAZ P-A (1782) 1922 *A Project of Universal and Perpetual Peace.* G. S. Eddy, New York
Reprinted 1973 Garland, New York

GENTZ F VON 1818 *Considerations on the Political System Now Existing in Europe.*
Reprinted in Cooper S (ed.) 1972 *Five Views on European Peace.* Garland, New York

GOLDSMITH R 1917 *A League to Enforce Peace.* Macmillan, New York
See also *Part 8: World Order and Internationalism*

GRIERSON P 1991 *Early Hellenistic Coinage from the Accession of Alexander to the Peace of Apamea (336-188 BC).* Cambridge UP

GROTIUS H (1625) 1922 *De Jure Belli ac Pacis* [The Law of War and Peace]. Sweet and Maxwell, London
Reprinted in Cook B W (ed.) 1972 *Peace Projects of the Seventeenth Century.* Garland, New York

GULICK S L 1915 *The Fight for Peace.* Revell, New York

GURNEY J J 1860 *War: Is it Lawful under the Christian Dispensation?* Society for the Promotion of a Permanent and Universal Peace, London
See also *Part 9.4: Peace and Religion*

HANCOCK T 1829 *Principles of Peace, Exemplified in the Conduct of the Society of Friends During the Rebellion of 1798.* Society for the Promotion of a Permanent and Universal Peace, London

HART H L 1918 *The Bulwarks of Peace.* Methuen, London

HEMLEBEN S 1943 *Plans for World Peace Through Six Centuries.* University of Chicago, Chicago, Illinois
Reprinted 1972 Garland, New York

HIRSH R-see *Part 1: Peace-General, including Peace Bibliographies*

HUGHES C E 1930 *Pan-American Peace Plans*. Yale University Press, New Haven, Connecticut

HUGO V (1849) 1914 *The United States of Europe*. World Peace Foundation, Boston, Massachusetts Reprinted in Cooper S (ed.) 1972 *Five Views on European Peace*. Garland, New York

HYDE H E 1919 *The International Solution*. Allen, London
See also *Part 8: World Order and Internationalism*

JACOB J R, JACOB M C (ed.) 1972 *Peace Projects of the Seventeenth Century*. Garland Pub., New York

JAMES W (1910) 1971 *The Moral Equivalent of War and Other Essays*. Harper and Row, New York

JAY W 1919 *War and Peace*. Oxford University Press, New York

JEFFERSON J 1832 *The Unlawfulness of War: A Discourse on Luke, ii, 14*. London
See also *Part 9.4: Peace and Religion*

JOHNSEN J E 1943 *World Peace Plans*. H. W. Wilson, New York

JORDAN D S 1914 *War and Waste*. Doubleday, Page, New York
Reprinted 1972 Garland, New York

KALLEN H M 1918 *Structure of Lasting Peace*. Jones, Marshall, USA

KANT I (1795) 1903 *Perpetual Peace*. Swan Sonnenschein, London
Reprinted 1972 Garland, New York

KANT I 1903 *Perpetual Peace*. Thommes Press

KELSEN H 1944 *Peace Through Law*. University of North Carolina Press, Chapel Hill, North Carolina

KEYNES J M 1979 *The Collected Writings of John Maynard Keynes: Vol. 24: Activities 1944-1946, the Transition to Peace*. Macmillan Press

KING M L 1964 *Strength to Love*. Hodder and Stoughton, London

KIRDY P 1971 *An American Peace Policy*. Garland Pub., New York

LADD W 1827 *The Essays of Philanthropos on Peace and War*. J. T. Burnham, Exeter, New Hampshire Reprinted 1971 Garland, New York

LADD W (1840) 1916 *An Essay on a Congress of Nations for the Adjustment of International Disputes Without Resort to Arms*. Oxford University Press, New York
See also *Part 8: World Order and Internationalism*

LEVI L 1855 *The Law of Nature and Nations as Affected by Divine Law*. London

LEVI L 1881 *War and its Consequences: With Proposals for Establishing a Court*. Partridge and Co., London

MACNAMARA H T J 1841 *Peace, Permanent and Universal: Its Practicability, Value and Consistency with Divine Revelation*. London

MARRIOTT J A R (Sir) 1937 *Commonwealth or Anarchy? A Survey of Projects of Peace from the Sixteenth to the Twentieth Century*. Philip Allan, London

MARRIOTT J A R 1981 *Commonwealth or Anarchy? A survey of Projects of Peace from the Sixteenth to the Twentieth Century*. Conn., Hyperion Press, Westport

MAZZINI G 1853 *Europe: Its Condition and Prospects*. Reprinted Cooper S (ed.) 1972 *Five Views on European Peace*. Garland, New York

MORRISON C C 1927 *The Outlawry of War*. Willett, Clark and Colby, Chicago, Illinois
Reprinted 1972 Garland, New York

MORROW D W 1919 *Society of Free States*. Harper, New York
See also *Part 8: World Order and Internationalism*

MOTT J 1814 *The Lawfulness of War for Christians Examined*. S. Wood, New York
Reprinted in Brock P (ed.) 1972 *The First American Peace Movement*. Garland, New York
See also *Part 9.4: Peace and Religion*

NOVICOW J 1901 *La Fédération de l'Europe.* Felix Alcan, Paris
Reprinted 1972 Garland, New York
See also *Part 8: World Order and Internationalism*

NOVIKOW J 1912 *War and its Alleged Benefits.* Heinemann, London
Reprinted 1971 Garland, New York

PAGE K 1925 *An American Peace Policy.* G. H. Doran, New York
Reprinted 1971 Garland, New York

PAGE K 1927 *Dollars and World Peace.* G. H. Doran, New York
Reprinted 1972 Garland, New York

PENN W (1693) 1912 *An Essay Towards the Present and Future Peace of Europe.* American Peace Society, Washington, DC
Reprinted in Cook B W (ed.) 1972 *Peace Projects of the Seventeenth Century.* Garland, New York

PODEBRAD J Z (1462-64) 1964 *The Universal Peace Organization of King George of Bohemia: A Fifteenth Century Plan for World Peace.* Czechoslovak Academy of Sciences, Prague
Reprinted 1972 Garland, New York

POLLARD A F 1919 *League of Nations: An Historical Argument.* Oxford, London
See also *Part 8: World Order and Internationalism*

ROBERTS S 1834 *Thoughts on War* ... London

ROUSSEAU J-J (1756) 1927 *A Project of Perpetual Peace.* Cobden-Sanderson, London
Reprinted in Cooper S (ed.) 1974 *Peace Projects of the Eighteenth Century.* Garland, New York

RUSKIN J 1895 *Unto This Last: Four Essays on the First Principles of Political Economy.* G. Allen, London

SACKS B 1962 *Peace Plans of the Seventeenth and Eighteenth Centuries.* Coronado Press, Sandoval, New Mexico

ST. AUGUSTINE 1931 *The City of God.* Dent, London
See also *Part 9.4: Peace and Religion*

SAINT-PIERRE C (Abbé de) (1738) 1927 *A Shorter Project for Perpetual Peace.* Sweet and Maxwell, London
Reprinted in Cooper S (ed.) 1974 *Peace Projects of the Eighteenth Century.* Garland, New York

SAINT-PIERRE C D 1974 *Peace Projects of the Eighteenth Century: Comprising A Shorter Project for Perpetual Peace.* Garland Pub., New York

SAINT-SIMON H (Comte de), THIERRY A 1814 *The Reorganization of the European Community.*
Reprinted in Cooper S (ed.) 1972 *Five Views on European Peace.* Garland, New York

SOMMERSTEIN A H 1985 *Aristophanes: "Peace".* Aris & Phillips

SOULEYMAN E V 1941 *The Vision of World Peace in Seventeenth and Eighteenth Century France.* G. P. Putnam's Sons, New York

SOULEYMAN E V 1972 *The Vision of World Peace in Seventeenth and Eighteenth-Century France.* Kennikat Press, Port Washington, NY

STOKES W 1861 *A Permanent European Congress in Lieu of War....* Author Publ., London
See also *Part 8: World Order and Internationalism*

SULLY M DE B (Duc De) 1921 *Grand Design of Henry IV.* Sweet and Maxwell, London
Reprinted in Cook B W (ed.) 1972 *Peace Projects of the Seventeenth Century.* Garland, New York

THOREAU H D (1848) 1963 *On the Duty of Civil Disobedience.* Peace News, London

TOLSTOY L 1993 *War & Peace (NCE).* W W Norton

TOLSTOY L 1995 *War and Peace.* W W Norton

TRUEBLOOD B F, MEAD E D 1972 *The Development of the Peace Idea, and other Essays.* J. S. Ozer, New York

UN 1990 *Science and Technology and the Implications for Peace and Security.* United Nations

VON SUTTNER B 1894 *Lay Down Your Arms.* Longmans, Green, New York
Reprinted 1972 Garland, New York

WELLOCK W 1949 *Rebuilding Britain: A New Peace Orientation.* Hallmark, London

WELLOCK W 1956 *New Horizons: Build the Future Now*. Housmans, London

WOOLF L S 1917 *The Framework of a Lasting Peace*. Allen, London
See also *Part 8: World Order and Internationalism*

WORCESTER N 1815 *A Solemn Review of the Custom of War*. Hartford, Connecticut
Reprinted in Brock P (ed.) 1972 *The First American Peace Movement*. Garland, New York

WRIGHT H C 1846 *Defensive War Proved to be a Denial of Christianity and the Government of God*. C. Gilpin, London
See also *Part 9.4: Peace and Religion*

WYNNER E, LLOYD G (eds.) 1946 *Searchlight on Peace Plans: Choose Your Road to World Government*. Dutton, New York

YORK E 1919 *Leagues of Nations: Ancient, Mediaeval and Modern*. Swarthmore, London
See also *Part 8: World Order and Internationalism*

Part 3

Peace Movement

3.1 History

ADDAMS J 1945 *Peace and Bread in Time of War.* King's Crown, New York
Reprinted 1971 Garland, New York

ADDAMS J, BALCH E, HAMILTON A 1915 *Women at The Hague.* Macmillan, New York
Reprinted 1972 Garland, New York

ALLEN D 1930 *The Fight for Peace*, 2 Vols. Macmillan, New York
Reprinted 1971 Garland, New York

AMIN J A 1993 *The Peace Corps in Cameroon.* Kent State UP

BACON M H 1992 *One Woman's Passion for Peace and Freedom.* Syracuse University

BEALES A C F 1931 *The History of Peace: A Short History of the Organised Movements for International Peace.* G. Bells and Sons, London

BIRN D S 1981 *The League of Nations Union, 1918-1945.* Clarendon Press, Oxford

BOURNE R S (comp.) 1916 *Towards An Enduring Peace: A Symposium of Peace Proposals and Programs 1914-1916.* American Association for International Conciliation, New York
Reprinted 1971 Garland, New York

BRITTAIN V 1964 *The Rebel Passion: A Short History of Some Pioneer Peace-makers.* Allen and Unwin, London

BREYMAN S 1996 *Why Movements Matter.* Westview Press

BROCK P 1968 *Pioneers of the Peaceable Kingdom.* Princeton University Press, Princeton, New Jersey
See also *Part 9.4: Peace and Religion*

BUSSEY G, TIMS M 1965 *Women's International League for Peace and Freedom 1915-1965: A Record of Fifty Years Work.* Allen and Unwin, London

CARSTEN F L 1982 *War Against War: British and German Radical Movements in the First World War.* Batsford, London

CARTER A 1992 *Peace Movements: International Protest and World Politics Since 1945.* Longman, London, New York

CARTER A 1992 *Peace Movements.* Longman

CATHALA D H 1990 *The Peace Movement in Israel, 1967-87.* Macmillan Press

CEADEL M - see *Part 6: Pacifism*

CHAMBERS J W II 1976 *The Eagle and the Dove: The American Peace Movement and United States Foreign Policy, 1900-1922.* Garland, New York

CHATFIELD C (ed.) 1973 *Peace Movements in America.* Schocken, New York

CHICKERING R 1975 *Imperial Germany and a World Without War: The Peace Movement and German Society 1892-1914.* Princeton University Press, Princeton, New Jersey

CONLIA J R 1968 1978 *American Anti-War Movements.* Glencoe Press, Beverly Hill

COOKSON J E 1982 *The Friends of Peace: Anti-war Liberalism in England 1973-1815.* Cambridge UP, Cambridge (Cambridgeshire), New York

CURTI M 1929 *The American Peace Crusade, 1815-1860.* Duke University Press, Durham, North Carolina

CURTI M 1936 *Peace or War: The American Struggle, 1636-1936*. Norton, New York
Reprinted 1972 Garland, New York

DAVIS C D 1962 *The United States and the First Hague Peace Conference*. Cornell University Press, Ithaca, New York

DAVIS H (ed.) 1907 *Among The World's Peacemakers*. Progressive Publishing, New York
Reprinted 1972 Garland, New York

DAY A J 1986 *Peace Movements of the World*. Longman, Harlow Essex UK

DEBENEDETTI C 1978 *Origins of the Modern American Peace Movement 1915-1929*. KTO Press, Millwood, New York

DEBENEDETTI C 1980 *The Peace Reform in American History*. Indiana University Press, Bloomington, Indiana

DEGEN M L 1939 *The History of the Woman's Peace Party*. Johns Hopkins Press, Baltimore, Maryland
Reprinted 1972 Garland, New York

DINGWALL E, HEARD E A 1937 *Pennsylvania 1681-1756: The State Without an Army: Successes and Failures of the Holy Experiment*. Daniel, London

DIVINE M J 1982 *The Peace Mission Movement: Founded*. Imperial Press, Philadelphia

DODGE D L 1972 *The First American Peace Movement: Comprising War Inconsistent with the Religion of Jesus Christ*. Garland Pub., New York

FABIAN L L 1985 *Andrew Carnegie's Peace Endowment*. Carnegie Endowment for International Peace, Washington, DC

FARRELL J C 1967 *Beloved Lady: A History of Jane Addams's Ideas on Reform and Peace*. Johns Hopkins Press, Baltimore, Maryland

FERRELL R H 1952 *Peace in Their Time: The Origins of the Kellogg-Briand Pact*. Yale University Press, New Haven, Connecticut

FRIED A H 1911 *Handbuch der Friedensbewegung, Vol. 1: Grundlagen, Inhalt und Ziele der Friedensbewegung* [Handbook on the Peace Movement: Foundations, Meaning and Aims of the Peace Movement]. Verlag der Friedens-Warte, Berlin/Leipzig
Reprinted 1972 Garland, New York

FRIED A H 1913 *Handbuch der Friedensbewegung, Vol. 2: Geschichte, Umfang und Organisation der Friedensbewegung* [Handbook on the Peace Movement: History, Extent and Organisation of the Peace Movement]. Verlag der Friedens-Warte, Berlin/Leipzig
Reprinted 1972 Garland, New York

FRANK L 1905 *Les Belges et la paix*. Lamertin, Brussels
Reprinted in Cooper S (ed.) 1972 *Peace Activities in Belgium and The Netherlands*. Garland, New York

GRUNEWALD G 1995 *Twentieth-Century Peace Movements*. Edwin Mellen Press

HOWARD M 1978 *War and the Liberal Conscience*. Temple Smith, London

HOWE F C 1916 *Why War?* C. Scribner's Sons, New York
Reprinted 1972 Garland, New York

HOWLETT C F, ZEIZER G 1985 *The American Peace Movement: History and Historiography*. American Historical Association, Washington, DC

HULL W I 1908 *The Two Hague Conferences and their Contributions to International Law*. Ginn, Boston, Massachusetts

JONG VAN BEEKEN DONK B DE 1915 *History of the Peace Movement in the Netherlands*. The Hague
Reprinted in Cooper S (comp.) 1972 *Peace Activities in Belgium and The Netherlands*. Garland, New York

JOYCE J A (ed.) 1959 *Red Cross International and the Strategy of Peace*. Oceana Pub., New York

KLANDERMANS B 1991 *International Social Movements Research*. JAI Press

KODAMA K 1990 *Towards a Comparative Analysis of Peace Movements*. Dartmouth

LA FONTAINE H-see *Part 1: Peace-General, including Peace Bibliographies*

LIBBY F 1969 *To End War: The Story of the National Council for Prevention of War.* Fellowship Publishing, Nyack, New York

LIEBKNECHT K 1917 *Militarism and Anti-militarism.* Socialist Labour Press, Glasgow
Reprinted 1973 Garland, New York

LIVINGSTONE A (Dame) 1935 *The Peace Ballot: The Official History.* Gollancz, London

LOEB P R 1987 *Hope in Hard Times: America's Peace Movement and the Reganera.* Lexington Books, Lexington, Mass

MARBURG T 1917 *League of Nations: A Chapter in the History of the Movement*, 2 Vols. Macmillan, New York
See also *Part 8: World Order and Internationalism*

MARCHAND C R 1972 *The American Peace Movement and Social Reform, 1898-1918.* Princeton University Press, Princeton, New Jersey

MARCHAND C R 1992 *The American Peace Movement and Social Reform, 1898-1918.* Princeton UP

MATTHEWS M A - see *Part 1: Peace-General, including Peace Bibliographies*

MOREL E D 1916 *Truth and the War.* National Labour Press, London
Reprinted 1972 Garland, New York

PASSY F 1909 *Pour la Paix: Notes et Documents* [For Peace: Notes And Documents]. Charpentier, Paris
Reprinted 1972 Garland, New York

PATTERSON D S 1976 *Toward a Warless World: The Travail of the American Peace Movement 1887-1914.* Indiana University Press, Bloomington, Indiana

PHILLIMORE W G F (Sir) 1918 *Three Centuries of Treaties of Peace.* Little, Brown, Boston, Massachusetts
Reprinted 1973 Garland, New York

PICKETT C E 1953 *For More Than Bread: An Autobiographical Account of Twenty-two Years Work with the American Friends Service Committee.* Little, Brown, Boston, Massachusetts

Proceedings of the Universal Peace Congress, July 1890. Office of the Congress, London

PUNSHON J 1984 *Portrait in Grey: A Short History of the Quakers.* Quaker Home Service, London
See also *Part 9.4: Peace and Religion*

Report of the Proceedings of the Second General Peace Congress, Held in Paris 1849. Charles Gilpin, London

Report of the Proceedings of the Third General Peace Congress, Held in Frankfort 1850-1851. Charles Gilpin, London

ROBBINS K 1976 *The Abolition of War: The 'Peace Movement' in Britain 1914-1919.* University of Wales Press, Cardiff

SCHLISSEL L (ed.) 1968 *Conscience in America: A Documentary History of Conscientious Objection in America, 1757-1967.* Dutton, New York

SCOTT J B 1909 *The Hague Peace Conferences of 1899 and 1907*, Vol. 1: *Conferences*, Vol. 2: *Documents.* Johns Hopkins Press, Baltimore, Maryland
Reprinted 1972 Garland, New York

STEAD W T 1899 *The United States of Europe on the Eve of the Parliament of Peace.* Doubleday and McClure, New York
Reprinted 1971 Garland, New York
See also *Part 8: World Order and Internationalism*

SWANWICK H M 1924 *Builders of Peace: Being Ten Years' History of the Union of Democratic Control.* Swarthmore, London
Reprinted 1973 Garland, New York

TEXTOR R B, MEAD M (ed.) 1966 *Cultural Frontiers of the Peace Corps.* Lambros Comitas Can (and others) M.I.T. Press, Cambridge

TRUEBLOOD B F (1901) 1932 *The Development of the Peace Idea and Other Essays.* World Peace Foundation, Boston, Massachusetts
Reprinted 1972 Garland, New York

VIPONT E 1960 *The Story of Quakerism: Through Three Centuries.* Bannisdale Press, London
See also *Part 9.4: Peace and Religion*

WANK S (ed.) 1978 *Doves and Diplomats: Foreign*

Offices and Peace Movements in Europe and America in the Twentieth Century. Greenwood Press, Westport, Connecticut

WEHR P E 1996 *The Persistent Activist.* Westview Press

WELLS H G 1918 *In the Fourth Year: Anticipations of a World Peace.* Chatto and Windus, London

WHITNEY E L 1928 *The American Peace Society: A Centennial History.* American Peace Society, Washington, DC

WILSON W 1917 *A League for Peace: Address of the President to the Senate.* GPO, Washington, DC
See also *Part 8: World Order and Internationalism*

3.2 Contemporary

ALTERNATIVE DEFENCE COMMISSION 1985 *Without the Bomb.* Paladin, London

AMERICAN FRIENDS SERVICE COMMITTEE 1966 *Peace in Vietnam: A New Approach in South-east Asia.* Hill and Wang, New York

BANNAN J F, BANNAN R S 1974 *Law, Morality and Vietnam: The Peace Militants and the Courts.* Indiana University Press, Bloomington, Indiana

BARNABY F, THOMAS G P 1982 *The Nuclear Arms Race: Control or Catastrophe.* Frances Pinter, London

BIGELOW A 1959 *The Voyage of the Golden Rule: An Experiment with Truth.* Doubleday, New York

BOULTON D (ed.) 1964 *Voices from the Crowd: Against the H-Bomb.* Peter Owen, London

CARTER A 1974 *Direct Action in a Liberal Democracy.* Routledge and Kegan Paul, London

COATES K 1984 *The Most Dangerous Decade: World Militarism and the New Non-aligned Peace Movement.* Spokesman, Nottingham

COOK A, KIRK G 1984 *Greenham Women Everywhere: Dreams, Ideas and Actions from the Women's Peace Movement.* Pluto Press, London

COONEY R, MICHALOWSKI H 1986 *The Power of the People.* New Society Publishers, Philadelphia, Pennsylvania

COX J 1981 *Overkill.* Penguin, Harmondsworth

DEUTSCH F (ed.) 1962 *Prisoners Against the Bomb:*

Prison Conditions for Unilateral Nuclear Disarmers. Committee of 100, London

DRIVER C 1964 *The Disarmers: A Study in Protest.* Hodder and Stoughton, London

DUFF P 1971 *Left, Left, Left.* Allison and Busby, London

FALL B 1967 *The Two Vietnams: A Political and Military Analysis.* Praeger, New York

GARRISON J 1980 *From Hiroshima to Harrisburg: The Unholy Alliance.* SCM Press, London

GETTLEMAN M E (ed.) 1966 *Vietnam.* Penguin, Harmondsworth

GLASSTONE S, DOLAN P J 1980 *The Effects of Nuclear Weapons.* Castle House, Tunbridge Wells

GOODWIN P 1981 *Nuclear War: The Facts on our Survival.* Ash and Grant, London

HACHIYA M 1955 *Hiroshima Diary.* University of North Carolina, Chapel Hill, North Carolina

HALSTEAD F 1978 *Out Now! A Participant's Account of the American Movement Against the Vietnam War.* Monad Press, New York

HERSEY J 1958 *Hiroshima.* Penguin, Harmondsworth

HERZOG A 1965 *The War/Peace Establishment.* Harper and Row, New York

HOLLIS E (ed.) 1967 *Peace is Possible: A Reader for Laymen.* Grossman, New York

HOWORTH J 1984 *France: The Politics of Peace.* European Nuclear Disarmament (END)/Merlin Press, London
See also *Part 9.2: Peace and Politics*

JUNGK R 1960 *Brighter Than a Thousand Suns: A Personal History of the Atomic Scientists.* Penguin, Harmondsworth

JUNGK R 1961 *Children of the Ashes: The Story of a Re-birth.* Heinemann, London

KENNAN G F 1984 *The Nuclear Delusion.* Hamish Hamilton, London

LIFTON R J 1968 *Death in Life: The Survivors of Hiroshima.* Weidenfeld and Nicholson, London

LYND A (coll.) 1968 *We Won't Go: Personal Accounts of War Objectors.* Beacon Press, Boston, Massachusetts

McREYNOLDS D 1970 *We Have Been Invaded by the 21st Century.* Grove Press, New York

MARTIN B 1984 *Uprooting War.* Freedom Press, London

MARTIN D, MULLEN P (eds.) 1983 *Unholy Warfare: The Church and the Bomb.* Basil Blackwell, Oxford
See also *Part 9.4: Peace and Religion*

MAYER P (ed.) 1966 *The Pacifist Conscience.* Holt, Rinehart and Winston, New York

MENON E P 1967 *Foot-prints on Friendly Roads: Story of the Global Peace March.* International Sarvodaya Centre, Bangalore

MINNION J, BOLSOVER P 1983 *The CND Story.* Allison and Busby, London

MUMFORD L 1954 *In the Name of Sanity.* Harcourt, Brace, New York

NAEVE V (ed.) 1963 *Changeover: The Drive for Peace.* Alan Swallow, Denver, Colorado

NIELD R 1981 *How to Make Your Mind Up About the Bomb.* Deutsch, London

NEWMAN J R 1962 *The Rule of Folly.* Allen and Unwin, London

OFFICE OF TECHNOLOGY ASSESSMENT 1980 *The Effects of Nuclear War.* Congress of the US/Croom Helm, London

OPPENSHAW S, STEADMAN P, GREENE O 1983 *Doomsday: Britain After Nuclear Attack.* Basil Blackwell, Oxford

O'ROURKE W 1973 *The Harrisburg 7 and the New Catholic Left.* Crowell, New York

OSTERGAARD G, CURRELL M 1971 *The Gentle Anarchists: A Study of the Leaders of the Sarvodaya Movement for Non-Violent Revolution in India.* Oxford University Press, Oxford

OVERY B 1980 *How Effective are Peace Movements? Peace Studies Paper No. 2.* School of Peace Studies/Housmans, Bradford

PAGE K 1946 *Now is the Time to Prevent a Third World War.* Kirby Page, La Habra, California

PARKIN F 1968 *Middle Class Radicalism: The Social Bases of the British Campaign for Nuclear Disarmament.* Manchester University Press, Manchester

PAULING L 1958 *No More War!* Dodd, Mead, New York

PRINS G (ed.) 1983 *Defended to Death.* Penguin, Harmondsworth

PRINS G (ed.) 1984 *The Choice: Nuclear Weapons Versus Security.* Chatto and Windus, London

RAPOPORT A 1964 *Strategy and Conscience.* Schocken, New York

REYNOLDS E 1975 *The Forbidden Voyage.* Greenwood, Westport, Connecticut

RICHARDS V 1981 *Protest without Illusions.* Freedom Press, London

ROGERS P, DANDO M, VAN DEN DUNGEN P 1981 *As Lambs to the Slaughter.* Arrow, London

ROUSSOPOULOS D (ed.) 1983 *Our Generation Against Nuclear War.* Black Rose, Montreal

RUSSELL B 1969 *The Autobiography of Bertrand Russell*, Vol. 3: *1944-1967.* Allen and Unwin, London

SCHEER R 1983 *With Enough Shovels: Reagan, Bush and Nuclear War*. Secker and Warburg, London

SCHWEITZER A 1958 *Peace of Atomic War*. Holt, New York

SIDER R J, TAYLOR R K 1983 *Nuclear Holocaust and Christian Hope*. Hodder and Stoughton, London

SMITH D 1980 *The Defence of the Realm in the 1980's*. Croom Helm, London

STEINWEG R (ed.) 1982 *Die Neue Friedensbewegung*. Suhrkamp, Frankfurt

STONE I F 1952 *Hidden History of the Korean War*. Monthly Review Press, New York

TAYLOR R, PRITCHARD C 1980 *The Protest Makers: The British Nuclear Disarmament Movement of 1958-1965, Twenty Years On*. Pergamon, Oxford

THICH NHAT HANH-see *Part 9.4: Peace and Religion*

THOMPSON D (ed.) 1983 *Over our Dead Bodies: Women Against the Bomb*. Virago, London

THOMPSON E P 1982 *Zero Option*. Merlin Press, London

THOMPSON E P, SMITH D (eds.) 1980 *Protest and Survive*. Penguin, Harmondsworth

USEEM M 1973 *Conscription, Protest and Social Conflict*. Wiley, New York

WALTERS R E 1974 *The Nuclear Trap: An Escape Route*. Penguin, Harmondsworth

WARBEY W 1965 *Vietnam: The Truth*. Merlin Press, London

WEINBERG A, WEINBERG L (eds.) 1963 *Instead of Violence: Writings by the Great Advocates of Peace Throughout History*. Grossman, New York

WITTNER L 1969 *Rebels Against War: The American Peace Movement 1941-1960*. Columbia University Press, New York

WOITO R S 1982 *To End War: A New Approach to International Conflict*. Pilgrim Press, New York

WOODSTONE N S 1970 *Up Against the War*. Tower Publications, New York

YORK H F 1970 *Race to Oblivion: A Participant's View of the Arms Race*. Simon and Schuster, New York

YOUNG N 1976 *War Resistance and the Nation State*. Ann Arbor, Michigan

YOUNG N 1977 *An Infantile Disorder? The Crisis and Decline of the New Left*. Routledge and Kegan Paul, London

Part 4

Disarmament and Arms Control

ABT C C et al. 1963 *Theoretical Aspects of Unilateral Arms Control*. Raytheon, Bedford, Massachusetts

ADAMS F G 1992 *The Macroeconomic Dimensions of Arms Reduction*. Westview Press

ALEXANDER A S et al. 1971 *The Control of Chemicals and Biological Weapons*. Carnegie Endowment for International Peace, New York

ALTERNATIVE DEFENCE COMMISSION 1983 *Defence Without the Bomb: The Report of the Alternative Defence Commission*. Taylor and Francis, London

APPLETON L 1900 *Fifty Years Historic Record of the Progress of Disarmament, 1849-1899*. London

ARKADYEV N N 1962 *General and Complete Disarmament: The Road to Peace*. Foreign Languages Publishing House, Moscow

ARNOLD-FORSTER W 1931 *The Disarmament Conference*. National Peace Council, London

AUTON G P 1989 *Arms Control and European Security*. Praeger Pub.

BARKER C A (ed.) 1963 *Problems of World Disarmament*. Houghton Mifflin, Boston, Massachusetts

BARNABY C F, BOSERUP A (eds.) 1969 *Implications of Anti-ballistic Missile Systems*. Souvenir Press, London

BARNABY C F, THOMAS G P 1982 *The Nuclear Arms Race: Control or Catastrophe?* Frances Pinter, London

BARNABY F, HUISKEN R 1975 *Arms Uncontrolled*. Harvard University Press, Cambridge, Massachusetts

BARNET R J - see *Part 9.1: Peace and Economics*

BARNET R J, FALK R A (eds.) 1965 *Security in Disar-* *mament*. Princeton University Press, Princeton, New Jersey

BARTON J H, WEILER L D (eds.) 1976 *International Arms Control: Issues and Agreements*. Stanford University Press, Stanford, California

BENOIT E, GLEDITSCH N P (eds.) - see *Part 9.1: Peace and Economics*

BERTRAM C (ed.) 1980 *Arms Control and Military Force*. Gower, Farnborough

BIRNBAUM K E 1980 *Arms Control in Europe: Problems and Prospects*. Austrian Institute for International Affairs, Laxenburg

BJERKHOLT O et al. 1980 *Disarmament and Development: A Study of Conversion in Norway*. International Peace Research Institute (PRIO), Oslo

BLOOMFIELD L P et al. 1966 *Khrushchev and the Arms Race: Soviet Interests in Arms Control and Disarmament, 1954-1964*. MIT Press, Cambridge, Massachusetts

BLUM L 1932 *Peace and Disarmament*. Cape, London

BOARDMAN G D 1899 *Disarmament of Nations: Or, Mankind One Body*. H. M. Jenkins, Philadelphia, Pennsylvania

BOLTE C 1956 *The Price of Peace*. Beacon, Boston, Massachusetts

BOLTON R E (ed.) - see *Part 9.1: Peace and Economics*

BOULDING K E (ed.) 1973 - see *Part 9.1: Peace and Economics*

BOULDING K E, BENOIT E (eds.) - see *Part 9.1: Peace and Economics*

BRAUER J 1992 *Economic Issues of Disarmament*. Macmillan Press

BREDOW W (ed.) 1975 *Economic and Social Aspects of Disarmament.* BBP Publications, Oslo
See also *Part 9.1: Peace and Economics*

BRENNAN D G (ed.) 1961 *Arms Control, Disarmament, and National Security.* Braziller, New York

BRENNAN D G (ed.) 1961 *Arms Control and Disarmament: American Views and Studies.* Cape, London

BROCKWAY F, MULLALLY F 1944 *Death Pays a Dividend.* Gollancz, London

BULL H 1965 *The Control of the Arms Race.* Praeger, New York

BURNS R D - see *Part 1: Peace-General, including Peace Bibliographies*

BURNS R D, URQUIDI D 1968 *Disarmament in Perspective: An Analysis of Selected Disarmament and Arms Control Agreements Between World War, 1919-1939*, 4 Vols. ACDA Report RS-55. GPO, Washington, DC

BURT R (ed.) 1982 *Arms Control and Defense Postures in the 1980's.* Croom Helm, London

BURTON J W 1962 *Peace Theory: Preconditions of Disarmament.* Knopf, New York

CARLTON D, SCHAERF O (eds.) 1977 *Arms Control and Technological Innovations.* Croom Helm, London

CARTER A (ed.) 1965 *Unilateral Disarmament: Its Theory and Policy from Different International Perspectives.* Housmans, London

CHATTERJI M 1992 *Disarmament, Economic Conversion, and Management of Peace.* Praeger Pub.

CHILTON P 1988 *Language and the Nuclear Arms Debate.* Pinter

CLEMENS W C JR 1965 - see *Part 1: Peace - General, including Peace Bibliographies*

CLEMENS W C JR 1973 *The Superpowers and Arms Control: From Cold War to Interdependence.* D. C. Heath, Lexington, Massachusetts

COATES K (ed.) 1981 *Eleventh Hour for Europe.* Spokesman, Nottingham

COFFEY J I 1979 *Arms Control and European Security: A Guide to East-West Negotiations.* Macmillan, London

COLLART Y - see *Part 1: Peace - General, including Peace Bibliographies*

CROSSLEY G 1984 *Disarmament Negotiations: The Way Forward.* CND Publs, London

DALLIN A et al. 1964 *The Soviet Union and Disarmament: An Appraisal of Soviet Attitudes and Intentions.* Praeger, New York

DEUTSCH K W 1967 *Arms Control and the Atlantic Alliance.* Wiley, New York

DHANAPALA J 1993 *Regional Approaches to Disarmament.* Dartmouth

DOUGHERTY J E, LEHMAN J F JR (eds.) 1965 *The Prospects for Arms Control.* MacFadden-Bartell, New York

DUMAS L J 1995 *The Socio-Economics of Conversion from War to Peace.* M E Sharpe

EDWARDS A J C 1986 *Nuclear Weapons, the Balance of Terror, the Quest for Peace.* Macmillan Press

EDWARDS D V 1969 *Arms Control in International Politics.* Holt, Rinehart and Winston, New York

EPSTEIN W 1976 *The Last Chance: Nuclear Proliferation and Arms Control.* Free Press, New York

EPSTEIN W, TOYODA T (eds.) 1977 *A New Design for Nuclear Disarmament.* Spokesman, Nottingham

EPSTEIN W, WEBSTER L (eds.) 1983 *We Can Avert a Nuclear War.* Oelgeschlager, Gunn and Hain, Cambridge, Massachusetts

FERGUSON J 1982 *Disarmament: The Unanswerable Case.* Heinemann, London

FINDLAY T 1991 *Chemical Weapons and Missile Proliferation.* Lynne Rienner

FISCHER D 1992 *Stopping the Spread of Nuclear Weapons.* Routledge

FORSBERG R 1996 *Arms Control in the New Era.* The MIT Press

GEYER A, WEILER L D 1982 *The Idea of Disarmament: Rethinking the Unthinkable.* Elgin III: Brethren Press, Churches' Center for Theology and Public Policy, Washington DC

GLEDITSCH N P 1989 *Arms Races: Technological and Political Dynamics.* Sage, London

GOLDBLAT J 1973 *The Implementation of International Disarmament Agreements.* Stockholm International Peace Research Institute (SIPRI), Stockholm.

GOLDBLAT J 1982 *Agreements for Arms Control.* Taylor and Francis, London

HAMPSCH G H, SOMERVILLE J 1988 *Preventing Nuclear Genocide: Essays on Peace and War.* P. Lang, New York

HEALD S 1932 *Memorandum on the Progress of Disarmament, 1919-1932.* Royal Institute of International Affairs, London

HELLMANN D C et al. 1971 *India and Japan: The Emerging Balance of Power in Asia and Opportunities for Arms Control 1970-1975*, 4 Vols. ACDA Report IR-170. Columbia University, New York

HENKIN L 1961 *Arms Control: Issues for the Public.* Prentice Hall, Englewood Cliffs, New Jersey

HIRST F W 1937 *Armaments: The Race and the Crisis.* Cobden-Sanderson, London

HOWARD 1983 *Nuclear, Weapons and the Preservation of Peace.* Liverpool UP

INOZEMTSEV N N et al. 1980 *Peace and Disarmament.* Progress, Moscow

ISARD W 1992 *Economics of Arms Reduction and the Peace Process.* North-Holland

ISARD W, SMITH C 1988 *Arms Races, Arms Control, and Conflict Analysis: Contributions from Peace Science and Peace Economics.* Cambridge UP, New York

ISARD W 1989 *Arms Races, Arms Control and Conflict Analysis.* Cambridge UP

JACK H A 1978 *Disarmament Workbook: The UN Special Session and Beyond.* World Conference on Religion and Peace, New York

JACK H 1983 *Disarm—or Die: The Second UN Special Session on Disarmament.* World Conference on Religion and Peace, New York

JOLLY R (ed.) 1978 - see *Part 9.1: Peace and Economics*

KAHAN J H 1975 *Security in the Nuclear Age.* Brookings Institution, Washington, DC

KALDOR M, EIDE A (eds.) 1979 *The World Military Order: The Impact of Military Technology on the Third World.* Macmillan, London

KALYADIN A, KADE G (eds.) 1976 *Detente and Disarmament: Problems and Perspectives.* Gazzetta, Vienna
See also *Part 9.2: Peace and Politics*

KARP R C 1991 *Security with Nuclear Weapons?* Oxford UP

KARSH E 1994 *Israel at the Crossroads.* British Academic

KOKOSKI R 1996 *Technology and the Proliferation of Nuclear Weapons.* Oxford UP

KOLOWICZ R, GALLAGHER M P, LAMBETH B S 1970 *The Soviet Union and Arms Control: A Superpower Dilemma.* Johns Hopkins, Baltimore, Maryland

LALL A S 1964 *Negotiating Disarmament: The 18 Nation Disarmament Conference: The First 2 Years 1962-1964.* Cornell University, Ithaca, New York

LATTER R 1993 *Controlling the Arms Trade.* HMSO

LEAGUE OF NATIONS LIBRARY - see *Part 1: Peace - General, including Peace Bibliographies*

LEFEVER E W (ed.) 1962 *Arms and Arms Control: A Symposium.* Praeger, New York

LEFEVER E W 1979 *Nuclear Arms in the Third World.* Brookings Institution, Washington, DC

LEMARCHAND G A 1988 *Scientists, Peace and Disarmament.* World Scientific

LLOYD L, SIMS N A - see *Part 1: Peace - General, including Peace Bibliographies*

LODGAARD S 1990 *Naval Arms Control.* Sage London

LUNDIN S J 1991 *Views on Possible Verification Measures for the Biological Weapons Convention.* Oxford UP

MACKAY L, FORNBACH D (ed.) 1983 *Nuclear-Free Defence: A Symposium.* Heretic Books, London

MCKERCHER B J C 1992 *Arms Limitation and Disarmament.* Praeger Pub.

MCKNIGHT A, SUTER K 1983 *The Forgotten Treaties: A Practical Plan for World Disarmament.* Law Council of Australia, Melbourne

MADARAGA S DE 1967 *Disarmament.* Kennikat Press, Port Washington, N.Y

MALCUZYNSKI K 1964 *The Gomulka Plan for a Nuclear Armaments Freeze in Central Europe.* Western Press Agency, Warsaw

MALLMANN W 1995 *Armament and Disarmament in the 1980s.* Berg

MAZARR M J 1994 *Toward a Nuclear Peace.* Macmillan Press

MELMAN S (ed.) 1958 *Inspection for Disarmament.* Columbia University Press, New York

MELMAN S 1962 *The Peace Race.* Gollancz, London

MELMAN S 1962 - see *Part 9.1: Peace and Economics*

MINTZ A 1992 *Defense, Welfare and Growth.* Routledge

MOCH J 1955 *Human Folly: To Disarm or Perish.* Gollancz, London

MYERS D P 1932 *World Disarmament: Its Problems and Prospects.* World Peace Foundation, Boston, Massachusetts

MYRDAL A 1976 *The Game of Disarmament: How the United States and Russia Run the Arms Race.* Pantheon Books, New York

NOEL-BAKER P 1927 *Disarmament.* Hogarth Press, London

NOEL-BAKER P 1958 *The Arms Race: A Programme For World Disarmament.* Atlantic Books, London

NOEL BAKER P 1979 *The First World Disarmament Conference 1932-33: And Why it Failed.* Pergamon, Oxford

NUTTING A 1959 *Disarmament: An Outline of the Negotiations.* Oxford University Press, London

PALME O et al. 1982 *Common Security: A Programme for Disarmament. The Report of the Independent Commission on Disarmament and Security Issues.* Pan, London

PERLO V 1963 *Militarism and Industry: Arms Profiteering in the Missile Age.* Lawrence and Wishart, London

PFALTZGRAFF R L (ed.) 1974 *Contrasting Approaches to Strategic Arms Control.* D. C. Heath, Lexington, Massachusetts

PRIMARKOV E et al. 1977 *International Detente and Disarmament: Contributions by Finnish and Soviet Scholars.* Tampere Peace Research Institute, Tampere
See also *Part 9.2: Peace and Politics*

PRINS G - see *Part 3.2: Peace Movement, Contemporary*

PURSELL C W JR (ed.) 1972 *The Military-Industrial Complex.* Harper and Row, New York

RAMBERG B 1993 *Arms Control without Negotiation: from the Cold War to the New World Order.* Lynne Rienner

RANA S (ed.) 1981 *Obstacles to Disarmament and Ways of Overcoming Them.* UNESCO Press, Paris

ROTBLAT J 1995 *A Nuclear-Weapon-Free World.* Westview Press

RUSSETT B 1970 *What Price Vigilance? The Burdens of National Defence.* Yale University Press, New Haven, Connecticut

SCHMIDT R K B, GRABOWSKY A (eds.) 1933 *The Problems of Disarmament.* Carl Haymanns, Berlin

SIBLEY M Q 1962 *Unilateral Initiatives and Disarmament.* American Friends Service Committee, Philadelphia, Pennsylvania

SIMS N A 1979 *Approaches to Disarmament: An Introductory Analysis.* Quaker Peace and Service, London

SINGER J D 1962 *Deterrence, Arms Control and Disarmament.* Ohio State University Press, Columbus, Ohio

SMITH R 1927 *General Disarmament or War?* Allen and Unwin, London

SOUTHWOOD P M 1990 *If Peace Breaks out, Disarming Military Industries.* Macmillan Press

STIPCICH S 1992 *The Nuclear Winter and the New Defense Systems: Problems and Perspectives.* World Scientific

STOCKHOLM INTERNATIONAL PEACE RESEARCH INSTITUTE (SIPRI) YEAR BOOKS - 1968/69 onwards. *World Armaments and Disarmament.* Shorter editions of the SIPRI Year Books Published as: *The Arms Race and Arms Control.* Taylor and Francis, London

SUR S 1991 *Disarmament Agreements and Negotiations.* Dartmouth

TALBOTT S 1979 *End Game: The Inside Story of SALT II.* Harper and Row, London

TATE M 1942 *The Disarmament Illusion: The Movement for a Limitation of Armaments to 1907.* Macmillan, New York

THEE M (ed.) 1981 *Armaments, Arms Control and Disarmament: A UNESCO Reader for Disarmament Education.* UNESCO Press, Paris

THORSSON I 1984 *In Pursuit of Disarmament: Conversion in Sweden*, Vol. 1. Liber, Stockholm See also *Part 9.1: Peace and Economics*

UN 1989 *The Prevention of Geographical Proliferation of Nuclear Weapons: Nuclear-Weapon-Free Zones and Zones of Peace in the Southern Hemisphere.* United Nations

UN 1993 *Disarmament New Realities.* United Nations

UN 1994 *Disarmament Topical Papers.* United Nations

UNITED NATIONS DEPARTMENT OF POLITICAL AND SECURITY COUNCIL AFFAIRS 1970 *The United Nations and Disarmament 1945-1970.* United Nations, New York

UNITED NATIONS SECRETARIAT - see *Part 1: Peace - General, including Peace Bibliographies*

UNITED STATES DEPARTMENT OF STATE - see *Part 1: Peace - General, including Peace Bibliographies*

UNITED STATES LIBRARY OF CONGRESS - see *Part 1: Peace - General, including Peace Bibliographies*

WALLENSTEEN P (ed.) 1978 *Experiences in Disarmament.* Department of Peace and Conflict Research, Uppsala University, Uppsala

WARBURG J P 1961 *Disarmament: the Challenge of the Nineteen Sixty.* New York

WESTON B (ed.) 1984 *Towards Nuclear Disarmament and Global Security.* Westview, Boulder, Colorado

WILLRICH M, RHINELANDER J B (eds.) 1974 *SALT: The Moscow Agreements and Beyond.* Free Press, New York

WILSON A 1983 *The Disarmers Handbook of Military Technology and Organization.* Penguin, Harmondsworth

YORK H F (ed.) 1974 *Arms Control.* W. H. Freeman, San Francisco, California

YORK H F - see *Part 3.2: Peace Movement, Contemporary*

YOUNG E 1972 *A Farewell to Arms Control?* Penguin, Harmondsworth

YOUNG W 1959 *Strategy for Survival: First Steps in Nuclear Disarmament.* Penguin, Harmondsworth

Part 5

Peace Advocates — Autobiographies and Biographies

ALEXANDER H 1984 *Gandhi Through Western Eyes.* New Society, Philadelphia, Pennsylvania

ANDREWS C F 1930 *Mahatma Gandhi: His Own Story.* Macmillan, New York

ANET D 1974 *Pierre Ceresole: Passionate Peacemaker.* Macmillan, Delhi

ANGELL N 1952 *After All: The Autobiography of Norman Angell.* Hamish Hamilton, London

APPLETON L 1889 *Memoirs of Henry Richard, The Apostle of Peace.* Trubner, London

ASHE G 1968 *Gandhi: A Study in Revolution.* Heinemann, London

BERRIGAN D 1973 *America is Hard to Find.* SPCK, London

BIRUKOFF P 1911 *The Life of Tolstoy.* Cassell, London

BRITTAIN V 1933 *Testament of Youth: Autobiography 1900-1925.* Gollancz, London

BRITTAIN V 1957 *Testament of Experience: Autobiography 1925-1950.* Gollancz, London

BROCKWAY F 1942 *Inside the Left.* Allen and Unwin, London

BROCKWAY F 1963 *Outside the Right.* Allen and Unwin, London

CHATFIELD C 1976 *Devere Allen, Life and Writings.* Garland Pub., New York

CHOUE Y S 1983 *Toward Oughtopia.* Institute of International Peace Studies, Kyung Hee University Press, Seoul

COVELL C 1997 *Kant, Peace & Liberalism.* Macmillan Press

CROZIER F P (Brig. Gen.) 1937 *The Men I Killed.* Michael Joseph, London

CURTI M 1937 *The Learned Blacksmith: The Letters and Journals of Elihu Burritt.* Wilson-Erickson, New York

DAVEY C J 1960 *Kagawa of Japan.* Epworth, London

DAVIS A F 1973 *American Heroine: The Life and Legend of Jane Addams.* Oxford University Press, New York

DAVIS A F 1976 *Jane Addams on Peace, War and International Understanding, 1988-1932.* Garland Pub., New York

DAY D 1963 *Loaves and Fishes.* Gollancz, London

DAY D 1972 *On Pilgrimage: The Sixties.* Curtis, New York

DEL VASTO L 1956 *Gandhi to Vinoba: The New Pilgrimage.* Rider, London

DERLETH A 1963 *Concord Rebel: A Life of Henry David Thoreau.* Chilton, Philadelphia, Pennsylvania

DUNGEN P V D 1990 *From Erasmus to Tolstoy.* Greenwood Press

DYER A S 1879 *A Hero from the Forge: A Biographical Sketch of Elihu Burritt.* Dyer Bros., London

EINSTEIN A 1949 *The World as I See it.* Watts, London

FOX G 1905 *Journal.* Pitman, London

FURLONG M 1980 *Merton: A Biography.* Collins, London

GALLIE W B 1978 *Philosophers of Peace and War: Kant, Clausewitz, Marx, Engels and Tolstoy.* Cambridge University Press, Cambridge, New York

GANDHI M K 1966 *The Story of My Experiments With Truth: An Autobiography.* Navajivan, Ahmedabad

GILLETT N 1965 *Men Against War.* Gollancz, London

GOWER J 1963 *The English Works of John Gower.* Early English Text

HENNACY A 1968 *The Book of Ammon.* Author publ., Salt Lake City, Utah

HENTOFF N 1963 *Peace Agitator: The Story of A. J. Muste.* Macmillan, New York

HENTOFF N (ed.) 1967 *The Essay of A. J. Muste.* Bobbs-Merrill, New York

HOPE M, YOUNG J 1977 *The Struggle for Humanity: Agents of Nonviolent Change in a Violent World.* Orbis, Maryknoll, New York

HUGHES W R 1964 *Indomitable Friend: The Life of Corder Catchpool 1883-1952.* Housmans, London

JONES T C 1972 *George Fox's Attitude Toward War.* Academic Fellowship, Annapolis, Maryland

KEYSERLINGK R W 1972 *Patriots of Peace: De Gasperi, Adenauer and Schuman.* C. Smythe, Gerrards Cross

KING C S 1970 *My Life With Martin Luther King Jr.* Hodder and Stoughton, London

LAMBAKIS S J 1993 *Winston Churchill—Architect of Peace.* Greenwood Press

LANSBURY G 1938 *My Quest for Peace.* Michael Joseph, London

LONDON J, ANDERSON H 1971 *So Shall Ye Reap: The Story of Cesar Chavez and the Farm Workers' Movement.* Cromwell, New York

LUTHULI A 1962 *Let My People Go: An Autobiography.* Collins, London

MCNEISH J 1965 *Fire Under the Ashes: The Life of Danilo Dolci.* Hodder and Stoughton, London

MILLER N C (ed.) 1973 *Sir Randal Cremer: His Life and Work.* Garland Pub., New York

MILLER W R 1968 *Martin Luther King Jr.* Weybright and Talley, New York

NARAYAN S 1970 *Vinoba: His Life and Work.* Popular Prakashan, Bombay

NATHAN O, NORDEN H (eds.) 1968 *Einstein on Peace.* Schocken, New York

NEARING S 1972 *The Making of a Radical: A Political Autobiography.* Harper and Row, New York

NORDHOLT J W S 1991 *Woodrow Wilson.* Univ. of California Press

PAYNE R 1969 *The Life and Death of Mahatma Gandhi.* Bodley Head, London

PIERCE E L 1881 *Memoir and Letters of Charles Sumner*, 4 vols. Roberts Bros. Boston, Massachusetts

PIRE D 1960 *Europe of The Heart: The Autobiography of Dominique Pire.* Hutchinson, London

PLAYNE C E 1936 *Bertha von Suttner and the Struggle to Avert World War.* Allen and Unwin, London

PLOWMAN M 1944 *Bridge into the Future: Letters of Max Plowman.* Andrew Dakers, London

PURI R S 1987 *Gandhi on War and Peace.* Praeger, New York

RANDALL M M 1964 *Improper Bostonian: Emily Greene Balch.* Twayne, New York

REYNOLDS R 1972 *The Wisdom of John Woolman.* Friends Home Service Committee, London

ROBINSON J A O 1981 *Abraham Went Out: A Biography of A. J. Muste.* Temple University Press, Philadelphia, Pennsylvania

RUSSELL B - see *Part 3.2: Peace Movement, Contemporary*

SAMPSON R V 1973 *Tolstoy: The Discovery of Peace.* Heinemann, London

SCHLESSINGER B S 1996 *The Who's Who of Nobel Prize Winners.* Oryx Press

SCHUCK H, SOHLMAN R 1929 *The Life of Alfred Nobel.* Heinemann, London

SCHWEITZER A 1935 *My Life and Thought: An Autobiography.* Allen and Unwin, London

SCOTT C 1977 *Dick Sheppard: A Biography.* Hodder and Stoughton, London

SOPER D 1984 *Calling for Action: An Autobiographical Enquiry.* Robson Books, London

TIMS M 1961 *Jane Addams of Hull House.* Allen and Unwin, London

TREVELYAN G M 1913 *The Life of John Bright.* Constable, London

TROYAT H 1970 *Tolstoy.* Pelican, Harmondsworth

TUCKERMAN B 1893 *William Jay and the Constitutional Movement for the Abolition of Slavery.* Dodd, Mead, New York

TWAIN M 1992 *Mark Twain's Weapons of Satire.* Syracuse University

VAN DEN DUNGEN P 1977 *A Bibliography of the Pacifist Writings of Jean De Bloch.* Housmans, London

VON SUTTNER B 1910 *Memoirs of Bertha von Suttner*, 2 vols. Ginn, Boston, Massachusetts Reprinted 1972 Garland, New York

WALWORTH A 1986 *Wilson and His Peacemakers.* W W North

WEBER T 1995 *Gandhi's Peace Army.* Syracuse UP

WEINBERG A, WEINBERG L (eds.) 1963 *Instead of Violence.* Grossman, New York

WELLOCK W 1961 *Off the Beaten Track: Adventures in the Art of Living.* Sarvodaya Prachuralaya, Tan Jore

WELSH J M 1995 *Edmund Burke and International Relations: the Commonwealth of Europe and the Crusade Against the French Revolution.* Houndmills, Basingstoke, Hampshire: Macmillan Press, New York, St. Martin's Press, in association with St. Antonys College, Oxford

Part 6

Pacifism

ALEXANDER H 1939 *The Growth of the Peace Testimony of the Society of Friends.* Friends Peace Committee, London

ALLEN C 1916 *Conscription and Conscience.* No Conscription Council, London

ALLEN D 1929 *Pacifism in the Modern World.* Doubleday, New York

AMERICAN FRIENDS SERVICE COMMITTEE 1955 *Speak Truth to Power.* AFSC, Philadelphia, Pennsylvania

BARRETT C 1987 *Peace Together: a Vision of Christian Pacifism.* James Clarke & Co

BEATON G 1943 *Four Years of War.* War Resisters' International, Enfield

BEEVOR H 1938 *Peace and Pacifism.* Centenary Press, London

BELL J (ed.) 1935 *We Did Not Fight.* Cobden Sanderson, London

BERKMAN J A 1967 *Pacifism in England: 1914-1939.* Ph.D Dissertation, Yale University, New Haven, Connecticut

BING H 1943 *Pacifists over the World: A Record of the Growth of a World Pacifist Fellowship.* Peace News, London

BING H 1972 *The Historical and Philosophical Background of Modern Pacifism.* War Resisters' International, London

BLAMIRES E P 1958 *War Tests the Church.* Fellowship of Reconciliation, London

BOULTON D 1967 *Objection Overruled.* MacGibbon and Kee, London

BRINTON H 1958 *The Peace Testimony of the Society of Friends.* American Friends Service Committee, Philadelphia, Pennsylvania

BRITTAIN V 1942 *Humiliation with Honour.* Andrew Dakers, London

BRITTAIN V 1964 *The Rebel Passion.* Allen and Unwin, London

BROCK P 1968 *Pacifism in the United States: From the Colonial Era to the First World War.* Princeton University Press, Princeton, New Jersey

BROCK P 1970 *Twentieth-Century Pacifism.* Van Nostrand Reinhold, New York

BROCK P 1972 *Pacifism in Europe to 1914.* Princeton University Press, Princeton, New Jersey

BROCK P 1981 *The Roots of War Resistance: Pacifism from the Early Church to Tolstoy.* Fellowship of Reconciliation, New York

CADOUX C J 1940 *Christian Pacifism Re-examined.* Blackwell, Oxford
See also *Part 9.4: Peace and Religion*

CATCHPOOL C 1941 *Letters of a Prisoner: For Conscience Sake.* Allen and Unwin, London

CEADEL M 1980 *Pacifism in Britain, 1914-1945.* Clarendon Press, Oxford

CHATFIELD C 1973 *For Peace and Justice: Pacifism in America 1914-1941.* Beacon Press, Boston, Massachusetts

CLARK R 1983 *Does the Bible Teach Pacifism?* Marshall Morgan and Scott, London
See also *Part 9.4: Peace and Religion*

COMFORT A (no date) *Peace and Disobedience.* Peace News, London

COMMUNITY SERVICE COMMITTEE 1938 *Community in Britain.* Community Service Committee, West Byfleet

COOPER S (ed.) 1973 *Voices of French Pacifism*. Garland, New York

CROMARTIE M 1990 *Peace Betrayed: Essays on Pacifism and Politics*. Ethics & Pub Policy

DAVIES G M L 1946 *Essays Towards Peace*. Sheppard Press, London

DONINGTON R, DONINGTON B 1936 *The Citizen Faces War*. Gollancz, London

DOTY H - see *Part 1: Peace - General, including Peace Bibliographies*

FAINLIGHT L 1960 *You Are Not Powerless*. Broadacre Books, Bradford

FERGUSON J (ed.) 1954 *Studies in Christian Social Commitment*. James Clarke, Cambridge

FINN J 1967 *Protest: Pacifism and Politics*. Random House, New York
See also *Part 9.2: Peace and Politics*

GANDHI M K 1949 *For Pacifists*. Navajivan, Ahmedabad

GRAHAM J W 1922 *Conscription and Conscience: A History 1916-1919*. Allen and Unwin, London

GRAY A H 1938 *Love: The One Solution*. Rich and Cowan, London

HASSLER A 1958 *Diary of a Self-Made Convict*. Fellowship of Reconciliation, New York

HAUGHAN J 1942 *Three Decades of War Resistance: The War Resisters' League*. War Resisters' League, New York

HAYES D 1949 *Challenge of Conscience*. Allen and Unwin, London

HAYES D 1949 *Conscription Conflict*. Sheppard Press, London

HEATH C *Pacifism in Time of War 1914-1948*. Headley Bros., London

HENGEL M 1971 *Was Jesus a Revolutionist?* Fortress Press, Philadelphia, Pennsylvania

HIBBERT G K (ed.) 1936 *The New Pacifism*. Allenson, London

HIRST M 1923 *The Quakers in Peace and War*. Swarthmore Press, London
See also *Part 9.4: Peace and Religion*

HOLL K (ed.) 1972 *Voices of German Pacifism*. Garland, New York

HOLL K, CHICKERING R (ed.) 1972 *Voices of German Pacifism*. Garland Pub., New York

HOLMES J H 1916 *New Wars for Old: Being a Statement of Radical Pacifism in Terms of Force vs Non-Resistance*. Dodd, Mead, New York

HORNUS J-M 1980 *It is Not Lawful for Me to Fight*. Herald Press, Scottsdale, Pennsylvania

HORSCH J 1931 *The Hutterian Brethren 1528-1931: A Story of Martyrdom and Loyalty*. Herald Press, Scottdale, Pennsylvania
See also *Part 9.4: Peace and Religion*

HORST S 1967 *Mennonites in the Confederacy: A Study of Pacifism during the Civil War*. Herald Press, Scottdale, Pennsylvania
See also *Part 9.4: Peace and Religion*

HOUSMAN L 1940 *The Preparation of Peace*. Cape, London

HUXLEY A 1936 *What Are You Going To Do About It?* Chatto and Windus, London

HUXLEY A 1937 *An Encyclopaedia of Pacifism*. Chatto and Windus, London

HYATT J - see *Part 1: Peace - General, including Peace Bibliographies*

INGRAM K 1939 *The Defeat of War: Can Pacifism Achieve It?* Allen and Unwin, London

JOAD C E M 1939 *Why War?* Penguin, Harmondsworth

KNOWLES G W (ed.) 1927 *Quakers and Peace*. Grotius Society, London
See also *Part 9.4: Peace and Religion*

LEE U - see *Part 9.4: Peace and Religion*

LEWIS J 1940 *The Case Against Pacifism.* Allen and Unwin, London

LITHERLAND A 1978 *War Under Judgment.* Fellowship of Reconciliation, London

LONG EL JR 1968 *War and Conscience in America.* Westminster, Philadelphia, Pennsylvania

MACGREGOR G H C 1960 *The New Testament Basis of Pacifism.* Fellowship of Reconciliation, New York
See also *Part 9.4: Peace and Religion*

MACLACHLAN L 1947 *Defeat Triumphant.* Fellowship of Reconciliation, London

MARTIN D A 1965 *Pacifism: A Historical and Sociological Study.* Routledge and Kegan Paul, London

MENDL W 1974 *Prophets and Reconcilers: Reflections on the Quaker Peace Testimony.* Friends Home Service, London
See also *Part 9.4: Peace and Religion*

MEYER P (ed.) 1966 *The Pacifist Conscience.* Rupert Hart-Davies Ltd, London

MILNE A A - see *Part 1: Peace - General, including Peace Bibliographies*

MORRISEY W 1996 *A Political Approach to Pacifism.* Edwin Mellen Press

MORRISON S 1962 *I Renounce War: The Story of the Peace Pledge Union.* Sheppard Press, London

MORRISON S 1952 *Plain Words on War.* Peace News, London

MUMFORD P S 1937 *An Introduction to Pacifism.* Cassell, London

MURRY J M 1937 *The Necessity of Pacifism.* Cape, London

MURRY J M 1940 *The Brotherhood of Peace.* Peace News, London

MUSTE A J 1947 *Not by Might.* Harper, London

NELSON J 1967 *Peace Prophets: American Pacifist Thought 1919-1941.* University of North Carolina, Chapel Hill, North Carolina

NIEBUHR R 1963 *Moral Man and Immoral Society.* SCM Press, London

NIEBUHR R 1940 *Why the Christian Church is Not Pacifist.* SCM Press, London

NORWEGIAN NOBEL INSTITUTE - see *Part 1: Peace - General, including Peace Bibliographies*

NUTTALL G F 1958 *Christian Pacifism in History.* Blackwell, Oxford
See also *Part 9.4: Peace and Religion*

PACIFIST RESEARCH BUREAU - see *Part 1: Peace - General, including Peace Bibliographies*

PAGE K 1937 *Must We Go To War?* Farrar and Rinehart, New York

PARTRIDGE F 1983 *A Pacifist's War.* Robin Clark, London

PEACE PLEDGE UNION 1940 *Pacifists at Bow Street: A Full Report of Proceedings Under the Defence Regulations Against Offices and Members of the PPU, June 1940.* Peace Pledge Union London

PEACE PLEDGE UNION 1958 *Pacifism: A Declaration of Policy and Principles Intended to Explain what Pacifists Believe and to Remove Prevailing Errors Regarding Pacifism.* Peace Pledge Union, London

PECK J 1969 *Underdogs Versus Upperdogs.* Greenleaf, New Hampshire

PLOWMAN M 1936 *The Faith Called Pacifism.* Dent, London

PLOWMAN M 1942 *The Right to Live.* Dakers, London

POLLARD F E 1953 *War and Human Values.* Peace News, London

RAE J 1970 *Conscience and Politics: The British Government and the Conscientious Objectors to Military Service 1916-1919.* Oxford University Press, London

RAVEN C 1938 *War and the Christian.* SCM Press, London

RAVEN C E 1951 *The Theological Basis of Christian Pacifism.* Fellowship of Reconciliation, New York
See also *Part 9.4: Peace and Religion*

RICHARDS L 1936 *The Christian's Alternative to War.* Student Christian Movement, London
See also *Part 9.4: Peace and Religion*

RICHARDS L 1948 *Christian Pacifism after Two World Wars.* Independent Press, London
See also *Part 9.4: Peace and Religion*

ROTH H - see *Part 1: Peace - General, including Peace Bibliographies*

RUSSELL B 1936 *Which Way to Peace?* Michael Joseph, London

SHEPPARD H R L 1935 *We Say No.* John Murray, London

SCHLISSEL L (ed.) - see *Part 3.1: Peace Movement, History*

SIBLEY M 1964 *Revolution and Violence.* Peace News, London

SIBLEY M 1971 *The Political Theories of Modern Pacifism.* Youth Association of Peace Pledge Union, London

SIBLEY M, JACOB P E 1952 *Conscription of Conscience.* Cornell University, Ithaca, New York

SKINNER J A - see *Part 7: Nonviolence*

SMITH C H (no date) *Christian Peace: 400 Years of Mennonite Peace Principles and Practice.* Mennonite Church of North America
See also *Part 9.4: Peace and Religion*

SPENCER S 1928 *Pacifism in Theory and Practice.* Henderson, Edinburgh

STEVENSON L 1929 *Towards a Christian International.* International Fellowship of Reconciliation, Paris

TAYLOR R 1988 *Against the Bomb.* Clarendon Press

TOLSTOI L 1951 *The Kingdom of God and Peace Essays.* Oxford University Press, London

TOWILL E S, FAULKER T E 1939 *Pacifism For Today and Tomorrow.* Peace Book Co., London

TURNER A - see *Part 1: Peace - General, including Peace Bibliographies*

UNDERHILL H 1971 *Pacifism: An Introductory Perspective.* Peace Pledge Union, London

WALKER F A 1940 *The Blunder of Pacifism.* Hodder and Stoughton, London

WELLOCK W 1916 *Pacifism.* Blackfriars, Manchester

WHITNEY N 1966 *Experiments in Community.* Pendle Hill, Wallingford, Pennsylvania

WOODCOCK G 1947 *The Basis of Communal Living.* Freedom Press, London

WOODCOCK G, AVAKUMOVIC I 1968 *The Doukhobours.* Faber, London

YODER J H 1981 *Nevertheless.* Herald Press, Scottsdale, Pennsylvania

Part 7

Nonviolence

AMERICAN FRIENDS SERVICE COMMITTEE 1967 *In Place of War: An Inquiry into Nonviolent National Defense.* Grossman, New York

ANDREWS C F 1930 *Mahatma Gandhi's Ideas Including Selections From His Writings.* Macmillan, New York

BALLOU A - see *Part 2: Peace Classics/Peace Plans*

BEDAU H A 1969 *Civil Disobedience Theory and Practice.* Pegasus, New York

BELL R G 1959 *Alternative to War.* James Clarke, London

BELL R G 1968 *Rhodesia: Outline of a Non-violent Strategy To Resolve the Crisis.* Housmans, London

BERGFELDT L - see *Part 1: Peace - General, including Peace Bibliographies*

BHAVE V 1958 *Swaraj Sastra: The Principles of a Nonviolent Political Order.* Sarva Seva Sangh, Varanasi

BHAVE V 1961 *Shanti Sena.* Sarva Seva Sangh, Varanasi

BOAS J H 1945 *Religious Resistance in Holland.* Allen and Unwin, London

BONDURANT J V 1971 *Conquest of Violence: The Gandhian Philosophy of Conflict.* University of California Press, Berkeley, California

BOSE N K 1947 *Studies in Gandhism.* Indian Associated, Calcutta

BOSERUP A, MACK A 1974 *War without Weapons: Non violence in National Defence.* Frances Pinter, London

BRANT S 1955 *The East German Uprising, 17th June 1953.* Thames and Hudson, London

BROCKWAY A F 1921 *Non-Cooperation in Other Lands.* Tagore, Madras

CAMARA H 1971 *Spiral of Violence.* Sheed and Ward, London

CARTER A 1962 *Direct Action.* Peace News, London

CARTER A, HOGGETT D, ROBERTS A - see *Part 1: Peace - General, including Peace Bibliographies*

CASE C M 1923 *Non-violent Coercion: A Study in Methods of Social Pressure.* Century, New York

CLARK H et al. 1984 *Preparing for Nonviolent Direct Action.* Peace News/Campaign for Nuclear Disarmament, Nottingham

CROOK W H 1931 *The General Strike: A Study of Labor's Tragic Weapon in Theory and Practice.* University of North Carolina Press, Chapel Hill, North Carolina

DASGUPTA S 1968 *A Great Society of Small Communities: The Story of India's Land Gift Movement.* Sarva Seva Sangh, Varanasi

DE JONG L, STOPPELMAN J W 1943 *The Lion Rampant: The Story of Holland's Resistance to the Nazis.* Querido, New York

DUNN T - see *Part 1: Peace - General, including Peace Bibliographies*

EBERT T 1970 *Gewaltfreier Aufstand: Alternative zum Bürgerkrieg* [Nonviolent Insurrection: Alternative to Civil War]. Fischer Bucherei, Frankfurt am Main

ERIKSON E H 1970 *Gandhi's Truth: On the Origins of Militant Nonviolence.* Faber and Faber, London

European Resistance Movements 1939-1945, Vol. 1: *1960 Proceedings of the First International Conference on the History of the Resistance Movements, September 1958.* Pergamon, Oxford

European Resistance Movements 1939-1945, Vol. 2: *1964 Proceedings of the Second International Conference on the History of the Resistance Movements, March 1961*. Pergamon, Oxford

FEN A 1943 *Nazis in Norway*. Penguin, Harmondsworth

FISCHER L (ed.) 1963 *The Essential Gandhi: An Anthology*. Allen and Unwin, London

FLENDER H 1963 *Rescue In Denmark*. W. H. Allen, London

FORTAS A 1968 *Concerning Dissent and Civil Disobedience*. New American Library, New York

FRY A R 1957 *Victories Without Violence*. Dobson, London

FULFORD R 1957 *Votes for Women: The Story of a Struggle*. Faber, London

GANDHI M K 1958 *Sarvodaya: The Welfare of All*. Navajivan, Ahmedabad

GANDHI M K 1958 *Satyagraha: Non-violent Resistance*. Navajivan, Ahmedabad

GANDHI M K 1960-1962 *Non-violence in Peace And War*, 2 Vols. Navajivan, Ahmedabad

GANDHI M K 1961 *Satyagraha In South Africa*. Navajivan, Ahmedabad

GEDYE G E R 1930 *The Revolver Republic: France's Bid for the Rhine*. Arrowsmith, London

GEERAERTS G (ed.) 1976 *Possibilities of Civilian Defense in Western Europe*. Polemological Centre of the Free University of Brussels, Brussels

GREGG R B 1959 *A Discipline For Nonviolence*. Navajivan, Ahmedabad

GREGG R B 1966 *The Power of Nonviolence*. Schocken Books, New York

HALBERSTAM D 1965 *The Making of a Quagmire*. Bodley Head, London

HALLIE P 1979 *Lest Innocent Blood be Shed*. Joseph, London

HARE A P, BLUMBERG H H (eds.) 1968 *Nonviolent Direct Action: American Cases: Social-Psychological Analyses*. Corpus Books, Washington, DC
See also *Part 9.5: Peace and Psychology*

HILLER E T 1928 *The Strike: A Study in Collective Action*. University of Chicago Press, Chicago, Illinois

HINSHAW C 1956 *Non-violent Resistance: A Nation's Way to Peace*. Pendle Hill, Wallingford, Pennsylvania

HOGGETT D - see *Part 1: Peace - General, including Peace Bibliographies*

HORSBURGH H J N 1968 *Non-violence and Aggression: A Study of Gandhi's Moral Equivalent of War*. Oxford University Press, London

HUGGON J - see *Part 1: Peace - General, including Peace Bibliographies*

KAHN T 1960 *Unfinished Revolution*. Igal Roodenko, New York

KING M L 1964 *Why We Can't Wait*. New American Library, New York

KING M L 1959 *Stride Toward Freedom: The Montgomery Story*. Gollancz, London

KING-HALL S (Sir) 1958 *Defence in the Nuclear Age*. Gollancz, London

KNOWLES K J C 1952 *Strikes: A Study in Industrial Conflict with Special Reference to British Experience Between 1911 and 1947*. Blackwell, Oxford

KOOL V K 1994 *Nonviolence*. Univ Press America

KUMARAPPA J C 1958 *Economy of Permanence: A Quest for a Social Order Based on Nonviolence*. Sarva Seva Sangh, Varanasi
See also *Part 9.1: Peace and Economics*

KUPER L 1956 *Passive Resistance in South Africa*. Cape, London

LAKEY G et al. 1969 *Nonviolent Responses in Social Conflict: A Manual for Trainers*. Friends Peace Committee, Philadelphia, Pennsylvania

LAKEY G 1973 *Strategy for a Living Revolution.* Freeman, San Francisco, California

LAMPE D 1957 *The Savage Canary: The Story of Resistance in Denmark.* Cassell, London

LASKY M H (ed.) 1957 *The Hungarian Revolution: A White Book.* Secker and Warburg, London

LINDBERG N JACOBSEN G, EHRLICH K 1937 *Kamp Uden Vaapen: Ikke-Vold Som Kampmiddel Mod Krig Og Undertrykkelse* [Fight Without Weapons: Nonviolence as a Means of Struggle Against War And Oppression]. Levin and Munksgaard, Copenhagen

LITTELL R (ed.) 1969 *The Czech Black Book Prepared by the Institute of History of the Czechoslovak Academy of Sciences.* Pall Mall Press, London

LONDON J, ANDERSON H - see *Part 5: Peace Advocates - Autobiographies and Biographies*

LUTHULI A 1962 *Let My People Go.* Collins, London

LYND S (ed.) 1966 *Nonviolence in America: A Documentary History.* Bobbs-Merrill, New York

LYTTLE B 1958 *National Defense Thru Nonviolent Resistance.* Regional Office of American Friends Service Committee, Chicago, Illinois

MANDELA N 1965 *No Easy Walk to Freedom: Articles, Speeches and Trial Addresses of Nelson Mandela.* Heinemann, London

MARTIN B - see *Part 3.2: Peace Movement, Contemporary*

MBEKI G 1964 *South Africa: The Peasant's Revolt.* Penguin, Harmondsworth

MILLER W R 1972 *Nonviolence: A Christian Interpretation.* Schocken Books, New York

MILLER W R - see *Part 1: Peace - General, including Peace Bibliographies*

MULLER J-M 1972 *Stratégie de l'action nonviolente* [Strategy of Nonviolent Action]. Fayard, Paris

MUSTE A J 1944 *Nonviolence in an Aggressive World.* Fellowship Publications, New York

NARAYAN J 1965 *Socialism, Sarvodaya and Democracy.* Asia Publishing, London
See also *Part 9.2: Peace and Politics*

OLSON T, CHRISTIANSEN G 1966 *The Grindstone Experiment: Thirty-one Hours.* Canadian Friends Service Committee, Toronto

OPPENHEIMER M, LAKEY G 1965 *A Manual for Direct Action: Strategy and Tactics for Civil Rights and All Other Nonviolent Protest Movements.* Quadrangle Books, Chicago, Illinois

PANKHURST C 1959 *Unshackled: The Story of How We Won the Vote.* Hutchinson, London

PAULLIN T 1944 *Introduction to Nonviolence.* Pacifist Research Bureau, Philadelphia, Pennsylvania

PAX CHRISTI INTERNATIONAL - see *Part 1: Peace - General, including Peace Bibliographies*

PECK J 1962 *Freedom Ride.* Grove Press, New York

PELTON L H 1974 *The Psychology of Nonviolence.* Pergamon, New York
See also *Part 9.5: Peace and Psychology*

PRASAD R 1949 *Satyagraha in Champaran.* Navajivan, Ahmedabad

PYARELAL 1959 *Gandhian Techniques in the Modern World.* Navajivan, Ahmedabad

RANDLE M, CARTER A et al. 1968 *Support Czechoslovakia.* Housmans, London

RAWLINSON R (no date) *The Battle of Larzac.* Fellowship of Reconciliation, New Malden

REGAMEY P 1966 *Nonviolence and the Christian Conscience.* Darton, Longman and Todd, London

ROBERTS A 1970 *Nonviolent Resistance as an Approach to Peace.* World Council of Churches, Geneva

ROBERTS A (ed.) 1969 *Civilian Resistance as a National Defence: Nonviolent Action against Aggression.* Penguin, Harmondsworth

SARVA SEVA SANGH 1957 *Planning for Sarvodaya.* Sarva Seva Sangh, Varanasi

SCHECHTER B 1963 *The Peaceable Revolution: The Story of Nonviolent Resistance.* Houghton Mifflin, Boston, Massachusetts

SCHOLMER J 1954 *Vorkuta.* Weidenfeld and Nicolson, London

SCHWARCZ E 1959 *Paths to Freedom Through Nonviolence: A Study of the East-West Conflict and the Methods of Nonviolent Resistance.* Sensen Verlag, Vienna

SEIFERT H 1965 *Conquest by Suffering: The Process and Prospects of Nonviolent Resistance.* Westminster Press, Philadelphia, Pennsylvania

SETH R 1956 *The Undaunted: The Story of Resistance in Western Europe,* Muller, London

SHARP G 1963 *Tyranny Could Not Quell Them: How Norway's Teachers Defeated Quisling During the Nazi Occupation and What it Means for Unarmed Defence Today.* Peace News, London

SHARP G 1963 *Non-violent Action: An Introductory Outline for Study Groups.* Friends Peace Committee, London

SHARP G 1970 *Exploring Nonviolent Alternatives.* Porter Sargent, Boston, Massachusetts

SHARP G 1973 *The Politics of Nonviolent Action, Part One: Power and Struggle.* Porter Sargent, Boston, Massachusetts

SHARP G 1973 *The Politics of Nonviolent Action, Part Two: The Methods of Nonviolent Action.* Porter Sargent, Boston, Massachusetts

SHARP G 1973 *The Politics of Nonviolent Action, Part Three: The Dynamics of Nonviolent Action.* Porter Sargent, Boston, Massachusetts

SHRIDHARANI K 1939 *War Without Violence: A Study of Gandhi's Method and its Accomplishments.* Gollancz, London

SIBLEY M Q (ed.) 1968 *The Quiet Battle: Writings on the Theory and Practice of Nonviolent Resistance.* Beacon Press, Boston, Massachusetts

SKINNER J A 1959 *Towards A Nonviolent Society.* Peace News, London

SPONSEL L E 1994 *The Anthropology of Peace and Nonviolence.* Lynne Rienner

STEERE D V 1953 *A Manual on the Need, the Organization and the Discipline of Cells for Peace.* Fellowship of Reconciliation, New York

STIEHM J 1972 *Nonviolent Power: Active And Passive Resistance in America.* D. C. Heath, Lexington, Massachusetts

SUHL Y (ed.) 1968 *They Fought Back: The Story of the Jewish Resistance in Nazi Europe.* MacGibbon and Kee, London

SYMONS J 1957 *The General Strike.* Cresset Press, London

TERKELSEN T M 1944 *Front Line in Denmark With a Postscript on D-Day and the 'People's Strike', June-July 1944.* Free Danish, London

THOREAU H D - see *Part 2: Peace Classics/Peace Plans*

TOLSTOY L 1968 *Tolstoy's Writings on Civil Disobedience and Nonviolence.* New American Library, New York

TOLSTOY L 1963 *Letter to a Hindu.* Peace News, London

TROUGHTON E R 1944 *It's Happening Again.* John Gifford, London

URQUHART C (ed.) 1963 *A Matter of Life.* Cape, London

WALKER C C 1961 *Organizing for Nonviolent Direct Action.* Author publ., Cheyney, Pennsylvania

WARBEY W 1945 *Look to Norway.* Secker and Warburg, London

WARMBRUNN W 1963 *The Dutch Under German Occupation, 1940-1945.* Oxford University Press, London

WAR RESISTERS' INTERNATIONAL 1966 *Training in Nonviolence: A Full Documentation of the WRI Study Conference.* War Resisters' International, Enfield

WAR RESISTERS' INTERNATIONAL 1972 *Manifesto for Nonviolent Revolution.* War Resisters' International, Sheffield

WESTIN A F (ed.) 1964 *Freedom Now! The Civil-Rights Struggle in America.* Basic Books, New York

WINDSOR P, ROBERTS A 1969 *Czechoslovakia 1968: Reform, Repression and Resistance.* Chatto and Windus, London

ZINN H 1965 *SNCC: The New Abolitionists.* Beacon Press, Boston, Massachusetts

Part 8

World Order and Internationalism

AKE C 1967 *A Theory of Political Integration.* Dorsey, Homewood, Illinois

ALBROW M 1990 *Globalization, Knowledge and Society.* Sage, London

ALGER C 1978 *The World in Your City, Your City in the World.* Mershon, Columbus, Ohio

ALKER H R 1996 *Rediscoveries and Reformulations.* Cambridge UP

AL N 1995 *International Legal Issues Arising Under the United Nations Decade of International Law.* Martinus Nijhoff

AMERICAN PEACE SOCIETY 1932 *World Affairs.* American Peace, Society, Washington D.C

AMSTUTZ M 1995 *International Conflict and Cooperation.* Wm C Brown

ANDERSON S 1968 *Planning for Diversity and Choice.* MIT Press, Cambridge, Massachusetts

ANGELL R C 1969 *Peace on the March: Transnational Participation.* Van Nostrand Reinhold, New York

ANGELL R C 1979 *The Quest for World Order.* University of Michigan Press, Ann Arbor, Michigan

ARNOLD T 1995 *Reforming the UN.* Royal Ins Int Affair

BAEHR P R 1994 *The United Nations in the 1990s.* Macmillan Press

BAILEY S D 1994 *The UN Security Council and Human Rights.* Macmillan Press

BAILEY S D 1994 *The United Nations.* Macmillan Press

BARTLETT C J 1994 *The Global Conflict.* Longman

BASSETT J S 1919 *Lost Fruits of Waterloo: Views on a League of Nations.* Macmillan, New York

BASSIOUNI M C 1992 *Crimes Against Humanity in International Criminal Law.* Martinus Nijhoff

BEITZ C R, HERMAN T - see *Part 9.2: Peace and Politics*

BENTWICH N 1946 *From Geneva to San Francisco: An Account of the International Organisation of the New Order.* Gollancz, London

BERES L R 1975 *Transforming World Politics: the National Roots of World Peace.* University of Denver, Denver

BERES L R 1981 *People, States and World Order.* F. E. Peacock, Itasca, Illinois

BERES L R, TARG H 1975 *Planning Alternative World Futures: Values, Methods and Models.* Praeger, New York

BERES L R, TARG H R 1978 *Constructing Alternative World Futures: Reordering the Planet.* Schenkman, Cambridge, Massachusetts

BERNIER I 1973 *International Legal Aspects of Federalism.* Longman, London

BERTSCH G K (ed.) 1982 *Global Policy Studies.* Sage, Beverly Hills, California

BHAGWATI J (ed.) 1972 *Economics and World Order from the 1970s to the 1990s.* Macmillan, New York

BLOOMFIELD L P 1964 *International Military Forces: The Question of Peacekeeping in an Armed and Disarming World.* Little, Brown, Boston, Massachusetts

BLOOMFIELD L P 1971 *The Power to Keep Peace, Today and in a World Without War.* World Without War Council, Berkeley, California

BONANATE L 1995 *Ethics and International Politics.* Polity Press

BOUCHER J 1987 *Ethnic Conflict.* Sage London

BOURANTONIS D 1995 *The United Nations in the New World Order.* Macmillan Press

BOURNE R 1964 *War and the Intellectuals.* New York

BOYD A 1992 *An Atlas of World Affairs.* Routledge

BRAUNTHAL J 1980 *History of the International: World Socialism, 1943-68.* Gollancz, London

BRIERLY J L 1963 *The Law of Nations.* Oxford UP

BROWN L 1972 *World Without Borders.* Vintage, New York

BROWN L R 1978 *Redefining National Security.* World Watch Institute, Washington, DC

BROWN M E 1993 *Ethnic Conflict and International Security.* Princeton UP

BROWN S 1974 *New Forces in World Politics.* Brookings Institution, Washington, DC

BUEHRIG E H, LASSWELL H D, LEPAWSKY A (eds.) 1971 *The Search for World Order.* Appleton-Century-Crofts, New York

BULL H 1977 *The Anarchical Society: A Study of Order in World Politics.* Columbia University Press, New York

BURTON J W 1965 *International Relations Theory.* Cambridge University Press, Cambridge

BURTON J W 1972 *World Society.* Cambridge University Press, London

CAMILLERI J A 1976 *Civilization in Crisis: Human Prospects in a Changing World.* Cambridge University Press, New York

CAMPS M 1974 *The Management of Independence.* Council on Foreign Relations, New York

CARNALL G 1965 *To Keep the Peace: The United Nations Peace Force.* Peace New, London

CARNEGIE ENDOWMENT FOR INTERNATIONAL PEACE. DIVISION OF INTERCOURSE AND EDUCATION 1909 *International Conciliation.* American Association for International Conciliation, New York

CHAMBERLIN T C 1918 *World Organization after the World-War: An Omninational Confederation.* University of Chicago Press, Chicago, Illinois

CHEEVER D S, HAVILAND H F JR 1954 *Organizing for Peace: International Organization in World Affairs.* Houghton Mifflin, Boston, Massachusetts

CHESTNUT H 1990 *International Conflict Resolution Using System Engineering.* Pergamon Press

CHOUCRI N, NORTH R C 1975 *Nations in Conflict: National Growth and International Violence.* W. H. Freeman, San Francisco, California

CHOUE Y S 1975 *Reconstruction of the Human Society.* Kyung Hee University Press, Seoul

CHOUE Y S 1979 *Oughtopia.* Kyung Hee University Press, Seoul

CHOUE Y S 1986 *Textbook on World Citizenship.* Kyung Hee University Press, Seoul

CHRISTOPHER P 1994 *Ethics of War and Peace.* Prentice Hall US

CLARK G, SOHN L B 1958 *World Peace Through World Law.* Harvard University Press, Cambridge, Massachusetts

CLARK G, SOHN L B (1960) 1966 *World Peace Through World Law: Two Alternative Plans.* Harvard University Press, Cambridge, Massachusetts

CLARK G, SOHN L B 1973 *Introduction to World Peace Through World Law.* World Without War Publications, Chicago, Illinois

CLAUDE I L 1962 *Power and International Relations.* Random House, New York

CLAUDE I L 1971 *Swords into Plowshares: The Problems and Progress of International Organization,* 4th edn. Random House, New York

CLEMENTS K 1995 *Building International Community.* Allen & Unwin

CLUTTERBUCK R 1993 *International Crisis and Conflict.* Macmillan Press

COBB R W, ELDER C 1970 *International Community: A Regional and Global Study.* Holt, Rinehart and Winston, New York

COMMISSION ON GLOBAL GOVERNANCE 1995 *Issues in Global Governance.* Kluwer Law Internat

COOPER S E (ed.) 1976 *Internationalism in Nineteenth-Century Europe.* Garland, New York

COOPER S E (ed.) 1976 *Internationalism in Nineteenth Century Europe: the Crisis of Ideas and Purpose.* Garland Pub., New York

CORDIER A W, MAXWELL K L (ed.) 1967 *Paths to World Order.* Columbia University Press, New York

CORNISH E 1977 *The Study of the Future.* World Future Society, Washington, DC

COTLER I 1995 *Nuremberg Forty Years Later.* McGill Q UP (UCL)

COUSINS N 1961 *In Place of Folly.* Harper, New York

DAHL N C, WEISNER J B (eds.) 1978 *World Change and World Security.* MIT Press, Cambridge, Massachusetts

DARBY W E 1899 *International Tribunals.* London Peace Society, London

DARBY W E 1904 *International Arbitration.* Dent, London

DEUTSCH K W 1957 *Political Community and the North Atlantic Area: International Organisation in the Light of Historical Experience.* Princeton University Press, Princeton, New Jersey

DICKINSON G L 1917 *The Choice Before Us.* Allen, London

DIEHL P F 1996 *The Politics of Global Governance.* Lynne Rienner

DINSTEIN Y 1996 *War Crimes in International Law.* Martinus Nijhoff

DOLMAN A J 1981 *Resources, Regimes, World Order.* Pergamon, New York

DOUGLAS W O 1971 *International Dissent: Six Steps to World Peace.* Random House, New York

DRAKE J A G 1994 *Integrated Pollution Control.* Royal Soc Chemistry

DUNCAN W R 1994 *Ethnic Nationalism and Regional Conflict.* Westview Press

DUPUY R J 1993 *The Development of the Role of the Security Council/Le Developement du Role du Conseil de Security.* Martinus Nijhoff

DURAS V H 1908 *Universal Peace: Universal Peace by International Government.* Broadway, New York

EASTWOOD P 1992 *Responding to Global Warming.* Berg

EDWARDS D V 1973 *Creating a New World Politics: From Conflict to Cooperation.* David McKay, New York

EKINS P 1992 *A New World Order: Grassroots Movements for Global Change.* Routledge

EL-AYOUTY Y 1994 *The Organization of African Unity After Thirty Years.* Praeger Pub

ELIAS T O 1992 *New Horizons in International Law.* Martinus Nijhoff

ETZIONI A 1962 *The Hard Way to Peace: A New Strategy.* Collier, New York

ETZIONI A 1965 *Political Unification.* Holt, Rinehart and Winston, New York

ETZIONI A, WENGLINSKY M (eds.) 1970 *War and its Prevention.* Harper and Row, New York

FABIAN L L 1971 *Soldiers Without Enemies.* Brookings Institution, Washington, DC

FALK R A 1968 *Legal Order in a Violent World.* Princeton University Press, Princeton, New Jersey

FALK R 1975 *A Study of Future Worlds.* Free Press, New York

FALK R A 1971 *This Endangered Planet: Prospects and Proposals for Human Survival.* Random House, New York

FALK R A 1978 *Nuclear Policy and World Order: Why Denuclearization.* W. H. Freeman, San Francisco, California

FALK R A 1991 *The United Nations and a Just World Order.* Westview Press

FALK R A, MENDLOVITZ S H (eds.) 1966a *The Strategy of World Order*, 4 Vols. Institute for World Order, New York

FALK R A, MENDLOVITZ S H (eds.) 1966b *Toward a Theory of War Prevention.* World Law Fund, New York

FALK R A, MENDLOVITZ S H (eds.) 1973 *Regional Politics and World Order.* W.H. Freeman, San Francisco, California

FALK R A, KIM S, MENDLOVITZ S H (eds.) 1981 *The Strategy of a Just World Order.* Westview Press, Boulder, Colorado

FALK R A, KRATOCHWIL F, MENDLOVITZ S H (eds.) 1981 *A Just World Order and International Law.* Westview Press, Boulder, Colorado

FALK R A, KIM S, MCNEMAR D, MENDLOWITZ S H (eds.) 1981 *United Nations and a Just World Order.* Westview Press, Boulder, Colorado

FELLER G 1981 *Peace and World Order Studies: a Curriculum Guide.* Transnational Academic Program Institute for World Order, New York

FERENCZ B B, KEYES K 1988 *Planethood: the Key to Your Survival and Prosperity.* Vision Book, Coos Bay OR

FERENCZ B B, KEYES K 1991 *Planethood: the Key to Your Future.* Love Line Books, Coos Bay OR

FERGUSON Y H, LAMPORT D E, MANSBACH R W 1976 *The Web of World Politics.* Prentice-Hall, Englewood Cliffs, New Jersey

FETHERSTON A B 1994 *Towards a Theory of United Nations Peacekeeping.* Macmillan Press

FLEMING D F 1961 *The Cold War and its Origins 1917-1960.* Allen and Unwin, London

FOSDICK R B et al. 1920 *The League of Nations Starts.* Macmillan, London

FRYDENBERG P (ed.) 1964 *Peace-Keeping: Experience and Evaluation.* Norwegian Institute of International Affairs, Oslo

FULLER B 1969 *Operating Manual for Spaceship Earth.* Bantam, New York

GAGLIONE A, YESELSON A 1974 *A Dangerous Place: The UN as a Weapon in World Politics.* Grossman, New York

GALTUNG J 1970 *Cooperation in Europe.* Universitetsforlaget, Oslo

GALTUNG J 1980 *The True Worlds: A Transnational Perspective.* Free Press, New York

GALTUNG J 1992 *Global Glasnost.* Hampton Press

GALTUNG J, ORNAUER H (eds.) 1976 *Images of the World in the Year 2000: A Comparative Ten-Nation Study.* Humanities Press, New Jersey

GAREAU F H (ed.) 1962 *The Balance of Power and Nuclear Deterrence.* Houghton Mifflin, Boston, Massachusetts

GARVIN J L 1919 *The Economic Foundations of Peace: Or, the Truer Basis of the League of Nations.* Macmillan, London

GERLE E 1995 *In Search of Global Ethics.* Chartwell-Bratt

GJELSTAD J 1995 *Nuclear Rivalry and International Order.* Sage London

GODOY H, LAGOS G 1977 *Revolution of Being: A Latin American View of the Future.* Free Press, New York

GOODMAN J 1996 *Nationalism and Transnationalism.* Avebury

GORDON W 1995 *The United Nations at the Crossroads of Reform.* M E Sharpe

GRAVES N J 1984 *Teaching for International Understanding, Peace and Human Rights.* UNESCO

GRAY R B (ed.) 1969 *International Security Systems: Concepts of Models of World Order.* Peacock, Itasca, Illinois

GREIG D W 1994 *International Law.* Butterworth Law

GRONOWICZ A, VILLARD O G (ed.) 1983 *Oswald Garrison Villard, the Dilemmas of the Absolute Pacifist in Two World Wars.* Garland Pub., New York

GURR T R 1994 *Ethnic Conflict in World Politics.* Westview Press

HAAS E B 1968 *Beyond the Nation-State: Functionalism and International Organisation.* Stanford University Press, Stanford, California

HANRIEDER W F (ed.) 1987 *Global Peace and Security: Trends and Challenges.* Westview Press, Boulder

HARBOTTLE M 1970 *The Impartial Soldier.* Oxford University Press, London

HARRIS E E 1966 *Annihilation and Utopia: The Principles of International Politics.* Allen and Unwin, London

HASTEDT G 1994 *One World, Many Voices.* Prentice Hall US

HAWLEY E W 1992 *The Great War and the Search for a Modern Order.* Saint Martin's Press

HEIBERG M 1994 *Subduing Sovereignty.* Pinter

HENKIN L 1978 *The Rights of Man Today.* Westview, Boulder, Colorado

HERMAN S 1969 *Eleven Against War: Studies in American Internationalist Thought 1898-1921.* Hoover Institution, Stanford, California
See also *Part 9.3: Peace and History*

HERZ J 1976 *The Nation-State and the Crisis of World Politics.* David McKay, New York

HILL S M 1996 *Peacekeeping and the United Nations.* Dartmouth

HINSLEY F H 1967 *Power and the Pursuit of Peace.* Cambridge University Press, Cambridge

HOBSON J A 1915 *Towards International Government.* Allen and Unwin, London
Reprinted 1971 Garland, New York

HOLLINS E J (ed.) 1966 *Peace is Possible.* Grossman, New York

HOLM H H 1995 *Whose World Order?* Westview Press

HORAK S N 1988 *The First Peace Treaty of World War I.* East Eur Monographs

HOWARD M 1981 *War and the Liberal Conscience.* Oxford University Press, Oxford

HUGHES B B 1993 *International Futures.* Westview Press

HUGHES B B 1993 *International Futures IBM Computer Simulation.* Westview Press

HUGHES H S 1962 *Approach to Peace and Other Essays.* Atheneum, New York

INTERNATIONAL PEACE ACADEMY 1978 *Peacekeeper's Handbook.* International Peace Academy, New York

JACOB P, TOSCANO J V (eds.) 1964 *The Integration of Political Communities.* Lippincott, Philadelphia, Pennsylvania

JACOBSON H 1979 *Networks of Interdependence: International Organisations and the Global Political System.* Knopf, New York

JAMES A 1990 *Peacekeeping in International Politics.* Macmillan Press

JANIS M W 1992 *International Courts for the 21st Century.* Martinus Nijhoff

JENKS C W 1958 *The Common Law of Mankind.* Stevens, London

JENKS C W 1967 *The World Beyond the Charter in Historical Perspective: A Tentative Synthesis of Four Stages of World Organisation.* Rustin House, London

JENKS C W, LARSON A 1965 *Sovereignty Within the Law*. Oceana, New York

JOHANSEN R C 1978 *Toward a Dependable Peace: A Proposal for an Appropriate Security System*. Institute for World Order, New York

JOHANSEN R C 1980 *The National Interest and the Human Interest*. Princeton University Press, Princeton, New Jersey

JOHANSEN R C 1983 *Toward an Alternative Security System*. World Policy Institute, New York

JOHNSEN J E 1941 *International Federation of Democracies (Proposed)*. Wilson, New York

JOLL J 1975 *The Second International, 1889-1914*. Routledge, London

KAHN H 1965 *Thinking about the Unthinkable*. Horizon, New York
See also *Part 10: Peace Research*

KEGLEY JR C W 1995 *The Global Agenda*. McGraw-Hill USA

KEOHANE R, NYE J 1970 *Transnational Relations and World Politics*. Harvard University Press, Cambridge, Massachusetts

KEOHANE T, NYE J 1977 *Power and Interdependence*. Little Brown, Boston, Massachusetts

KHAN L A 1996 *The Extinction of Nation-states*. Kluwer Lay Internat

KIANG J 1992 *One World: the Approach to Permanent Peace*. Ind: One World Pub., Notre Dame

KIM S 1979 *China, the United Nations, and World Order*. Princeton University Press, Princeton, New Jersey

KLARE M T 1994 *Peace and World Security Studies: a Curriculum Guide*. Lynne Rienner

KLEIN B S 1994 *Strategic Studies and World Order*. Cambridge UP

KNORR K, VERBA S 1961 *The International System*. Princeton University Press, Princeton, New Jersey

KOTHARI R 1975 *Footsteps into the Future*. Free Press, New York

KRIESBERG L 1992 *International Conflict Resolution*. Yale UP

KUEHL W F 1969 *Seeking World Order: The United States and International Organization to 1920*. Vanderbilt University Press, Nashville, Tennessee
See also *Part 9.3: Peace and History*

LACKEY D P 1989 *The Ethics of War and Peace*. Prentice Hall US

LADON-LEDERER J J 1963 *International Non-Governmental Organizations*. Sijthoff, Leyden

LALL A 1966 *Modern International Negotiation: Principles and Practice*. Columbia University Press, New York

LANDHEER B, LOENEN J, POLAK F 1971 *World Society*. Martinus Nijhoff, The Hague

LARSON A 1961 *When Nations Disagree: A Handbook on Peace Through Law*. Louisiana State University Press, London

LASZLO E 1974 *A Strategy for the Future: The Systems Approach to World Order*. Braziller, New York

LAUTERPACHT H 1950 *International Law and Human Rights*. Praeger, New York

LAUTERPACHT 1975 *International Law 2 Pt1 Law of Peace*. Cambridge UP

LAWSON S 1996 *The New Agenda for Global Security*. Allen & Unwin

LEAGUE OF NATIONS ASSOCIATION 1932 *A Study Course on the League of Nations*. League of Nations Association, Education Committee, New York

LEAGUE OF NATIONS SECRETARIAT 1930 *Ten Years of World Co-operation*. League of Nations, Geneva

LEE D C 1992 *Toward a Sound World Order*. Greenwood Press

LENTZ T F 1976 *Humatriotism*. Futures Press, St. Louis, Missouri

LEVERMORE C H 1919 *Synopsis of Plans for International Organisation. American Peace Society,* Washington, DC

LLOYD G, WYNNER E 1944 *Searchlight on Peace Plans: Choose Your Road to World Government.* Dutton, New York
Reprinted 1949 in new enlarged edition
See also *Part 2: Peace Classics/Peace Plans*

LONG D 1995 *Towards a New Liberal Internationalism.* Cambridge UP

LOPEZ-REYES R - see *Part 9.5: Peace and Psychology*

LOVELL J P 1974 *The Search for Peace: An Appraisal of Alternative Approaches.* International Studies Association, Pittsburgh, Pennsylvania

LUARD D E T 1968 *Conflict and Peace in the Modern International System.* Little, Brown, Boston, Massachusetts
(Originally published in 1962 as *Peace and Opinion*)

LUARD D E T (ed.) 1970 *International Regulation of Frontier Disputes.* Praeger, New York

LUARD D E T 1977 *International Agencies: The Emerging Framework of Interdependence.* Macmillan, London

LUARD E 1994 *The United Nations.* Macmillan Press

LUNDESTAD G 1994 *The Fall of Great Powers.* Scandinavian UP

LYNN-JONES S M 1995 *Global Dangers.* MIT Press

MACKAY R W G 1940 *Federal Europe.* Michael Joseph, London

MANDLOVITZ S H 1987 *Towards a Just World Peace.* Butterworth Heineman

MCKINLEY R D, LITTLE R 1986 *Global Problems and World Order.* Frances Pinter, London

MCWHINNEY E 1981 *Conflict and Compromise: International Law and World Order in a Revolutionary Age.* Holmes and Meier, New York

MARK M 1965 *Beyond Sovereignty.* Public Affairs Press, Washington DC

MATTER J A - see *Part 9.5: Peace and Psychology*

MATTHEWS R O 1989 *International Conflict and Conflict Management.* Prentice Hall US

MAZRUI A A 1975 *A World Federation of Cultures.* Free Press, New York

MEAD L 1971 *Swords and Ploughshares.* S. Ozer, New York

MEDLOVITZ S H 1975 *On the Creation of a just World Order.* The Free Press, New York

MEEHAN E 1993 *Citizenship and the European Community.* Sage, London

MENDLOVITZ S H (ed.) 1962 *Legal and Political Problems of World Order.* World Law Fund, New York

MENDLOVITZ S H (ed.) 1975 *On the Creation of a Just World Order.* Free Press, New York

MENEGAZZI G 1975 *Laws and Models for a Vital Order and Mutual Development of Peoples.* Palazzo Giuliari, Verona

MENNIS B, SAUVANT K P 1976 *Emerging Forms of Transnational Community.* Lexington Books, Lexington, Massachusetts

MILLARD E L 1961 *Freedom in a Federal World.* CURE (Conference Upon Research and Education in World Government.) Oceana, Dobbs Ferry, New York

MILLER L 1972 *Organizing Mankind.* Holbrook Press, Boston, Massachusetts

MILLIS W 1965 *An End To Arms.* Atheneum, New York

MILLIS W, REAL J 1963 *The Abolition of War.* Macmillan, New York

MINGST K A 1995 *The United Nations in the Post-Cold War Era.* Westview Press

MISCHE P 1978 *Women and World Order.* Global Education Associates, East Orange, New Jersey

MISCHE G, MISCHE P 1977 *Towards a Human World Order.* Paulist Press, New York

MITRANY D 1966 *A Working Peace System.* Quadrangle Books, Chicago, Illinois

MODELSKI G 1972 *Principles of World Politics.* Free Press, New York

MODELSKI G (ed.) 1973 *Multinational Corporations and World Order.* Sage, Beverly Hills, California

MOHAN B 1992 *Global Development.* Praeger Pub

MOLINARI G DE 1904 *The Society of Tomorrow: A Forecast of its Political and Economic Organization.* Putnam's Sons, New York

MORRISON C C 1972 *The Outlawry of War: a Constructive Policy for World Peace.* Garland Pub., New York

MYERS N (ed.) 1985 *The Gaia Atlas of Planet Management.* Pan Books, London

NARDIN T 1996 *Ethics of War and Peace.* Princeton UP

NELSEN B F 1994 *The European Union: Readings on the Theory and Practice of European Integration.* Lynne Rienner

NELSEN B F 1995 *The European Union.* Macmillan Press

NEWCOMBE H 1980 *World Unification Plans and Analyses.* Ont: Peace Research Institate Dundas, Dundas

NEWMAN S 1996 *Ethnoregional Conflict in Democracies.* Greenwood Press

NORTHROP F S C 1953 *The Taming of Nations.* Macmillan, New York

NYE J S JR 1971 *Peace in Parts: Intergration and Conflict in Regional Organization.* Little, Brown, Boston, Massachusetts

OAKESHOTT M 1975 *On Human Conflict.* Oxford University Press, New York

O'LEARY J P 1978 *Systems Theory and Regional Integration: The "Market Model" of International Politics.* University Press of America, Washington, DC

ORR D W, SOROOS M S (eds.) 1979 *The Global Predicament: Ecological Perspectives on World Order.* University of North Carolina Press, Chapel Hill, North Carolina

OSKAMP S 1985 *International Conflict and National Public Policy Issues.* Sage, London

PECK C 1996 *The United Nations as a Dispute Settlement System.* Kluwer Law Internat

PETTMAN R 1975 *Human Behavior and World Politics.* St. Martin's Press, New York

PHELPS E S - see *Part 9.5: Peace and Psychology*

PHILLIPS R L 1995 *Humanitarian Intervention.* Rowman & Littlefield

PIRAGES D 1978 *The New Concept for International Relations: Global Ecopolitics.* Duxbury Press, No. Scituate, Massachusetts

PLANO J C, RIGGS R E 1967 *Forging World Order.* Macmillan, New York

POTTER P B 1928 *An Introduction to the Study of International Organization.* Century, New York

RAFFO P 1974 *The League of Nations.* Historical Association, London

REISMAN M, WESTON B H (eds.) 1976 *toward World Order and Human Dignity.* Free Press, New York

RENTELN A D 1990 *International Human Rights: Universalism Versus Relativism.* Sage London

RENWICK S R 1996 *Fighting with Allies.* Macmillan Press

REVES E 1945 *Anatomy of Peace.* Harper, New York

RIGHTER R 1994 *Utopia Lost: the United Nations and World Order.* Brookings Inst

RIKHYE I J 1990 *The United Nations and Peacekeeping-Results, Limitations and Prospects, the Lessons of 40 Years of Experience.* Macmillan Press

RITTBERGER V 1973 *Evolution and International Organisation: Toward a New Level of Sociopolitical Integration.* Martinus Nijhoff, The Hague

ROBERTS A 1993 *United Nations, Divided World.* Clarendon Press

ROBERTS B 1996 *A Reconstructed World.* McGill Q UP (UCL)

ROSENAU J 1976 *World Politics.* Free Press, New York

ROSENAU J (ed.) 1961 *International Politics and Foreign Policy.* Free Press, New York

ROSENAU J (ed.) 1969 *Linkage Politics.* Free Press, New York

ROSS A 1966 *The United Nations: Peace and Progress.* Bedminster, Totowa, New Jersey

ROSTOW V 1968 *Law Power, and the Pursuit of Peace.* University of Nebraska Press, Lincoln

RUECKERT G L 1993 *Global Double Zero.* Greenwood Press

RUSSELL B 1971 *Principles of Social Reconstruction.* Allen and Unwin, London

RUSSETT B 1963 *Community and Contention: Britain and America in the Twentieth Century.* MIT Press, Cambridge, Massachusetts

RYAN S 1995 *Ethnic Conflict and International Relations.* Dartmouth

SAKHAROV A D 1968 *Progress, Coexistence and Intellectual Freedom.* Norton, New York

SAROOSHI D 1994 *Humanitarian Intervention and International Humanitarian Assistance.* HMSO

SAYRE F B 1919 *Experiments in International Administration.* Harper, New York

SCHOFIELD C H 1994 *Global Boundaries.* Routledge

SCHURMANN F 1974 *The Logic of World Power: An Inquiry into the Origins, Currents, and Contradictions of World Politics.* Pantheon, New York

SCOTT W A, WITHEY S B 1958 *The United States and the United Nations: The Public View, 1945-1955.* Manhattan Publishing Co., New York

SHARP G 1981 *Making the Abolition of War a Realistic Goal.* World Policy Institute, New York

SILVA K M DE 1993 *Internationalization of Ethnic Conflict.* Pinter

SIMMEL G 1955 *Conflict and the Web of Group Affiliations.* Free Press, New York

SIMONI A 1972 *Beyond Repair: The Urgent Need for a New World Body.* Collier-Macmillan, Ontario

SINGER D J (ed.) 1963 *Weapons Management in World Politics.* University of Michigan Press, Ann Arbor, Michigan

SINGER J D *Models, Methods, and Progress in World Politics.* Westview Press

SINGER M 1996 *The Real World Order: Zones of Peace/Zones of Turmoil.* Chatham House

SPROUT H, SPROUT M 1971 *Towards a Politics of the Planet Earth.* Van Nostrand Reinhold, New York

STALEY II R S 1992 *The Wave of the Future: the United Nations and Naval Peacekeeping.* Lynne Rienner

STEPHENSON C M (ed.) 1982 *Alternative Methods for International Security.* University Press of America, Washington, DC

STERN G 1995 *The Structure of International Society.* Pinter

STONE J 1958 *Aggression and World Order.* University of California Press, California

STRAUSS S (ed.) 1915 *Towards International Government.* Macmillan, New York

STRAUSS S (ed.) 1971 *Towards International Goverment.* Garland Pub., New York

SUBEDI S 1996 *Land and Maritime Zones of Peace in International Law.* Clarendon Press

SUNDELIUS B 1978 *Managing Transnationalism in Northern Europe.* Westview, Boulder, Colorado

SUNGA L S 1992 *Individual Responsibility in International Law for Serious Human Rights Violations.* Martinus Nijhoff

SUR S 1992 *Security Council Resolution 687 of 3 April 1991 in the Gulf Affair.* United Nations

SUTTERLIN J S 1995 *The United Nations and the Maintenance of International Security.* Praeger Pub

TACSAN J 1991 *The Dynamics of International Law in Conflict Resolution.* Martinus Nijhoff

TAYLOR P 1990 *International Institutions at Work.* Pinter

TEHRANIAN K 1992 *Restructuring for World Peace.* Hampton Press

TER MEULEN J 1917 *Der Gedanke der Internationalen Organisation in Seiner Entwicklung, 1300-1800* [The Evolution of the Idea of International Organisation]. Nijhoff, The Hague

THOMAS D C, KLARE M T (ed.) 1989 *Peace and World Order Studies: a Curriculum Guide.* Westview Press, Boulder

TIVEY L (ed.) 1981 *The Nation State: The Formation of Modern Politics.* Martin Robertson, London

TOMUSCHAT C 1995 *The United Nations at Age Fifty.* Kluwer Law Internat

TRUEBLOOD B F 1899 *The Federation of the World.* Houghton Mifflin, Boston, Massachusetts

UN 1991 *Teaching about the United Nations and Peace Keeping.* United Nations

UNESCO 1981 *Unesco Yearbook on Peace and Conflict Studies.* Greewood Press, Paris

UNESCO 1991 *Unesco Yearbook on Peace and Conflict Studies 1988.* UNESCO

UNITED NATIONS 1992 *Yearbook of the United Nations.* Marinus Nijhoff, New York, USA

UNITED NATIONS 1992 *Yearbook of the United Nations.* Kluwer

UNITED NATIONS 1994 *Yearbook of the United Nations.* 1992. Martinus Nijhoff, New York, USA

UNITED NATIONS 1995 *Yearbook of the United Nations.* Martinus Nijhoff, New York, USA

UNITED NATIONS 1996 *Yearbook of the United Nations.* Martinus Nijhoff, New York, USA

UNITED NATIONS EDUCATIONAL, SCIENTIFIC, AND CULTURAL ORGANIZATION 1990 *Unesco Yearbook on Peace and Conflict Studies 1988.* Greenwood Press

VAUX K L 1992 *Ethics and the Gulf War.* Westview Press

VEBLEN T (1917) 1964 *An Inquiry into the Nature of Peace and the Terms of its Perpetuation.* Kelly, Clifton, New Jersey

VERNON R 1971 *Sovereignty at Bay.* Basic Books, New York

WAGAR W W 1971 *Building the City of Man.* Grossman and W.H. Freeman, New York/San Francisco, California

WALKER R B J 1988 *One World, Many Worlds: Struggles for a Just World Peace.* Rienner Pub., Boulder: L

WALL L, BRIMMER B 1962 *Guide to the Use of United Nations Documents.* Oceana, Dobbs ferry, New York

WALLACE M D 1973 *War and Rank Among Nations.* Lexington Books, Toronto

WARD B 1966 *Spaceship Earth.* Columbia University Press, New York

WASKOW A 1967 *Towards a Peacemaker's Academy.* World Association of World Federalists, New York

WEATHERFORD R 1993 *World Peace and the Human Family.* Routledge, London, New York

WEISS T G 1993 *Humanitarianism Across Borders: Sustaining Civilians in Times of War.* Lynne Rienner

WEISS T G 1994 *The United Nations and Changing World Politics.* Westview Press

WESTON B et al. 1980 *International Law and World Order*. West Publishing, St. Paul, Minnesota

WHITTAKER D J 1995 *The United Nations in Action*. UCL Press

WILLIAM L 1972 *European Socialism and the Problem of Internationalism before World War I*. Garland Pub., New York

WOITO R 1982 *To End War: A New Approach to International Conflict*. Pilgrim, New York
See also *Part 3.2: Contemporary*

WOLFRUM R 1995 *United Nations: Law, Policies and Practice*. Martinus Nijhoff

WOOLF L S 1916 *International Government*. Brentano's, New York
Reprinted 1971 Garland, New York

WORLD POLICY INSTITUTE 1984 *The Security Project: The First Report*. World Policy Institute, New York

WRIGHT Q 1935 *The Causes of War and the Conditions of Peace*. Longmans, London

WRIGHT Q 1961a *International Law and the United Nations*. Taplinger, New York

WRIGHT Q 1961b *The Role of International Law in the Elimination of War*. Oceana, New York

WRIGHT Q 1962 *Essays on Espionage and International Law*. Ohio State University Press, Columbus, Ohio

WRIGHT Q (ed.) 1948 *The World Community*. University of Chicago Press, Chicago, Illinois

WRIGHT Q, EVAN W M, DEUTSCH M (eds.) 1962 *Preventing World War III: Some Proposals*. Simon and Schuster, New York

YARROW C H M 1978 *Quaker Experiences in International Conciliation*. Yale University Press, New Haven, Connecticut

YASUAKI O 1993 *A Normative Approach to War*. Clarendon Press

YODER A 1993 *Evolution of the United Nations System*. Taylor & Francis

YOST C 1968 *The Insecurity of Nations*. Praeger, New York

YOUNG N 1970 *On War, National Liberation and the State*. Christian Action, London

ZONNEVELD L 1985 *Humanity's Quest for Unity: a United Nations Teilhard Colloquium*. Mirananda, Wassenaar [Netherlands]

Part 9

Peace and ...

9.1 Economics

ADAMS G 1981 *The Iron Triangle: The Politics of Defense Contracting.* Council on Economic Priorities, New York

ANDERSON M 1980 *Converting the Work Force: Where the Jobs Would Be.* Employment Research Associates, East Lansing, Michigan

ANDERSON M 1981 *Bombs or Bread: Black Unemployment and the Pentagon Budget.* Employment Research Associates, East Lansing, Michigan

ANDERSON M 1982 *The Empty Pork Barrel: Unemployment and the Pentagon Budget.* Employment Research Associates, East Lansing, Michigan

ANDERSON M 1982 *Neither Jobs nor Security: Women's Unemployment and the Pentagon Budget.* Employment Research Associates, East Lansing, Michigan

ARCHIBUGI D 1995 *Cosmopolitan Democracy.* Polity Press

ART R J, WALTZ K N (ed.) 1983 *The Use of Force: International Politics and Foreign Policy.* University Press of America, Lanham

ASHLEY R K 1980 *The Political Economy of War and Peace: The Sino-Soviet-American Triangle and the Modern Security Problematique.* Nicholas, New York

ASPIN L, KEMP J 1976 *How Much Defense Spending is Enough?* American Enterprise Institute for Public Policy Research, Washington, DC

BARNET R J 1969 *The Economy of Death.* Atheneum, New York

BARTON J H 1981 *The Politics of Peace.* Stanford UP (CUP)

BENOIT E 1973 *Defense and Economic Growth in Developing Countries.* Lexington books, Lexington, Massachusetts

BENOIT E, GLEDITSCH N P (eds.) 1967 *Disarmament and World Economic Interdependence.* Columbia University Press, New York

BERKOWITZ M 1970 *The Conversion of Military-Orientated Research and Development to Civilian Uses.* Praeger, New York

BESS M 1993 *Realism, Utopia, and the Mushroom Cloud.* Univ. of Chicago Press

BLALOCK H M 1989 *Power and Conflict.* Sage London

BOLTON R E (ed.) 1966 *Defense and Disarmament: The Economics of Transition.* Prentice-Hall, Englewood Cliffs, New Jersey

BOOTH K 1995 *International Relations Theory Today.* Polity Press

BOSTON STUDY GROUP 1979 *The Price of Defense: A New Strategy for Military Spending.* Times Books, New York

BOULDING K 1992 *Towards a New Economics.* Edward Elgar

BOULDING K E 1945 *The Economics of Peace.* Prentice-Hall, New York

BOULDING K E (ed.) 1973 *Peace and the War Industry,* 2nd edn. Transaction Books, New Brunswick, New Jersey

BOULDING K E, BENOIT E (eds.) 1963 *Disarmament and the Economy.* Harper and Row, New York

BOYCE J K 1996 *Economic Policy for Building Peace.* Lynne Rienner

BROWN M E 1996 *Debating the Democratic Peace.* MIT Press

BRUCE W J (ed.) 1973 *Three Centuries of Treaties of Peace and Their Teaching.* Garland Pub., New York

CABLE J 1989 *Navies in Violent Peace.* Macmillan Press

CASSESE A 1994 *The Tokyo Trial and Beyond.* Polity Press

CHAE M S 1992 *Peace Under Heaven.* M E Sharpe

CHOUCRI N, NORTH R C 1975 *Nations in Conflict: National Growth and International Violence.* W. H. Freeman, San Francisco

COOPER S E 1972 *Militarism.* Garland Pub., New York

DAVIES C S L 1995 *Peace, Print and Protestantism.* Fontana

DEGRASSE R JR 1982 *The Costs and Consequences of Reagan's Military Build-up.* Council on Economic Priorities, New York

DIAMOND L 1993 *Nationalism, Ethnic Conflict, and Democracy.* Johns Hopkins UP

DIGOU A C 1939 *The Political Economy of War.* A new and revised edition, Cambridge

DINSTEIN Y 1992 *The Protection of Minorities and Human Rights.* Martinus Nijhoff

DUMAS L (ed.) 1982 *The Political Economy of Arms Reduction: Reversing Economic Decay.* Westview, Boulder, Colorado

DYER H C 1989 *The Study of International Relations.* Macmillan Press

ECONOMIST INTELLIGENCE UNIT, LONDON 1963 *The Economic Effects of Disarmament.* United World Trust, London

EDELSTEIN M 1977 *The Economic Impact of Military Spending.* Council on Economic Priorities, New York

EHRLICH R 1987 *Contribution in Military Study.* Greenwood Press

ELLIOTT D, KALDOR M, SMITH D, SMITH R 1977 *Alternative Work for Military Industries.* Richardson Institute for Conflict and Peace Research, London

ELOWITZ L 1994 *International Relations.* Harper Reference

ELSHTAIN J B 1992 *Just War Theory.* Blackwell Pub

ENZ J J 1972 *The Christian and Warfare: the Roots of Pacifism in the Old Testament.* Herald Press, Scottdale, Pa

FALK R A, MENDLOVITZ S H (eds.) 1966 *Disarmament and Economic Development.* World Law Fund, New York

FATHER ALEXANDER F C WEBSTER 1993 *The Price of Prophecy.* Ethics & Pub., Policy

FISCHER S 1993 *The Economics of Middle East Peace.* MIT Press

GABRIEL J M 1994 *Worldviews and Theories of International Relations.* Macmillan Press

GEISEMAN O A 1943 *God's Answer: Sermons for Sundays and Holy Days from Advent to Pentecost.* Ernest Kayfmann, New York

GLAD B 1991 *Psychological Dimensions of War.* Sage, London

GLAGOLEV I 1961 *Economic Probems of Disarmament.* Moscow

GLAGOLEV I 1964 *The Effect of Disarmament on the Economy: Militarisation and the Expected Consequences of Disarmament.* Nauka, Moscow

GURTOV M 1991 *Global Politics in the Human Interest.* Lynne Rienner

GUSTO R G 1993 *Catholic Peacemakers: a Documentary History.* Garland Pub.

HAHN W 1993 *Paying the Premium: a Military Insurance Policy for Peace and Freedom.* Greenwood Press

HARRIS A 1989 *Rocking the Ship of State: Toward a Feminist Peace Politics.* Westview Press

HARTLEY K 1990 *The Economics of Defence, Disarmament and Peace.* Edward Elgar

HINSLEY F H 1967 *Power and the Pursuit of Peace: Theory and Practice in the History of Relations Between States.* Cambridge U.P., London

HOSELITZ B F (ed.) 1965 *Economics and the Idea of Mankind.* Columbia University Press, New York

JACOBS M S 1989 *American Psychology in the Quest for Nuclear Peace.* Praeger Pub.

JOHNSON D H 1994 *Newer Prophets.* Clarendon Press

JOLLY R (ed.) 1978 *Disarmament and World Development.* Pergamon, Oxford

KAMINER R 1995 *The Politics of Protest.* Sussex Aca, Drake Int

KEGLEY C W JR 1995 *World Politics 5th Edition.* Macmillan Press

KELSAY J 1991 *Just War and Jihad.* Greenwood Press

KENNEDY G 1956 *The Christian and his America.* Harper & Brothers, New York

KENNEDY G 1975 *The Economics of Defence.* Faber and Faber, London

KLIOT N 1993 *The Political Geography of Conflict and Peace.* John Wiley Ltd

KREHBIEL E 1973 *Nationalism, War and Society.* Garland Pub., New York

LALL B G 1977 *Prosperity Without Guns: The Economic Impact of Reductions in Defense Spending.* Institute for World Order, New York

LARSEN K S 1993 *Conflict and Social Psychology.* Sage London

LEE A A 1985 *Circle of Peace: Reflections on the Bahai Teachings.* Kalimat Press, Los Angeles

LEVINE H M 1992 *World Politics Debated.* McGraw-Hill USA

MAHAN A T 1972 *Unilateral Force in International Relations: Comprising Some Neglected Aspects of War.* Garland Pub., New York

MAHBUB UL HAQ 1996 *Reflections on Human Development.* Oxford UP

MARK H 1988 *Energy in Physics, War and Peace: a Festschrift Celebrating Edward Teller's 80th Birthday.* Kluwer

MARKS III F 1993 *Power and Peace.* Praeger Pub

McDOUGALL W 1972 *Janus: the Conquest of War: a Psychological Inquiry.* Garland Pub., New York

McPHERSON J M 1991 *Ordeal by Fire.* McGraw-Hill USA

MELMAN S 1964 *Elements of the Industrial Conversion Problem.* Columbia University Press, New York

MELMAN S 1965 *Our Depleted Society.* Rinehart and Winston, New York

MELMAN S 1970 *Pentagon Capitalism: The Political Economy of War.* McGraw-Hill, New York

MELMAN S (ed.) 1962 *Disarmament: Its Politics and Economics.* American Academy of Arts and Sciences, Houston, Texas

MELMAN S (ed.) 1970 *The Defense Economy.* Praeger, New York

MELMAN S (ed.) 1971 *The War Economy of the U.S.* St. Martin's Press, New York

MERCIER M 1995 *Crimes Without Punishment.* Pluto Press

MIKO YARROW C H 1978 *Quaker Experiences in International Conciliation.* Yale University Press, New Haven, Conn

MINOR P E 1971 *The Enconomic Bases of Peace.* Kennilcat Press, Washington, N.Y

MORGAN P 1996 *Ethical Issues in Six Religious Traditions.* Edinburgh UP

NACHMIAS N 1988 *Contributions in Military Studies.* Greenwood Press

NESTER W 1995 *International Relations.* Longman

O'CONNELL J 1994 *A Theology of Peace.* Geoffrey Chapman

PAPACOSMA S V 1994 *NATO in the Post-Cold War Era.* Macmillan Press

PARKER R A C 1990 *Struggle for Survival: the History of the Second World War.* Oxford Paperbacks

PETER W 1995 *Arbitration and Renegotiation of International Investment Agreements.* Kluwer Law Internat

QUINNEY R 1991 *The Problem of Crime.* Wm C Brown

RAMSBOTHAM O 1996 *Muslim/Christian Appr War & Peace.* Macmillan Press

RICHARDS P 1996 *Fighting for the the Rain Forest.* James Currey Pub.

RILEY-SMITH J 1992 *What Were the Crusades?* Macmillan Press

RUSSETT B 1995 *Grasping the Democratic Peace.* Princeton UP

RUSSETT B 1995 *World Politics.* W H Freeman

SANDLER T 1995 *The Economics of Defence.* Cambridge UP

SARSAR S 1995 *World Politics.* Univ Press America

SCALAPINO R A 1988 *Peace, Politics and Economics in Asia.* Brassey's US

SCHMIDT C 1987 *Peace, Defence and Economic Analysis.* Macmillan Press

SHARP A 1991 *The Versailles Settlement.* Macmillan Press

SHIRLEY G 1990 *West of Hell's Fringe: Crime, Criminals, and the Federal Peace Officer in Oklahoma Territory, 1889-1907.* Univ Oklahoma Press

SHIVA V 1991 *Ecology and the Politics of Survival.* Sage, London

SIVARD R L 1979 *World Military and Social Expenditures 1979.* World Priorities Inc., Leesburg, Virginia
(Edns. available for each subsequent year)

SMITH D (ed.) 1977 *Alternative Work for Military Industries.* Richardson Institute for Conflict and Peace Research, London

STANTON J, PEARTON M 1972 *The International Trade in Arms.* Chatto and Windus, London

TAJIMA M 1988 *Peace Through Economic Justice: Essays in Memory of Manuel Perez-Guerrero.* Japan, (s.n.)

TELHAMI S 1992 *Power and Leadership in International Bargaining.* Columbia UP

TEMPERLEY H W V 1969 *A History of the Peace Conference of Paris.* Oxford UP

THOMAS N M 1972 *War: No Glory, No Profit, No Need: and the Challenge of War, an Economic Interpretation.* Garland Pub., New York

TRUE M 1995 *An Energy Field more Intense than War.* Syracuse University

TULLOCK G 1974 *The Social Dilemma: The Economics of War and Revolution.* University Publications, Blacksburg, Virginia

UDIS B (ed.) 1973 *The Economic Consequences of Reduced Military Spending.* Lexington-Heath, Lexington, Massachusetts

UDIS B 1978 *From Guns to Butter.* Ballinger, Cambridge, Massachusetts

UNITED NATIONS 1978 *Economic and Social Consequences of the Arms Race and Military Expenditure.* United Nations, New York

UNITED STATES 1978 *The Economic Impact of Reductions in Defense Spending.* US Arms Control and Disarmament Agency, Washington, DC

UNITED STATES ARMS CONTROL AND DISARMAMENT AGENCY 1962 *Economic Impacts of Disarmament.* US Government Printing Office, Washington, DC

VERWEY W 1972 *Economic Development, Peace and International Law.* Humanities Press, New York See also *Part 9.2: Peace and Politics*

VERWAY W D 1972 *Economic Development, Peace, and International Law.* Gorcum Assen: Van

WALLIS J (ed.) 1983 *Peacemakers Christian Voices from the New Abolitionist Movement.* Harper & Row, San Francisco

WEIDENBAUM M 1974 *The Economics of Peacetime Defense.* Praeger, New York

WEIZSACLCER G F 1978 *The Politics of Peril: Economics, Society and the Prevention of War.* Seabury Press, New York

WILLIAMS H 1991 *International Relations in Political Theory.* Open UP

ZIEGLER D W 1984 *War, Peace and International Politics.* Little, Brown, Boston

ZIEGLER 1991 *War, Peace and International Politics.* Longman

ZISK B H 1992 *The Politics of Transformation.* Praeger Pub.

9.2 Politics

ALKER H R JR, RUSSETT B M 1965 *World Politics in the General Assembly.* Yale University Press, New Haven, Connecticut

ANDEMICAEL B 1972 *Peaceful Settlement Among African States: Roles of the United Nations and the Organisation of African Unity.* United Nations Institute for Training and Research (UNITAR), New York

ANDPRESKI S 1968 *Military Organisation and Society.* University of California Press, Berkeley, California

ARENDT H 1963 *On Revolution.* Viking, New York

ARON R 1958 *On War: Atomic Weapons and Global Diplomacy.* Doubleday, New York

ASHLEY R K - see *Part 9.1: Peace and Economics*

BARBUSSE H (ed.) 1929 *The Soviet Union and Peace.* International, New York

BARGHOORN F C 1976 *Detente and the Democratic Movement in the USSR.* Free Press, Riverside, New Jersey

BARNET R J 1972 *Roots of War.* Atheneum, New York

BARNETT F R, MOTT W C, NEF J C (eds.) 1965 *Peace and War in the Modern Age: Premises, Myths and Realities.* Anchor, New York

BEER F A 1981 *Peace Against War: The Ecology of International Violence.* W. H. Freeman, San Francisco, California

BEITZ C R, HERMAN T (eds.) 1973 *Peace and War.* Freeman, San Francisco, California

BIENEN H (ed.) 1971 *The Military and Modernization.* Aldine/Atherton, Chicago, Illinois

BLAINEY G 1973 *The Causes of War.* Macmillan, London

BLUMBERG H H, HARE A P 1977 *Liberation Without Violence: A Third Party Approach.* Rex Collings, London

CANTRIL H (ed.) 1950 *Tensions that Cause Wars.* University of Illinois Press, Urbana, Illinois

CHATFIELD C, COOK B, COOPER S (eds.) 1971 *Five Views on European Peace.* Garland, New York

CLARKSON J C, COCHRAN T 1941 *War as a Social Institution.* Columbia University Press, New York

CLAUSEWITZ C VON 1962 *War, Politics and Power.*

Henry Regnery, Chicago, Illinois

CLAUSEWITZ C VON 1977 *On War*. Princeton University Press, Princeton, New Jersey

COOK F J 1962 *The Warfare State*. Jonathan Cape, New York
(Also 1963 Jonathan Cape, London)

CORTESE C F 1976 *Modernization, Threat, and the Power of the Military*. Sage, Beverly Hills, California

DAVIES J C (ed.) 1971 *When Men Revolt - And Why*. Free Press, New York

DONOVAN J S 1970 *Militarism USA*. Scribner's, New York

EGGE B, HARBOTTLE M, RIKHYE I J 1974 *The Thin Blue Line: International Peacekeeping and its Future*. Yale University Press, New Haven, Connecticut

FALK R A, LIFTON R J - see *Part 9.5: Peace and Psychology*

FRYDENBERG P (ed.) 1964 *Peacekeeping, Experience and Evaluation*. Norwegian Institute of International Affairs, Oslo

GIVENS R C, NETTLESHIP A, NETTLESHIP M A (eds.) 1975 *War: Its Causes and Correlates*. Mouton, The Hague

GURR T R 1970 *Why Men Rebel*. Princeton University Press, Princeton, New Jersey

HERZOG A 1965 *The War-Peace Establishment*. Harper and Row, New York

HOLCOMBE A N 1967 *A Strategy of Peace in a Changing World*. Harvard University Press, Cambridge, Massachusetts

HOROWITZ I L 1963 *The War Game*. Ballantine, New York

HOWARD M *Studies in War and Peace*. Viking, New York

IKLE F C 1964 *How Nations Negotiate*. Harper and Row, New York

IKLE F C 1971 *Every War Must End*. Columbia University Press, New York

INTERNATIONAL SOCIOLOGICAL ASSOCIATION - see *Part 10: Peace Research*

JACKSON E 1952 *Meeting of Minds: A Way to Peace Through Mediation*. McGraw-Hill, New York

JAMES A 1969 *The Politics of Peacekeeping*. Praeger, New York

KRUSHCHEV N A 1961 *On Peaceful Co-Existence*. Foreign Languages Publishing House, Moscow

LENIN V I 1966 *Lenin on War and Peace*. Foreign Languages Press, Peking

LEVINE R A 1963 *The Arms Debate*. Oxford University Press, London

MELMAN S - see *Part 9.1: Peace and Economics*

MIDLARSKY M I 1975 *On War: Political Violence in the International System*. Free Press, New York

MILLS C W 1958 *The Causes of World War III*. Ballantine Books, New York
(Also 1959 Secker and Warburg, London)

NEWHOUSE J 1973 *Cold Dawn: The Story of SALT*. Holt, Rinehart and Winston, New York

OSGOOD C E 1962 *An Alternative to War or Surrender*. University of Illinois Press, Urbana, Illinois

OSGOOD R E 1967 *Force, Order, and Justice*. Johns Hopkins Press, Baltimore, Maryland

PECHOTA V 1971 *Complementary Structures of Third-Party Settlement of International Disputes*. United Nations Institute for Training and Research (UNITAR), New York

PECHOTA V 1972 *The Quiet Approach*. United Nations Institute for Training and Research (UNITAR), New York

PROUDHON P-J (1861) 1971 *La Guerre et la Paix*. Garland, New York

PRUITT D G, SNYDER R C (eds.) 1969 *Theory and Research on the Causes of War*. Prentice-Hall,

Englewood Cliffs, New Jersey

RANDLE R F 1973 *The Origins of Peace.* Free Press, New York

REARDON B 1985 *Sexism and the War System.* Teachers College Press, New York

ROSECRANCE R (ed.) 1972 *The Future of the International Strategic System.* Chandler, San Francisco, California

RUSSELL B (1917) 1971 *Why Men Fight: A Method of Abolishing the International Duel.* Garland, New York

SMITH C G (ed.) 1971 *Conflict Resolution: Contributions of the Behavioral Sciences.* University of Notre Dame Press, Notre Dame, Indiana

SMITH D S (ed.) 1974 *From War to Peace: Essays in Peacemaking and War Termination.* Columbia University Press, New York

SPEIER H (1952) 1969 *Social Order and the Risks of War.* MIT Press, Cambridge, Massachusetts

STANFORD B (ed.) 1976 *Peacemaking: A Guide to Conflict Resolution for Individuals, Groups and Nations.* Bantam, New York

STOESSINGER J G 1971 *Why Nations Go To War.* St. Martin's Press, New York

TANTER R 1974 *Modelling and Managing International Conflict: The Berlin Crisis.* Sage, Beverly Hills, California

UNITED NATIONS 1970 *Peaceful Settlement of Disputes.* United Nations Institute for Training and Research (UNITAR), New York

UNITED NATIONS - see *Part 9.5: Peace and Psychology*

VERWEY W - see *Part 9.1: Peace and Economics*

WAINHOUSE D W 1973 *International Peacekeeping at the Crossroads.* Johns Hopkins Press, Baltimore, Maryland

WAINHOUSE D W et al. 1966 *International Peace Observation: A History and Forecast.* Johns Hopkins Press, Baltimore, Maryland

WASKOW A I 1962 *The Limits of Defense.* Doubleday, New York

WELCH C E JR (ed.) 1976 *Civilian Control of the Military.* State University of New York Press, Albany, New York

YORK H 1970 *Race to Oblivion.* Simon and Schuster, New York

YOUNG O R 1967 *The Intermediaries.* Princeton University Press, Princeton, New Jersey

YOUNG O R (ed.) 1975 *Bargaining: Formal Theories of Negotiation.* University of Illinois Press, Chicago, Illinois

9.3 History

ARON R 1955 *The Century of Total War.* Beacon, Boston, Massachusetts

BOGUE D D 1869 *On Universal Peace: Extracts from a Discourse Delivered in October 1813.* Peace Association of Friends in America, New Vienna, Ohio

BOZEMAN A 1960 *Politics and Culture in International History.* Princeton University Press, Princeton, New Jersey

CADOUX C J - see *Part 9.4: Peace and Religion*

COBLENTZ S A 1953 *From Arrow to Atom Bomb.* Beechhurst, New York

DAVIE M R 1929 *The Evolution of War: A Study of its Role in Early Societies.* Yale University Press, New Haven, Connecticut

FITZGERALD A 1931 *Peace and War in Antiquity.* Scolartis Press

GALLIE W B 1978 *Philosophers of Peace and War.* Cambridge University Press, New York

Garland Library of War and Peace. 1971 Garland, New York

GROTIUS H (1925) 1957 *Prolegomena to the Law of War and Peace.* Bobbs-Merrill, Indianapolis, Indiana

HIGGINS R 1970 *United Nations Peacekeeping 1946-67: Documents and Commentary.* Oxford University Press, New York

JAMES S 1963 *A People among People: Quaker Benevolence in 18th Century America.* Harvard University Press, Cambridge, Massachusetts
See also *Part 9.4: Peace and Religion*

JOHNSON J T 1975 *Ideology, Reason and the Limitations of War: Religious and Secular Concepts 1299-1740.* Princeton University Press, Princeton, New Jersey

JONES M H 1937 *Swords into Ploughshares: An Account of the American Friends Service Committee 1917-37.* Macmillan, New York
See also *Part 9.4: Peace and Religion*

JONES R 1962 *Quakers in the American Colonies.* Norton, New York
See also *Part 9.4: Peace and Religion*

KANT I (1795) 1971 *Perpetual Peace: A Philosophic Essay.* Garland, New York

LAPP R E 1968 *The Western Culture.* Norton, New York

MACHIAVELLI N 1965 *The Arts of War.* Bobbs-Merrill, Indianapolis, Indiana

MELKO M 1973 *52 Peaceful Societies.* Canadian Peace Research Institute, Oakville, Ontario

NEF J U 1968 *War and Human Progress.* Norton, New York

RUSSELL B 1969 *The Autobiography of Bertrand Russell.* Simon and Schuster, New York

SOROKIN P A 1937 *Social and Cultural Dynamics.* American Book, New York

STAWELL F M 1929 *The Growth of International Thought.* Thornton Butterworth, London

TOLSTOY L 1970 *The Law of Love and the Law of Violence.* Holt, Rinehart and Winston, New York

TOLSTOY L (1926) 1971 *War-Patriotism-Peace.* Garland, New York

TOMKINSON L - see *Part 9.4: Peace and Religion*

TOYNBEE A 1956 *A Study of History.* London

TOYNBEE A 1950 *War and Civilization: Selections from a Study of History.* Oxford University Press, New York

WALKER C C 1969 *Peacekeeping.* Friends Peace Committee, Philadelphia, Pennsylvania

WELDON T D 1963 *States and Morals.* John Murray

ZAMPAGLIONE G 1973 *The Idea of Peace in Antiquity.* University of Notre Dame Press, Notre Dame, Indiana

9.4 Religion

ABERCROMBIE C L 1977 *The Military Chaplain.* Sage, Beverly Hills, California

ABU ZAHRA S (no date) *The Concept of War in Islam.* Ministry of Waqfs, Cairo

ANDREWS E 1953 *The People Called Shakers.* Dover, New York

AVAKUMOVIC I, WOODCOCK G 1968 *The Doukhobours.*

Faber, London
See also *Part 6: Pacifism*

BAINTON R H 1960 *Christian Attitudes to War and Peace.* Abingdon, New York

BEALES A C F 1941 *The Catholic Church and International Order.* Penguin, Harmondsworth

BETHUNE-BAKER J F 1888 *The Influence of Christianity*

on War. Cambridge University Press, Cambridge

BORAM C D H 1941 *Which Kingdom: The Challenge of Pacifism to the Church*. Daniel, London

BOWMAN R D 1944 *The Church of the Brethren and War*. Brethren Press, Elgin, Illinois

BRAITHWAITE W 1955 *The Beginnings of Quakerism*. Cambridge University Press, Cambridge

BURROUGHS W 1931 *The Christian Church and War*. Nisbet, London

BYRD R O 1960 *Quaker Ways in Foreign Policy*. University of Toronto Press, Toronto

CADOUX C J 1919 *The Early Christian Attitude to War*. Headley, London

CADOUX C J 1925 *The Early Church and the World*. Clark, Edinburgh
See also *Part 9.3: Peace and History*

CAMARA H 1971 *Revolution Through Peace*. Harper and Row, New York

CHAN W T 1963 *The Way of Lao Tzu*. Bobbs-Merrill, Indianapolis, Indiana

CHURCH PEACE MISSION 1951 *The Christian Conscience and War*. Church Peace Mission

CLAVIER H 1956 *The Duty and Right of Resistance According to the Bible and the Church*. Blackwell, Oxford

CREEL H G 1962 *Chinese Thought*. Methuen, London

DAKIN D M 1956 *Peace and Brotherhood in the Old Testament*. Bannisdale

DYMOND J 1838 *Observations on the Applicability of the Pacific Principles of the New Testament to the Conduct of States and on the Limitations which Principles Impose on the Rights on Self Defense*. Society for the Promotion of Permanent and Universal Peace, London

DYMOND J (1823) 1915 *War, its Causes, Consequences, Lawfulness, etc.* Peace Committee of the Society of Friends, London

FANG Y-L 1937 *A History of Chinese Philosophy*. Vetch, Beijing

FERGUSON 1973 *The Politics of Love*. James Clarke, Cambridge

FERGUSON J 1977 *War and Peace in the World's Religions*. Sheldon Press, London

FINN J 1965 *Peace, the Churches and the Bomb*. Council on Religious and International Affairs, New York

FRANTE C 1957 *The Doukhobours, Sons of Freedom*. Portland State College

FREEMAN R 1947 *Quakers and Peace*. Pacifist Research Bureau, Ithaca, New York

GANDHI M K 1948-49 *Nonviolence in Peace and War*, 2 vols. Navajivan, Ahmedabad

See also *Part 7: Nonviolence*

GINGERICH M 1949 *Service for Peace: A History of Mennonite Civilian Public Service*. Mennonite Central Committee, Akron, Pennsylvania

GORGEN C 1963 *Catholic Conscientious Objectors*. Allied Printing Co., San Francisco, California

GRAHAM J W 1912 *The Passing of War*. Macmillan, London

HAGUE S A (no date) *Islam's Contribution to the Peace of the World*. Ahmadiya, Cairo

HEERING G J 1928 *The Fall of Christianity*. Allen and Unwin, London

HIRSCH R G 1974 *Thy Most Precious Gift: Peace in Jewish Tradition*. Union of American Hebrew Congregations, New York

HIRST M - see *Part 6: Pacifism*

HORSCH J - see *Part 6: Pacifism*

HORST S - see *Part 6: Pacifism*

HOYLAND J S 1928 *The Warfare of Reconciliation*. Allen and Unwin, London

JACK H (ed.) 1966 *Religion and Peace.* Bobbs-Merrill, New York

JAMES S - see *Part 9.3: Peace and History*

JOHNSON A 1930 *Christianity and War.* James Clarke, London

JONES M H - see *Part 9.3: Peace and History*

JONES R - see *Part 9.3: Peace and History*

KHADDURI M 1955 *War and Peace in the Law of Islam.* Johns Hopkins University Press, Baltimore, Maryland

LEE U 1943 *The Historic Church and Modern Pacifism.* Abingdon Cokesbury, Nashville, Tennessee

MASSYNGBAERDE FORD J 1984 *My Enemy is My Guest: Jesus and Violence in Luke.* Orbis Press, Maryknoll, New York

MATHESON P 1977 *Profile of Love.* Christian Journals, Belfast

MOELLERING R 1956 *Modern War and the American Churches.* American Press, New York

RAMSEY P 1961 *War and the Christian Conscience.* Duke University Press, Durham, North Carolina

RAMSEY P 1968 *The Just War.* Scribner, New York

RAPOPORT A 1936 *The Gauntlet Against the Gospel.* Skeffington and Son, London

ROWNTREE M 1939 *Mankind Set Free.* Cape, London

RUSSELL F H 1975 *The Just War in the Middle Ages.* Cambridge University Press, Cambridge

SAUNDERS A 1967 *Christianity and Peace.* Canadian Peace Research Institute, Oakville, Ontario

SCOTT-CARIG T S K 1938 *Christian Attitudes to War and Peace.* Oliver and Boyd, London

SHOGHI EFFENDI 1955 *The World Order of Baha'u'llah.* Bahai, Wilmette, Illinois

SMITH D H 1968 *Chinese Religions.* Weidenfeld, London

STRATMAN F 1929 *The Church and War.* Sheed and Ward, London

STURZO L 1939 *Church and State.* BLES, London

TENDULKAR D G 1967 *Abdul Ghaffar Khan: Faith is a Battle.* Popular Pakasham, Bombay

THICH NHAT HANH 1967 *Vietnam: The Lotus in the Sea of Fire.* SCM Press, London

TOMKINSON L 1940 *Studies in the Theory and Practice of Peace and War in Chinese History and Literature.* Christian Literature Society, China See also *Part 9.3: Peace and History*

TOOKE J D 1965 *The Just War in Aquinas and Grotius.* SPCK, London

VAN KIRK W 1934 *Religion Renounces War.* Willet and Clark, New York

WINDASS S 1964 *Christianity versus Violence.* Sheed and Ward, London

9.5 Psychology

ADORNO T W, FRENKEL-BRUNSWICK E, LEVINSON D J, SANFORD R N 1961 *The Authoritarian Personality.* Harper, New York

ALCOCK N Z 1971 *The Logic of Love.* Canadian Peace Research Institute, Oakville, Ontario

BERKOWITZ L 1962 *Aggression: A Social Psychological Analysis.* McGraw-Hill, New York

BROWN B R, RUBIN J Z 1975 *The Social Psychology of Bargaining and Negotiation.* Academic Press, New York

DOLLARD J, DOBB L, MILLER N E, MOWRER A H, SEARS R R 1939 *Frustration and Aggression.* Yale University Press, New Haven, Connecticut

FALK R A, LIFTON R J 1982 *Indefensible Weapons:*

The Political and Psychological Case Against Militarism. Basic Books, New York
See also *Part 9.2: Peace and Politics*

FORNARI F 1975 *The Psychoanalysis of War.* Indiana University Press, Bloomington, Indiana

FRANK J D 1967 *Sanity and Survival.* Vintage, New York

FREUD S 1915 *Reflections on War and Death.* Encyclopedia Britannica Inc., Vol. 54
(Also 1961 Doubleday, New York, Vol. II)

FREUD S 1933 *Why War? Great Political Thinkers.* Rinehart, New York

FREUD S 1962 *Civilisation and its Discontents.* Norton, New York

FREUD S 1968 *Civilisation, War and Death.* Hogarth, London

FROMM E 1973 *The Anatomy of Human Destructiveness.* Holt, Rinehart and Winston, New York

GOLDMAN N, SEGAL D R (eds.) 1976 *The Social Psychology of Military Service.* Sage, Beverly Hills, California

HOKANSON J E, MEGARGEE E I (eds.) 1970 *The Dynamics of Aggression: Individual, Group and International Analyses.* Harper and Row, New York

KAUFMANN H 1970 *Aggression and Altruism: A Psychological Analysis.* Holt, Rinehart and Winston, New York

KELMAN H C (ed.) 1965 *International Behavior: A Social-Psychological Analysis.* Holt, Rinehart and Winston, New York

LARSON O N (ed.) 1968 *Violence and the Mass Media.* Harper, New York

LOPEZ-REYES R 1971 *Power and Immortality: Essays on Strategy, War Psychology and War Control.* Exposition, New York

LORENZ K 1966 *On Aggression.* Harcourt, Brace and World, New York
(Also 1963 Methuen, London)

MARWELL G, SCHMIDT D R 1975 *Cooperation: An Experimental Analysis.* Academic, New York

MASSERMAN J H (ed.) 1963 *Violence and War: Science and Psychoanalysis.* Grune and Stratton, New York

MATTER J A 1974 *Love, Altruism and World Crisis: The Challenge of Pitirim Sorokin.* Nelson-Hall, Chicago, Illinois

MAY R 1972 *Power and Innocence: A Search for the Sources of Violence.* Norton, New York

MCLELLAND D C 1975 *Power: The Inner Experience.* Halsted, New York

NCNEILL W H 1976 *Plagues and Peoples.* Anchor Books, Garden City, New York

MILGRAM S 1974 *Obedience to Authority.* Harper and Row, New York

MONTAGU A 1976 *The Nature of Human Aggression.* Oxford University Press, New York

MONTAGU A (ed.) (1968) 1973 *Man and Aggression.* Oxford University Press, New York

MURPHY G (ed.) 1945 *Human Nature and Enduring Peace.* Houghton Mifflin, Boston, Massachusetts

NICOLAI G F 1918 *The Biology of War.* Century, New York

NIEBURG H L 1969 *Political Violence: The Behavioral Process.* St Martin's Press, New York

PEAR T H (ed.) 1950 *Psychological Factors of Peace and War.* Philosophical Library, New York

PELTON L H 1974 *The Psychology of Nonviolence.* Pergamon, New York

PHELPS E S (ed.) 1975 *Altruism, Morality, and Economic Theory.* Sage, Beverly Hills, California
See also *Part 8: World Order and Internationalism*

RUMMEL R J 1976 *Understanding Conflict and War, Vol. 1: The Dynamic Psychological Field.* Wiley, New York

SCHWEBEL M (ed.) 1965 *Behavioral Science and*

Human Survival. Science and Behavior Books, Palo Alto, California

SHERIF M 1966 *In Common Predicament: Social Psychology of Inter-Group Conflict and Cooperation.* Houghton Mifflin, Boston, Massachusetts
See also *Part 10: Peace Research*

SINGER J L (ed.) 1971 *The Control of Aggression and Violence.* Academic Press, New York

SOROKIN P A 1941 *The Crisis of our Age: The Social and Cultural Outlook.* Dutton, New York
See also *Part 10: Peace Research*

STAGNER R 1967 *Psychological Aspects of International Conflict.* Brooks/Cole Division, Wadsworth, Monterey, California

STORR A 1968 *Human Aggression.* Atheneum, New York

STRACHEY A 1957 *The Unconscious Motives of War.* International Universities Press, New York

TOCH H M 1969 *Violent Men: An Inquiry into the Psychology of Violence.* Aldine, Chicago, Illinois

UNITED NATIONS 1970 *Social Psychological Techniques and the Peaceful Settlement of International Disputes.* United Nations Institute for Training and Research (UNITAR), New York
See also *Part 9.2: Peace and Politics*

WATSON P 1978 *War on the Mind: The Military Uses and Abuses of Psychology.* Basic Books, New York

Part 10

Peace Research

ADLER M J 1944 *How to Think about War and Peace.* Simon and Schuster, New York

AKKERMAN R J, VAN KRIEKEN P J, PANNENBORG C O (eds.) 1977 *Declarations on Principles: A Quest for Universal Peace.* Sijthoff, Leyden

ALCOCK N Z 1961 *The Bridge of Reason.* Canadian Peace Research Institute, Oakville, Ontario

ALCOCK N Z 1977 *The Emperor's New Clothes.* Canadian Peace Research Institute, Oakville, Ontario

ALCOCK N Z 1977 *The War Disease.* Canadian Peace Research Institute, Oakville, Ontario

ANGELL R C 1960 *Value Systems, Foreign Policy and Soviet-American Coexistence.* University of Michigan Press, Ann Arbor, Michigan

ARENDT H 1955 *On Violence.* Harcourt, Brace and World, New York

AZAR E E 1973 *The Review of Peace Science*, Vol. 1. Canadian Peace Research Institute, Oakville, Ontario

BARRINGER R E, RAMERS R K 1972 *War: Patterns of Conflict.* MIT Press, Cambridge, Massachusetts

BEITZ C R, HERMAN T (eds.) 1973 *Peace and War.* W. H. Freeman, San Francisco, California

BERNARD L L 1944 *War and its Causes.* Henry Holt, New York

BOASSON C 1971 *A Prologue to Peace Research.* Israel Universities Press, Jerusalem/Amsterdam

BOASSON C (ed.) 1973 *The Changing International Community: Some Problems of its Laws, Structures, Peace Research and the Middle East Conflict.* Mouton, The Hague

BOASSON C, DUNGEN P VAN DEN 1991 *In Search of Peace Research.* London, Macmillan

BOHANNAN P (ed.) 1967 *Law and Warfare: Studies in the Antropology of Conflict.* Natural History Press, New York

BOND J E 1974 *The Rules of Riot: Internal Conflict and the Law of War.* Princeton University Press, Princeton, New Jersey

BOOTH K, WRIGHT M (eds.) 1978 *American Thinking about Peace and War.* Harvester Press, Brighton

BOULDING E 1992 *New Agendas for Peace Research.* Lynne Rienner

BOULDING K E 1961 *Conflict and Defense: A General Theory.* Harper, New York

BOULDING K E 1964 *The Meaning of the Twentieth Century: The Great Transition.* Harper and Row, New York

BOULDING K E 1969 *The Image.* University of Michigan Press, Ann Arbor, Michigan

BOULDING K E 1970 *A Primer on Social Dynamics: History as Dialectics and Development.* Free Press, New York

BOULDING K E 1975 *Collected Papers*, Vol. 5. Colorado Associated University Press, Boulder, Colorado

BOULDING K E 1978 *Stable Peace.* University of Texas Press, Austin, Texas

BOUTHOUL G 1962 *Le Phénomène - Guerre.* Prentice-Hall, New York

BOUTHOUL G 1970 *Traité de Polémologie.* Payot, Paris (1st edn. 1951 *Les Guerres*)

BOUTHOUL G, CARRERE R 1976 *Le Défi de la Guerre, 1740-1974.* Presses Universitaires de France, Paris

BRAMSON L, GOETHALS G W (eds.) 1968 *War: Studies from Psychology, Sociology, Anthropology.* Basic Books, New York

CARLTON D, SCHAERF C (ed.) 1975 *The Dynamics of the Arms Race.* Croom Helm, London

CHILD J 1987 *International Peace Academy Report.* Kluwer

CHOUE Y S 1983 *Peace Studies.* Kyung Hee University Press, Seoul Korea

CLARKE R 1971 *The Science of War and Peace.* Jonathan Cape, London

CURLE A 1975 *Making Peace.* Tavistock, London

DASGUPTA S 1974 *Problems of Peace Research: A Third World View.* Indian Council of Peace Research, New Delhi

DEDRING J 1976 *Recent Advances in Peace and Conflict Research: A Critical Survey.* Sage, Beverly Hills, California

DURKEE K 1976 *Peace Research: Definitions and Objectives: A Bibliography.* Center for the Study of Armament and Disarmament, California State University, Los Angeles, California

ECKHARDT W 1963 *Foreign Politics, Prejudice and Religion.* Peace Research Group, Des Moines, Iowa

FEIERABEND I K, FEIERABEND R L, GURR T R (eds.) 1972 *Anger, Violence and Politics: Theories and Research.* Prentice-Hall, New York

FINE M, STEVEN P M, INSTITUTE FOR DEFENSE AND DISARMAMENT STUDIES (U.S.) (ed.) 1984 *American Peace Directory.* Ballinger Pub., Cambridge, Mass.

FISHER R (ed.) 1964 *International Conflict and Behavioral Science.* Basic Books, New York

FREEDMAN R O 1993 *The Middle East After Iraq's Invasion of Kuwait.* Univ. Florida Press

GALTUNG J 1973 *The European Community: A Superpower in the Making.* Allen and Unwin, London

GALTUNG J 1974 *A Structural Theory of Revolutions.* University Press, Rotterdam

GALTUNG J 1975 *Peace: Research Education Action.* Ejlers, Copenhagen

GALTUNG J 1975-80 *Essays in Peace Research*, 5 Vols. Christian Ejlers, Copenhagen

GALTUNG, J, JUNGK R (eds.) 1969 *Mankind 2000.* Allen and Unwin, London

GALTUNG J - see *Part 8: World Order and Internationalism*

GLEDITSCH N P et al. 1980 *Johan Galtung: A Bibliography of his Scholarly and Popular Writings, 1951-80.* International Peace Research Institute (PRIO), Oslo

GOPINATHAN S (ed.) 1977 *Man and Peace.* Federal Publications/UNESCO, Singapore

GUETZKOW H, ALGER C F, BRODY R A, NOEL R C, SNYDER R C 1963 *Simulation in International Relations.* Prentice-Hall, Englewood Cliffs, New Jersey

HOROWITZ I L 1967 *The Rise and Fall of Project Camelot.* MIT Press, Cambridge, Massachusetts

HOROWITZ I L 1974 *War and Peace in Contemporary Social Theory.* Humanities Press, New York

INDIAN COUNCIL FOR HISTORICAL RESEARCH, DELHI 1995 *We Fought Together for Freedom.* Oxford UP India

INDIAN COUNCIL OF PEACE RESEARCH 1972 *Peace Research for Peace Action.* Indian Council of Peace Research, New Delhi

INSTITUTE OF INTERNATIONAL PEACE STUDIES 1983 *A Road to World Peace.* Kyung Hee University Press, Seoul

INSTITUTE OF INTERNATIONAL PEACE STUDIES 1988 *Search for Causes of International Conflicts and Ways to the Resolutions.* Kyung Hee University Press, Seoul

INTERNATIONAL SOCIOLOGICAL ASSOCIATION 1957 *The Nature of Conflict: Studies on the Sociological*

Aspects of International Tension. United Nations Educational, Scientific and Cultural Organization (UNESCO), Paris
See also *Part 9.2: Peace and Politics*

JOHNSON L G 1976 *Conflicting Concepts of Peace in Contemporary Peace Studies.* Sage, Beverly Hills, California

KAHN H - see *Part 8: World Order and Internationalism*

KAHN H, WIENER A J 1967 *The Year 2000: A Framework for Speculation on the Next Thirty-Three Years.* Macmillan, New York

KAISER K 1970 *Friedensforschung in der Bundesrepublik* [Peace Research in the Federal Republic]. Vandenhoeck and Ruprecht, Gottingen

KERMAN C E 1974 *Creative Tension: The Life and Thought of Kenneth Boulding.* University of Michigan Press, Ann Arbor, Michigan

KLINEBERG O 1964 *The Human Dimension in International Relations.* Holt, Rinehart and Winston, New York

KOHLER G 1974 *Events Research and War/Peace Prediction.* Canadian Peace Research Institute, Oakville, Ontario

KRIESBERG L 1992 *Research in Social Movements, Conflicts and Change.* JAI Press

KUMAR M 1968 *Current Peace Research and India.* Gandhian Institute of Studies, Rajghat, Varanasi

LANG J 1971 *Military Institutions and the Sociology of War.* Sage, Beverly Hills, California

LASZLO E, YOO J Y 1985 *Peace Through Global Transformation: Hope for a New World in the Late 20th Century.* The Institute of International Peace Studies, Kyung Hee University, Seoul

LAWLER P 1995 *A Question of Values: Johan Galtung's Peace Research.* Lynne Rienner

LENTZ T F 1955 *Towards a Science of Peace.* Halcyon Press, London

LENTZ T F 1972 *Towards a Technology of Peace.*

Peace Research Laboratory, St. Louis, Minnesota

LOPEZ G A 1989 *Peace Studies: Past and Future.* Sage London

MacQUARRIE J 1973 *The Concept of Peace.* SCM Press, London

MORGENTHAU H 1967 *Scientific Man versus Power Politics.* University of Chicago Press, Chicago, Illinois

NEHNEVAJSA J 1963 *Futures of the Cold War.* University of Pittsburgh Press, Pittsburgh, Pennsylvania

NEWCOMBE A, NEWCOMBE H 1969 *Peace Research Around the World.* Canadian Peace Research Institute, Oakville, Ontario

NEWCOMBE A G, WERT J 1972 *An Inter-Nation Tensiometer for the Prediction of War.* Canadian Peace Research Institute, Oakville, Ontario

NICHOLSON M 1970 *Conflict Analysis.* English Universities Press, London

NIEZING J 1970 *Sociology, War and Disarmament: Studies in Peace Research.* Rotterdam University Press, Rotterdam

NOACK P 1970 *Friedensforsching: Ein Signal der Hoffnung?* Eurobuch A. Lutzeyer, Freudenstadt

O'CONNELL J 1989 *Making the Future: Peace Studies.* Trentham Books

PARDESI G (ed.) 1982 *Contemporary Peace Research.* Humanities Press, Atlantic Highlands, N.J

PAUL J, LAULICHT J 1963 *In your Opinion: Leaders' and Voters' Attitudes to Defense and Disarmament.* Canadian Peace Research Institute, Oakville, Ontario

RAPOPORT A 1960 *Fights, Games and Debates.* University of Michigan Press, Ann Arbor, Michigan

RAPOPORT A 1964 *Strategy and Conscience.* Harper and Row, New York

RAPOPORT A 1965 *Prisoner's Dilemma: A Study in Conflict and Co-operation.* University of Michigan Press, Ann Arbor, Michigan

RAPOPORT A 1971 *The Big Two: Soviet-American Perceptions of Foreign Policy*. Bobbs-Merrill, New York

RAPOPORT A 1974 *Conflict in Man-Made Environment*. Penguin, Harmondsworth

Review of Research Trends and an Annotated Bibliography: Social and Economic Consequences of the Arms Race and of Disarmament. 1978. UNESCO, Paris

RICHARDSON L F 1960 *Arms and Insecurity: A Mathematical Study of the Causes and Origins of War*. Quadrangle Books, Chicago, Illinois

RICHARDSON L F 1960 *Statistics of Deadly Quarrels*. Quadrangle Books, Chicago, Illinois

RUSSETT B M (ed.) 1972 *Peace, War and Numbers*. Sage, Beverly Hills, California

SCHELLING T C 1960 *The Strategy of Conflict*. Harvard University Press, Cambridge, Massachusetts

SHAW M 1984 *War, State and Society*. Macmillan, London

SHERIF M, SHERIF C 1953 *Groups in Harmony and Tension*. Harper, New York

SHERIF M - see *Part 9.5: Peace and Psychology*

SINGELL L D (ed.) 1974 *Kenneth E. Boulding: Collected Papers*. Colorado Associated University Press, Boulder, Colorado

SOROKIN P A - see *Part 9.5: Peace and Psychology*

STAGNER R 1967 *The Dimensions of Human Conflict*. Wayne State University Press, Detroit, Michigan

STARKE J G 1968 *An Introduction to the Science of Peace (Irenology)*. Sijthoff, Leyden

STOCKHOLM INTERNATIONAL PEACE RESEARCH INSTITUTE (SIPRI), TURNER J 1985 *Arms in the 80s*. Taylor and Francis, London

STRATEGY FOR PEACE CONFERENCE 1969-1978 *Strategy for Peace Conference Report*. Stanley Foundation, Muscadine, Iowa

SWINGLE P G (ed.) 1970 *The Structure of Conflict*. Academic Press, New York

UN 1989 *Participation of Women in Decisionmaking for Peace, Case Study of Sweden/e 89 IV 7*, United Nations

UNESCO 1981 *World Directory of Peace Research Institutions*. Distributed by Uni pub., Paris, UNESCO, New York, N.Y

UNESCO 1988 *World Directory of Peace Research and Training Institutions*. Berg

UNESCO 1988 *World Directory of Peace Research and Training Institutions*. UNESCO, New York, NY, U.S.A., Berg, Paris, France

UNESCO 1991 *World Directory of Peace Research and Training Institutions 1991*, New York

UNESCO 1995 *World Directory of Peace Research and Training Institutions*. Blackwell Pub.

VAN DEN DUNGEN P 1980 *Foundations of Peace Research*. School of Peace Studies, University of Bradford/Housmans, London

WALLENSTEEN P 1988 *Peace Research*. Westview Press

WALLENSTEEN P (ed.) 1988 *Peace Research: Achievements and Challenges*. Westview Press, Boulder

WALTZ K N 1965 *Man, the State, and War*. Columbia University Press, New York

WEHR P 1978 *Conflict Regulation*. Westview, Boulder, Colorado

WRIGHT Q 1942 *A Study of War*. University of Chicago Press, Chicago, Illinois

ZINNES D A 1976 *Contemporary Research in International Relations*. Free Press, New York

Part 11

Peace Education

ABRAMS G, SCHMIDT F 1972 *Learning Peace: A Resource Unit*. Jane Addams Peace Association, Philadelphia, Pennsylvania

ABRAMS G, SCHMIDT F 1973 *Social Studies: Peace in the Twentieth Century*. Jane Addams Peace Association, Philadelphia, Pennsylvania

ABRAMS G C, SCHMIDT F C (ed.) 1974 *Learning Peace a Resource Unit*. Jane Addams Peace Association, Philadelphia

AMERICAN FRIENDS SERVICE COMMITTEE 1973 *Workbook to End War*. American Friends Service Committee, Philadelphia, Pennsylvania

ASCD 1973 *Yearbook Committee; George Henderson, Chairman and editor 1973 Education for Peace: Focus on Mankind*. Association for Supervision and Curriculum Development, Washington

BROCK B 1985 *Educating for Peace: a Feminist Perspective*. Teachers College

BROCK-UTNE B 1986 *Educating for Peace: A Feminist Perspective*. Pergamon, New York

BROCK-UTNE B 1992 *Feminist Perspectives on Peace and Education*. Teachers College

CALLEJA J 1994 *International Education and the University*. Jessica Kingsley

CARPENTER S (ed.) 1977 *Repertoire of Peacemaking Skills*. Author Pub., Boulder, Colorado (Distributed by Consortium on Peace Research, Education and Development)

CURLE A 1975 *The Scope and Dilemmas of Peace Studies*. University of Bradford, Bradford

DAVIS U, MIDDLETON L 1982 *A Learning Community? The School of Peace Studies at the University of Bradford: A Critical Documentary History*. Fourth Idea Bookshop Collective, Bradford

DIABLO VALLEY EDUCATION PROJECT 1971 *Selected War/Peace Curriculum Units Available for High School Teaching*. Diablo Valley Education Project, Orinda, California

DOUGALL L 1973 *The War/Peace Film Guide*. World Without War Publications, Chicago, Illinois

GALTUNG J 1975 *Peace Research, Education, Action*. Humanities Press, New York

GRIFFITH P, REARDON B 1972 *Let us Examine our Attitude Toward Peace*. Social Studies School Series, Culver City, California

HAAVELSRUD M 1981 *Approaching Disarmament Education*. Butterworth, Woburn, Massachusetts

HAAVELSRUD M (ed.) 1974 *Education for Peace*. University of Keele, Keele
(Also 1976 IPC Science and Technology Press, Guildford)

HEATER D B 1984 *Peace Through Education: the Contribution of the Council for Education in World Citizenship*. Falmer Press, London, Philadelphia

HENDERSON G (ed.) 1973 *Education for Peace: Focus on Mankind*. Association for Supervision and Curriculum Development, Washington, DC

HICKS D 1982 *Studying Peace: The Educational Rationale*. Peace Studies Centre, Lancaster

HICKS D 1988 *Education for Peace*. Routledge

INSTITUTE FOR WORLD ORDER 1981 *Peace and World Order Studies: A Curriculum Guide*. Institute for World Order, New York

JUDSON S (ed.) 1976 *A Manual on Nonviolence and Children*. Nonviolence and Children Program, Friends Peace Committee, Philadelphia, Pennsylvania

KING D C 1973 *Patterns of Human Conflict*. Schloat Productions, Pleasantville, New York

KIRKLAND O 1970 *On Conflict: A Curriculum Unit with Comments*. Diablo Valley Education Project, Orinda, California

LAKEWOOD PUBLIC SCHOOLS 1971 *A Curriculum to Help Students Deal With Frustration and Aggression*. Lakewood Public Schools, Lakewood, Ohio

LASLEY II T J 1994 *Teaching Peace*. Bergin & Garvey

LAUTER P 1965 *Teaching about Peace Issues: A Peace Education Kit*. American Friends Service Committee, Philadelphia, Pennsylvania

McGINNIS J B 1977 *A Strategy Guide for Schools and School Systems in Education for Peace and Justice*. Institute for Education in Peace and Justice, St. Louis, Missouri

McGINNIS K, McGINNIS J B, McGIVERN M A, SCHINZEL L 1976 *Education for Peace and Justice: A Manual for Teachers*, 5th edn. Institute for Education in Peace and Justice, St. Louis, Missouri

McKAY B 1971 *Training for Nonviolent Action for High School Students: A Handbook*. Friends Peace Committee, Philadelphia, Pennsylvania

MONTESSORI M 1949 (1972) *Education and Peace*. Henry Regnery, Chicago, Illinois

MUDD S (ed.) 1966 *Conflict Resolution and World Education*. W. Junk, The Hague

MURRAY A M 1980 *Peace and Conflict Studies as Applied Liberal Arts: A Theoretical Framework for Curriculum Development*. Juniata College, Huntington, Philadelphia, Pennsylvania

NESBITT W A 1971 *Teaching about War and War Prevention*. Thomas Y. Crowell, New York

NESBITT W, ABRAMOVITZ N, BLOOMSTEIN C 1973 *Teaching Youth about Conflict and War*. National Council for the Social Studies, Washington, DC

READ H 1950 *Education for Peace*. Routledge and Kegan Paul, London

REARDON B 1982 *Militarization, Security and Peace Education: A Guide for Concerned Citizens*. United Ministries in Education, New York

RICHARDSON R (ed.) 1976 *Learning for Change in World Society*. World Studies Project, London

SLOAN D (ed.) 1984 *Education for Peace and Disarmament: Toward a Living World*. Teachers College Press, New York

TAYLOR H 1969 *The World as Teacher*. Doubleday, Garden City, New York

THORPE G L 1968 *A Suggested Procedure for Teaching a Twelve Week Unit on Problems of Peace and War in the Modern World*. Institute for World Order, New York

ULICH R 1964 *Education and the Idea of Mankind*. Harcourt, Brace and World, New York

WALTER V A 1993 *War and Peace Literature for Children and Young Adults*. Oryx Press

WASHBURN M, WEHR P 1976 *Peace and World Order Systems: Teaching and Research*. Sage, Beverly Hills, California

WOLF-WASSERMAN M, HUTCHINSON L 1978 *Teaching Human Dignity*. Education Exploration Center, Minneapolis, Minnesota

WORLD POLICY INSTITUTE 1984 *Peace and World Order Studies: A Curriculum Guide*. World Policy Institute, New York

WORLD POLICY INSTITUTE 1981 *Elements of a Network to Educate for World Security*. World Policy Institute, New York

WREN B 1977 *Education for Justice*. Orbis Books, Maryknoll, New York

WULF C (ed.) 1974 *Handbook on Peace Education*. International Peace Research Association, Oslo

YOUNG N 1983 *The Contemporary Peace Education Movement*. International Peace Research Institute (PRIO), Oslo

YOUNG N 1985 *Studying Peace: Problems and Possibilities*. Housmans, London

Part 12

Local/Regional Conflict and Peace

ABUL-HUSN L 1996 *The Lebanese Conflict.* Lynne Rienner

AHRARI M E 1996 *Change and Continuity in the Middle East.* Macmillan Press

ALAGAPPA M 1989 *In Search of Peace: Confidence Building and Conflict Reduction in the Pacific.* Kegan Paul

ALLAN J A 1996 *Water, Peace and the Middle East.* Tauris Acad Studies

ALPHER J *War in the Gulf.* Westview Press

ANDERSON M S 1995 *The War of the Austrian Succession, 1740-1748.* Longman

ANTHONY I 1994 *The Future of the Defence Industries in Central and Eastern Europe.* Oxford UP

ARNETT R C 1980 *Dwell in Peace: Applying Nonviolence to Everyday Relationships.* Brethren Press, Elgin, Ill

BAILEY S D 1990 *Four Arab-Israeli Wars and the Peace Process.* Macmillan Press

BEN G 1994 *Confidence Building in the Middle East.* Westview Press

BERGER E 1993 *Peace for Palestine: First Lost Opportunity.* Univ. Florida Press

BERUFF J R 1991 *Conflict, Peace and Development in the Caribbean.* Macmillan Press

BERUFF J R 1996 *Security Problems and Policies in the Post-Cold War Caribbean.* Macmillan Press

BERUFF J R, FIGUEROA J P, GREENE J E 1991 (eds.) *Conflict, Peace and Development in the Caribbean.* St Martinis Press, New York

BIRNBAUM K E 1991 *Towards a Future European Peace Order?* Macmillan Press

BOULDING E 1993 *Building Peace in the Middle East.* Lynne Rienner

BOZEMAN A B 1992 *Conflict in Africa.* Princeton UP

BRADBURY M 1994 *The Somali Conflict, Prospects for Peace.* Oxfam

BRAZIER C 1991 *Vietnam.* Oxfam

BRYAN A T 1990 *Peace, Development and Security in the Caribbean.* Macmillan Press

BUCKLAND P 1993 *The Arab-Israeli Conflict.* Blackwell Pub.

CHILD J 1986 *Conflict in Central America.* C Hurst & Co.

CHILD J 1992 *The Central American Peace Process, 1983-1991.* Lynne Rienner

CLARK R P 1991 *Negotiating with ETA.* Un Nevada Press

CLEMENTS K 1993 *Peace and Security in the Asia Pacific Region.* United Nations Univ.

COLEMAN K M 1991 *Understanding the Central American Crisis.* Scholarly Resources

COLLINGS, DEIRDRE (Research Associate, Political Science Department, Carleton University, USA) 1994 *Peace for Lebanon?* Lynne Rienner

CONTAMINE P 1986 *War in the Middle Ages.* Blackwell Pub.

COOPER S E 1972 *Five Views on European Peace.* Garland Pub., New York

CORDESMAN A H 1991 *Weapons of Mass Destruction in the Middle East.* Brassey's UK

COTRAN E 1996 *The Arab-Israeli Accords.* Kluwer Law Internat

CROCKER C A 1993 *High Noon in Sothern Africa.* W W Norton

CRUCE E 1972 *The New Cineas.* Garland Pub., New York

DALTON R 1992 *Winning Peace in the Gulf.* Royal Ins. Int. Affair

DANFORTH L N 1995 *The Macedonian Conflict.* Princeton UP

DEALY G C 1988 *An Honorable Peace in Central America.* Brooks Cole

DEAN J 1994 *Ending Europe's Wars: the Continuing Search for Peace and Security.* Brookings Inst.

DENG F M 1991 *Conflict Resolution in Africa.* Brookings Inst.

DOORNBOS M 1992 *Beyond Conflict in the Horn: the Prospects for Peace, Recovery and Development in Ethiopia, Eritrea, Somalia and Sudan.* James Currey Pub.

DOYLE M W 1995 *UN Peacekeeping in Cambodia: UNTAC's Civilian Mandate.* Lynne Rienner

DUNKERLEY J 1994 *The Pacification of Central America.* Verso

DUNNIGAN J P 1995 *Deep-rooted Conflict and the IRA Cease-fire.* Univ Press America

EVRON Y 1994 *Israel's Nuclear Dilemma.* Routledge

FARLY O W 1995 *Conflict in Africa.* Tauris Acad Studies

FAUST D G 1994 *Southern Stories.* Univ. Missouri Press

FELD W J 1993 *The Future of European Security and Defense Policy.* Adamantine Press

FISCHER S 1994 *Securing Peace in the Middle East.* MIT Press

FLAMHAFT Z 1995 *Israel on the Road to Peace.* Westview Press

FORUM FOR PEACE AND RECONCILIATION 1996 *Building Trust in Ireland.* Blackstaff Press

FRASER T G 1995 *The Arab-Israeli Conflict.* Macmillan Press

FREEDMAN L 1994 *The Gulf Conflict 1990-1991.* Princeton UP

GEDDES C L 1991 *A Documentary History of the Arab-Israeli Conflict.* Praeger Pub.

GEORGE L 1972 *Why Pacifists Should be Socialists.* Garland Pub., New York

GLICKMAN H 1990 *Toward Peace and Security in Southern Africa.* Gordon & Breach

GREEN M 1995 *Arming Japan.* Columbia UP

GUELKE A 1994 *New Perspectives on the Northern Ireland Conflict.* Avebury

HAAS M 1989 *The Asian Way to Peace: a Story of Regional Co-operation.* Praeger Pub.

HARLOW N 1982 *California Conquered.* Univ California Press

HARLOW N 1992 *California Conquered: War and Peace on the Pacific, 1846-1850.* Univ California Press

HAYES P 1996 *Peace and Security in Northeast Asia.* M E Sharpe

HEUSER B 1991 *Securing Peace in Europe.* Macmillan Press

HOWLETT C F 1993 *Brookwood Labor College and the Struggle for Peace and Social Justice in America.* Edwin Mellen Press

INBAR E 1991 *War and Peace in Israeli Politics.* Lynne Rienner

INSTITUTE FOR PALESTINIAN STUDIES 1994 *The Palestinian-Israeli Peace Agreement.* Inst. Palestine Study Washington, DC

INTERNATIONAL CONFERENCE ON PEACE AND SECURITY IN SOUTH-EAST ASIA 1988 *Security in South-East Asia and the South-West Pacific.* Kluwer

ISAAC J 1994 *Water and Peace in the Middle East.* Elsevier

KARSH E 1993 *Non-Conventional Weapons Proliferation in the Middle East.* Clarendon Press

KAUFMAN E 1993 *Democracy, Peace and the Israeli-Palestinian Conflict.* Lynne Rienner

KEINLE E 1996 *Contemporary Syria.* Tauris Acad Studies

KEMP G 1992 *The Control of the Middle East Arms Race.* Brookings Inst.

KEMP G 1994 *Arab-Israeli Security Agreements: Negotiating Asymmetric Reciprocity.* Brookings Inst.

KEOGH D 1994 *Northern Ireland and the Politics of Reconciliation.* Cambridge UP

KERNAN T P 1990 *The Future of Peace.* Philosophical Library, New York

KIM H K 1995 *The Division of Korea and the Alliance Making Process.* Univ Press America

KIMCHE D 1988 *The Last Option: the Quest for Peace in the Middle East.* Weidenfeld & Nicholsn

KING P 1996 *Peace Building in the Asia Pacific Region.* Allen & Unwin

LAPIDOTH R 1992 *The Arab-Israel Conflict and its Resolution: Selected Documents.* Martinus Nijhoff

LUKACS Y 1996 *Israel, Jordan and the Peace Process.* Syracuse University

MAKINDA S 1993 *Seeking Peace from Chaos: Humanitarian Intervention in Somalia.* Lynne Rienner

MARSON G S 1988 *Hidden in Plain View.* Scolar Press

MARWICK A 1990 *Europe on the Eve of War 1900-1914.* Open UP

McCLEAN A 1993 *Security, Arms Control, and Conflict Reduction in East Asia and the Pacific.* Greenwood Press

MESTROVIC S G 1995 *Genocide after Emotion: the Postemotional Balkan War.* Routledge

MILLAR T B 1978 *Australia in Peace and War.* C Hurst & Co.

MOLLER B 1991 *Resolving the Security Dilemma in Europe.* Brassey's UK

MOLVAER R K 1993 *Environmental Cooperation and Confidence Building in the Horn of Africa.* Sage London

MOORE J N 1992 *The Arab-Israeli Conflict.* Princeton UP

MORENA D 1994 *The Struggle for Peace in Central America.* Univ Florida Press

MUNSKE B 1995 *The Two Plus Four Negotiations from a German-German Perspective.* Westview Press

MURAKAMI M 1995 *Managing Water for Peace in the Middle East.* United Nations Univ.

OAKLEY S P 1993 *War and Peace in the Baltic, 1560-1790.* Routledge

OBERG J 1992 *Nordic Security in the 1990s.* Pinter

OLSEN E A 1996 *The Major Powers in Northeast Asia.* Lynne Rienner

OWEN D 1995 *Balkan Odyssey.* Victor Gollancz

OZ A 1994 *Israel, Palestine and Peace: Essays.* Vintage

PELEG I 1995 *Human Rights in the West Bank and Gaza.* Syracuse University

PRUCHA F P 1995 *Indian Peace Medals in American History.* Univ Oklahoma Press

PRUNIER G 1995 *The Rwanda Crisis, 1954-1994.* C Hurst & Co.

PUGH M C 1991 *European Security—towards 2000.* Manchester UP

QUANDT W B 1993 *Peace Process: American Diplomacy and the Arab-Israeli Conflict Since 1967.* Brookings Inst.

RASHID MAM 1993 *Jordan the United States and the Middle East Peace Process, 1974-1991*. Cambridge UP

REICH B 1995 *Arab-Israeli Conflict and Conciliation*. Greenwood Press

REMAK J 1993 *A Very Civil War*. Westview Press

RESEARCH INSTITUTE FOR PEACE STUDIES 1994 *Asian Security*. Brassey's UK

ROBERTS P L 1994 *Teaching Peace Through Children's Literature*. Libraries Unlimited

ROGERS J P 1992 *The Future of European Security*. Macmillan Press

ROGERS P 1988 *Guide to Nuclear Weapons*. Berg

RUANE J 1996 *The Dynamics of Conflict in Northern Ireland*. Cambridge UP

RUANE K 1996 *War and Revolution in Vietnam*. UCL Press

RUBIN B R 1995 *The Search for Peace in Afghanistan*. Yale UP

RUEL S 1995 *Promoting a Culture for Peace in the Middle East*. United Nations

RUPESINGHE K 1992 *Internal Conflict and Governance*. Mcmillan Press

RUPESINGHE K 1996 *Internal Conflicts in South Asia*. Sage, London

RYAN M 1994 *War and Peace in Ireland*. Pluto Press

SALEM E 1994 *Violence and Diplomacy in Lebanon*. I B Tauris

SATO S 1993 *Security Challenges for Japan and Europe in a Post-Cold War World*. Brookings Inst.

SERBIN A 1990 *Caribbean Geopolitics*. Lynne Rienner

SHALEV A 1994 *Israel and Syria*. Westview Press

SHLAIM A 1996 *War and a Peace in the Middle East*. Penguin

SHON J S 1991 *Peace and Unification of Korea*. Seoul Computer Press

SKOLD N 1996 *United Nations Peacekeeping After Suez*. C Hurst & Co.

SOHN J S 1994 *Peace in Northeast Asia: Toward Greater Regional Cooperation*. Seoul, Kyung Hee University Press

SICHERMAN H 1993 *Palestinian Self-Government, Autonomy, and Peace*. Westview Press

SINGH J 1993 *Security in Third World Countries*. Dartmouth

SMITH C D 1996 *Palestine and the Arab-Israeli Conflict*. Macmillan Press

SPIEGEL S 1992 *Conflict Management in the Middle East*. Pinter

SPIEGEL S L 1992 *The Arab-Isreali Search for Peace in the Middle East*. Lynne Rienner

SPENCER C 1995 *Prospects for an Arab-Israeli Peace*. HMSO

STIPCICH S 1992 *The Technical Basis for Peace*. World Scientific

STJERNFELT B 1992 *The Sinai Peace Front*. C Hurst & Co.

STOCKHOLM INTERNATIONAL PEACE RESEARCH INSTITUTE (SIPRI) 1993 *SIPRI Yearbook*. Oxford UP

SWATUK L A 1991 *Prospects for Peace and Development in Southern Africa in the 1990s: Canadian and Comparative Perspectives*. Univ Press America

TAYLOR M A 1995 *Prerequisites for Peace in the Middle East*. United Nations

TIBI B 1992 *Conflict and War in the Middle East, 1967-91*. Macmillan Press

TSCHIRGI D 1989 *The American Search for Mideast Peace*. Praeger Pub.

UN 1993 *The United Nations in Cambodia*. United Nations

UN 1993 *Workshop on the Role of Border Problems in African Peace and Security*. United Nations

USHER G 1995 *Palestine in Crisis*. Pluto Press

VAROUFAKIS Y 1991 *Rational Conflict*. Blackwell Pub.

WALSH J 1995 *The Gulf War did not Happen*. Arena

WELLER M 1994 *Regional Peace-Keeping and International Enforcement: the Liberian Crisis*. Cambridge UP

WELLMAN C 1994 *The Baltic Sea Region: Conflict or Cooperation*. Westview Press

WOODWARD S L 1994 *Balkan Tragedy: Chaos and Dissolution After the Cold War*. Brookings Inst.

WOODWARD P 1994 *Conflict and Peace in the Horn of Africa*. Dartmouth

WRIGLEY C 1992 *David Lloyd George and the British Labour Movement*. Gregg Revivals

ZOUBIR Y H 1993 *International Dimensions of the Western Sahara Conflict*. Praeger Pub.

JOURNALS

This section comprises basic data on the journals published in the field.

The entries are listed alphabetically by country of origin (including a special section on journals generated through the United Nations) and then by journal title. Entries include a publisher's (or distributor's) address, date of first issue, details of frequency of publication, and a circulation figure whenever this is available. Additional information—for example, details of indices and former titles—are supplied where appropriate.

In this expansion job, exhaustive use was made of computer data base in the library of Kyung Hee University.

Journals

ARGENTINA

Paz y Justicia
Subject: Peace Activism
Published by: (Fellowship of Reconciliation), c/o
  Adolfo Pérez Esquivel, Espana 890, San Isidro
First Issue: 1973
Frequency: Monthly
Circulation: 6,000

Paz y Justicia
Subject: Peace Activism
Published by: Nuevo Mundo, S.A., Caldas 1348,
  Buenos Aires
First Issue: 1983
Frequency: Monthly
Circulation: 1,500

AUSTRALIA

Peace Plans
Subject: Peace Research
Published by: Libertarian Microfiche Publishing, 7
  Oxley St., Berrima, NSW 2577
First Issue: 1964
Frequency: Irregular
Circulation: 750
Published in microfiche form

The Australian Year Book of International Law
Subject: LAW—International Law
Published by: Centre for International and Public Law
  Australian National University, Canberra ACT 0200
  Australia
First Issue: 1965
Frequency: 1/year
Added/Corp: Australian National University. Faculty
  of Law
Subs Addr: Bibliotech, Australian National University,
  Canberra ACT 0200 Australia
Editor(s): Don Greig
ISSN: 0084-7658

Telephone: 011 61 6 2490454
Fax: 61 6 2490150

Working Paper
Subject: Political Science—International Relations
Published by: Peace Research Centre Australian
  National University, GPO Box 4, Canberra Aus-
  tralian Capital Territory 2601 Australia
First Issue: 1986
Frequency: Irregular
Added/Corp: Australian National University. Peace
  Research Centre
ISSN: 0817-1831
Telephone: 011 61 6 2493098
E-mail: peace@coombs.anu.edu.au
Fax: 61 6 2490174

World Review
Subject: International Relations
Published by: Australian Institute of International
  Affairs, Queensland Branch, Box 279, Indooroopil-
  ly, QLD 4068
First Issue: 1962
Frequency: 4/year
Circulation: 2,000

AUSTRIA

Kampf Dem Krieg
Subject: Peace Activism
Published by: Suttner-Gesellschaft, Oesterreichische
  Friedensgesellschaft, Landstr. Hauptstr. 14/5, A-
  1030 Vienna
First Issue: 1967
Frequency: 4/year
Circulation: 1,000

Peace and the Sciences
Subject: Political Science—International Relations
Published by: International Institute for Peace Moell-
  waldplatz 5, A-1040 Vienna, Austria
First Issue: (July/Sept. 1964)
Frequency: 4/year

Added/Corp: International Institute for Peace
Editor(s): Lev Voronkov
Telephone: 43 1 50464370
Fax: 43 1 5053236

Wiener Blätter zur Friedensforschung
Subject: Peace Research
Published by: Universitätszentrum für Friedens-forschung, Schottenring 21, A-1010 Vienna
First Issue: 1974
Frequency: 4/year
Circulation: 500

BELGIUM

Disarmament Campaigns
Subject: Military and Defense
Published by: Peace Press International 22 rue de Toulouse, 1040 Brussels, Belgium
First Issue: 1980?
Frequency: Monthly
Telephone: 32 2 2301621

IRG Bulletin
Subject: Peace Activism
see: **Nonviolence et Société**

Nonviolence et Société
Subject: Peace Activism
Published by: W. R. I. Belgian Section, Mouvement International de la Reconciliation, Van Elewyck-straat 35, 1050 Brussels (Or: 59 rue de Loriot, 1170 Brussels)
First Issue: 1947
Frequency: Bi-monthly
Circulation: 1,000

Peace Action News
Subject: Peace Activism
Published by: Non-Violent Alternatives, Antwerp
First Issue: 1978
Frequency: 5/year

International Associations
Subject: International Relations
see: **Transnational Associations**

Transnational Associations
Subject: International Relations
Published by: Union of International Associations, 1 Rue Aux Laines, B-1000 Brussels
First Issue: 1949

Frequency: Monthly
Text in English and French

CANADA

Armed Conflicts Report
Subject: Political Science
Published by: Project Ploughshares Conrad Grebel College, Waterloo ONT N2L 3G6 Canada
First Issue: 1994
Frequency: One time a year
Telephone: (519) 888-6541
E-mail: plough@watservl. uwaterloo.ca
Fax: (519) 885-0014

B.C. Peace News
Subject: Political Science—International Relations
Published by: British Columbia Peace Council 712-207 West Hastings Road, Vancouver British, Columbia V6B 1H7 Canada
First Issue: (Sept. 1978)
Frequency: 4/year
Added/Corp: B.C. Peace Council
Editor(s): Rosaleen Ross and Dorothy Morrison
ISSN: 0708-0859
Telephone: (604) 685-9958

Concern International
Subject: International Relations
Published by: Box 2086, Thunder Bay, ONT P7B SE7
First Issue: 1974
Frequency: Bi-monthly
Circulation: 2,500

Conflict Quarterly
Subject: International Relations
Published by: University of New Brunswick, Center for Conflict Studies, Fredericton, NB E3B 5A3
First Issue: 1980
Frequency: 4/year
Circulation: 425

Journal of Conflict Studies
Subject: Political Science—International Relations
Published by: University of New Brunswick Centre for Conflict Studies PO Box 4400, Fredericton NB E3B 5A3 Canada
First Issue: 199?
Frequency: 2/year
ISSN: 1198-8614
Telephone: (506) 453-4587
E-mail: acadnsis@unb.ca
Fax: (506) 453-4599

International Insights: A Dalhousie Journal on International Affairs

Subject: Political Science—International Relations
Published by: Dalhousie Law School Dalhousie University, Halifax Nova Scotia B3H 4H9 Canada
First Issue: Vol. 1, No. 1 (Spring Issue 1985)
Frequency: 2/year (Apr., and Oct.)
Added/Corp: Dalhousie University. Faculty of Law. John E. Read International Law Society
Editor(s): Ann Griffiths
ISSN: 0829-321X
Telephone: (902) 494-6639

International Perspectives

Subject: Political Science—International Relations
Published by: Baxter Publishing Company 310 Dupont Street, Toronto Ontario M5R 1V9 Canada
First Issue: (Jan./Feb. 1972)-(Jan. 1991)
.ISSN: 0381-4874
Telephone: (416)968-7252
E-mail: ctp@baxter.net
Internet: http://www.baxter.net
Fax: (416)968-2377

Middle East Focus

Subject: International Relations
Published by: Canadian Academic Foundation for Peace in the Middle East, 491 Lawrence Avenue W, Suite 307, Toronto, ONT M5M 1C7
First Issue: 1978
Frequency: Bi-monthly
Circulation: 4,000

Nuclear Free Press

Subject: Peace Activism
Published by: Ontario Public Interest Research Group, Trent University, Peterborough, ONT K9J 7B8
First Issue: 1978
Frequency: 4/year
Circulation: 4,000

Open Road

Subject: Peace Activism
Published by: Box 6135, Station G, Vancouver, BC V6R 4G5
First Issue: 1976
Frequency: 4/year
Circulation: 8,000

Peace and Environment News/Ottawa Peace and Environment Resource Centre

Subject: Environmental Issues
Published by: Ottawa Peace and Environment Resource Centre PO Box 4075, Station E, Ottawa Ontario K1S 5B1 Canada
First Issue: Vol. 5, No. 9 (Nov. 1990)
Frequency: Monthly
Added/Corp: Ottawa Peace and Environment Resource Centre
ISSN: 1181-9391

Peacekeeping & International Relations

Subject: Political Science—International Relations
Published by: Pearson Peacekeeping Center Cornwallis Park, PO Box 100, Clementsport NS B0S 1A0 Canada
First Issue: Vol. 20, No. 2 (Mar./Apr. 1991)
Frequency: 6/year
Editor(s): James Kiras
ISSN: 1187-3485
Telephone: (902)638-8611
E-mail: jkiras@ppc.edupeacekeeping.ns.ca
Fax: (902) 638-8888

Peace Magazine

Subject: Political Science—International Relations
Published by: Canadian Disarmament Information Service 736 Bathurst Street, Toronto Ontario M5S 2R4 Canada
First Issue: Vol. 1 Issue 1 (March 1985)
Frequency: 6/year
Added/Corp: Canadian Disarmament Information Service
Editor(s): Metta Spencer
ISSN: 0826-9521
Telephone: (416) 533-7581
E-mail: mspencer@web.net
Fax: (416) 531-6214

Peace Research

Subject: Peace Research
Published by: Canadian Peace Research Institute, 119 Thomas Street, Oakville, ONT
First Issue: 1969
Frequency: Monthly
Circulation: 1,600

Peace Research

Subject: Political Science—International Relations
Published by: Brandon University 270 18th Street, Brandon Manitoba R7A 6A9 Canada
First Issue: Vol. 1 (Nov. 1969)
Frequency: 4/year (Feb., May, Aug., Nov.)
Added/Corp: Canadian Peace Research Institute. Canadian Peace Research and Education Association

Editor(s): M. V. Naidu
ISSN: 0008-4697
Telephone: (204) 727-9720, (204) 729-9010
E-mail: naidu@docker.com
Fax: (204) 726-4573, (204) 728-4492

Peace Research Abstracts Journal

Subject: Peace Research
Published by: Peace Research Institute-Dundas, 25
    Dundana Ave., Dundas, ONT L9H 4E5
First Issue: 1964
Frequency: Monthly
Circulation: 400

Peace Research Reviews

Subject: Political Science
Published by: Peace Research Institute 25 Dundana
    Avenue, Dundas, Ontario L9H 4E5 Canada
First Issue: Vol. 1, No. 1 (1967)
Frequency: 6/year
Added/Corp: Peace Research Institute-Dundas. Cana-
    dian Peace Research Institute
Editor(s): Hanna Newcombe
ISSN: 0553-4283
Telephone: (905) 628-2356
E-mail: newcombe-pride@freenet.hamilton.on.ca
Fax: (905) 628-1830

Ploughshares Monitor

Subject: Political Science—International Relations
Published by: The Institute of Peace & Conflict Studies
    Conrad Grebel College, Waterloo, Ontario N2L
    3G6 Canada
First Issue: Vol. 1 (Apr. 1977)
Frequency: 4/year
Added/Corp: Project Ploughshares
Editor(s): Ernie Regehr
ISSN: 0703-1866
Telephone: (519) 888-6541
Fax: (519) 885-0014

Quaker Concern

Subject: Peace Activism
Published by: Canadian Friends Service Committee, 60
    Lowther Ave., Toronto ONT MSR 1C7
First Issue: 1977
Frequency: 4/year
Circulation: 2,300

Solidarites

Subject: Religions and Theology
Added/Corp: Canadian Catholic Organization for
    Development and Peace

Published by: Canadian Catholic Organization for
    Development and Peace 211 Center Street, Montre-
    al, Quebec H3K 1J5 Canada
First Issue: Vol. 1 (Oct. 1976)
Frequency: 5/year
ISSN: 0383-6711
Telephone: (514) 932-5136

The Canadian Yearbook of International Law (Annuaire Canadien De Droit International)

Subject: Law—International Law
Published by: University of British Columbia Press
    6344 Memorial Road, Vancouver, British Colum-
    bia V6T 1Z2 Canada
First Issue: Vol. 1 (1963)
Frequency: 1/year
Added/Corp: International Law Association, Canadian
    Branch
Editor(s): C.B. Bourne
ISSN: 0069-0058
Telephone: (604) 228-3259
Fax: (604) 228-6083

The Global Village Voice

Subject: Business and Economics—Economic Assis-
    tance and Development
Published by: Canadian Catholic Organization for
    Development and Peace 211 Center Street, Montre-
    al, Quebec H3K 1J5 Canada
First Issue: Vol. 1 (Oct. 1976)-Vol. 12 No. 3 (1988)
Added/Corp: Canadian Catholic Organization for
    Development and Peace
ISSN: 0383-6703
Telephone: (514) 932-5136

The Peace Arch News Weekender

Subject: Newspapers
Published by: The Peace Arch News Weekender PO
    Box 131, White Rock, British Columbia V4B 4Z7
    Canada
First Issue: Vol. 1, No. 1 (Sept. 12, 1982)
Frequency: 1/year
ISSN: 0821-5251

CHINA, REPUBLIC OF

International Journal of Peace Studies

Subject: Political Science
Published by: Grassroots Publishing Company PO Box
    26-447, Taipei 106 Taiwan
First Issue: Vol. 1, No. 1 (Jan. 1996)
Frequency: 2/year (Jan., July)

Editor(s): Cheng-Feng Shih
ISSN: 1085-7494
Telephone: 886 2 7060962
Fax: 886 2 7077965

DENMARK

Ikkevold
Subject: Peace Activism
Published by: Aldrig Mere Krig, Thorsgade 79, 2200
    Copenhagen N
First Issue: 1933
Frequency: 9/year
Circulation: 1,300
War Resisters' International publication

FINLAND

Disarmament Forum
Subject: Peace Activism
Published by: World Peace Council, WPC Information
    Centre, Box 18114, 00181 Helsinki 18
First Issue: 1982
Frequency: Monthly

Instant Research on Peace and Violence
Subject: Peace Research
See: **Current Research on Peace and Violence**

International Mobilisation
Subject: Political Science—Civil Rights
Published by: World Peace Council Lonnrotinkatu 25
    A 5 KRS, PO Box 114, 00181 Helsinki 18 Finland
First Issue: Jan. 1980
Added/Corp: World Peace Council. United Nations
    Centre Against Apartheid
Telephone: 358 6931044, 358 6933667

List of Members-World Peace Council
Subject: Law—International Law
Published by: World Peace Council Lonnrotinkatu 25
    A 5 krs, PO Box 114, 00181 Helsinki 18 Finland
First Issue: 19??
Main/Corp: World Peace Council
Telephone: 358 6931044, 358 6933667

New Perspectives
Subject: Peace Activism
Published by: World Peace Council, Lonnrotinkatu
    25a, Box 18114, Helsinki 18
First Issue: 1970

Frequency: Bi-monthly
Circulation: 15,000
English, French, German, and Spanish editions

Peace Courier
Subject: Political Science—International Relations
Published by: World Peace Council Lonnrotinkatu 25
    A 5 KRS, PO Box 114, 00181 Helsinki 18 Finland
First Issue: No. 1 (Sept. 1, 1970)
Frequency: 2/year
Added/Corp: World Peace Council
ISSN: 0031-594X
Telephone: 358 6931044, 358 6933667

FRANCE

Alerte Atomique
Subject: Peace Activism
Published by: Mouvement pour le Désarmement, La
    Paix et la Liberté, 25 rue de la Reynie, 75 Paris
    (1er)
Frequency: Bi-monthly

Alternatives Non Violentes
Subject: Peace Research
Published by: A.N.V., Craintilleux, 42210 Montrond
First Issue: 1973
Frequency: 4/year

Cahiers de Combat Pour La Paix
Subject: Peace Activism
Published by: Mouvement de la Paix, 35 rue de Clichy,
    75009 Paris
First Issue: 1952
Frequency: 4/year
Circulation: 10-15,000

Cahiers de la Reconciliation
Subject: Peace Activism
Published by: Mouvement International de la Recon-
    ciliation, BP 369, 75625 Paris Cedex 13
First Issue: 1923
Frequency: Monthly
Circulation: 1,800
Fellowship of Reconciliation Publication

Combat Non Violent
Subject: Peace Activism
Published by: Communauté Non Violente, 50 rue
    d'Illiers, 4500 Orleans
First Issue: 1971
Frequency: Weekly
Circulation: 4,000

Combat Pour La Paix
Subject: Peace Activism
See: **Cahiers de Combat Pour la Paix**

Cultures Et Conflits
Subject: Political Science—International Relations
Published by: L'Harmatten 7 rue de L'Ecole-Polytech-
nique, 75005 Paris France
First Issue: No. 1 (Winter 1991)
Frequency: 4/year
Added/Corp: Centre d'Etude des Conflits (Paris, France)
ISSN: 1157-996X
Telephone: 33 1 43257651

Elan
Subject: Peace Activism
Published by: Louis Lippens, 31 rue Foch, 59126 Lin-
selles
First Issue: 1955
Frequency: Quarterly

The ICC International Court of Arbitration Bulletin
Subject: Law—International Law
Published by: International Chamber of Commerce 38
Cours Albert 1 ER, 75009 Paris, France
First Issue: Vol. 1, No. 1 (June 1990)
Frequency: 2/year
Added/Corp: International Chamber of Commerce.
Court of Arbitration
Editor(s): Jean Francois Bourdue
ISSN: 1017-284X
Telephone: 011 33 1 49532828, 011 33 1 49532023
Fax: 33 1 45623456

UNESCO Prize for Peace Education
Subject: Political Science—International Relations
Published by: UNESCO/France 31 rue Francois Bonvin,
75732 Paris Cedex 15 France
First Issue: 1981
Frequency: Irregular
Added/Corp: UNESCO
Telephone: 33 1 45684564, 33 1 45684565
Fax: 33 1 45685745

GERMANY

Antimilitarismus Information
Subject: Peace Activism
Published by: AMI-Verlag G.B.R., Deidesheimer Str. 3,
D-1000 Berlin 33
First Issue: 1971
Frequency: Monthly

Circulation: 3,800
War Resisters' International publication

Aussenpolitik
Subject: International Relations
Published by: Interpress Verlag Gmbh, Holsteinis-
cheskamp 14, 2000 Hamburg 76
First Issue: 1950
Frequency: 4/year
Circulation: 6,800 (English edn.); 2800 (German edn.)
Editions in English and German

Blätter für Deutsche und Internationale Politik
Subject: International Relations
Published by: Pahl-Rugenstein Verlag, Gottesweg 54,
5000 Cologne 51
First Issue: 1956
Frequency: Monthly
Circulation: 18,000

Europa-Archiv
Subject: International Relations
Published by: (Deutsche Gesellschaft für Auswärtige
Politik e.V.) Verlag für Internationale Politik
Gmbh, Bachstr. 32, Postfach 1529, 5300 Bonn
First Issue: 1946
Frequency: Bi-monthly
Circulation: 3,900
Cumulative indexes: 1946-65, 1966-70, 1971-75,
1976-80

Friedens-Warte
Subject: Peace Research
Published by: Berlin Verlag Arno Spitz, Pacelliallee 5,
1000 Berlin 33
First Issue: 1899
Frequency: 4/year
Publication ceased during the Second World War

German Yearbook of International Law
Subject: Law—International Law
Published by: Duncker und Humblot Verlag Postfach
410329, D-12113 Berlin, Germany
First Issue: Vol. 19 (1976)
Frequency: 1/year
Added/Corp: Universitaet Kiel. Institut fuer Interna-
tionales Recht
ISSN: 0344-3094
Telephone: 49 30 79000612, 011 49 30 79000613
Fax: 49 30 79000631

Gewalt Freie Aktion
Subject: Peace Activism

Published by: Versoehnungsbund E.V., Jochen-Klep-
per-Str., 2082 Uetersen
First Issue: 1969
Frequency: 4/year
Circulation: 6,000

International Law of Arms Control

Subject: Political Science—International Relations
Published by: Berlin Verlag Arno Spitz Pacelliallee 5,
W-100 Berlin 33 Germany
First Issue: 19??
Frequency: Irregular
Editor(s): Gundolf Fahl

IPRA Studies in Peace Research

Subject: Political Science—International Relations
Published by: International Peace Research Associa-
tion/ Germany Wurzerstrasse 136, D 53175 Bonn
Germany
First Issue: 1960
Frequency: Irregular
Main/Corp: International Peace Research Association
ISSN: 0074-7289
Telephone: 49 228 353603
E-mail: afb@iz-bonn. gesis.d400.de
Fax: 49 228 353603

Public International Law

Subject: Law—International Law
Published by: Springer-Verlag GmbH & Company KG
Heidelberger Platz 3, D-14197 Berlin Germany
First Issue: Vol. 1 (1975)
Frequency: 2/year
Added/Corp: Max-Planck-Institut fuer Auslandisches
Offentliches Recht und Volkerrecht
Subs Addr: Springer-Verlag New York Inc./North
America, PO Box 2485, Journal Fulfillment, Secau-
cus, NJ, 07096. Telephone: (201)348-4033,
(800)777-4643. Fax: (201)348-4505
Editor(s): R. Bernhardt, K. Doehring, and J.A. Frowein
ISSN: 0340-7349
Telephone: 49 30 82787492
E-mail: order@spring.de
Fax: 49 30 82787448

Zivil Courage

Subject: Peace Activism
Published by: Deutsche Friedensgesellschaft-Vere-
inigte Kriegsdienstgegner (DFG-VK), Haserstr. 6,
5000 Cologne 21
First Issue: 1975
Frequency: Monthly
Circulation: 20,000

INDIA

Gandhian Perspectives

Subject: Peace Research
Published by: Gandhian Institute of Studies, Rajghat,
Varanasi 221001
First Issue: 1978
Frequency: Semi-annually
Text in English

Gandhi Marg

Subject: Political Science—International Relations
Published by: Gandhi Peace Foundation 221-223 Deen
Dayal Upadhyaya Marg, New Delhi 110002 India
First Issue: Vol. 1 (April 1979)
Frequency: 4/year
Added/Corp: Gandhi Peace Foundation (New Delhi,
India)
ISSN: 0016-4437

Gandhi Peace Foundation Lecture

Subject: History—History of Asia
Published by: Gandhi Peace Foundation 221-223 Deen
Dayal Upadhyaya Marg, New Delhi 110002 India
First Issue: 1975
Frequency: Irregular

Journal of Gandhian Studies

Subject: Peace Research
Published by: Institute of Gandhian Thought and Peace
Studies, University of Allahabad, Gandhi Bhawan,
Allahabad
First Issue: 1973
Frequency: 4/year
Circulation: 500
Text in English

Peace: A Monthly Journal Devoted to Peace and Illumination

Subject: Religions and Theology—Hinduism
Published by: Peace Sri Swami Nirvanananda, Sri
Lanka
First Issue: 19??
Frequency: 12/year

The Indian Journal of International Law

Subject: Law—International Law
Published by: Indian Society of International Law 7-8
Scindia H/Kasturba Gandhi M, New Delhi 110001
India
First Issue: Vol. 1, No. 1 (July 1960)
Frequency: 4/year

Added/Corp: Indian Society of International Law
Subs Addr: Prints India, 11 Darya Ganj, New Delhi
110002 India. Telephone: 91 11 3268645
ISSN: 0019-5294
Fax: 91 11 6475450

The Indian Year Book of International Affairs
Subject: Political Science—International Relations
Published by: University of Madras Registrar Universi-
ty Building Chepauk, Madras 600 005 India
First Issue: Vol. 1 (1952)
Frequency: Monthly
Added/Corp: University of Madras, Indian Study
Group of International Affairs
ISSN: 0537-2704

IRELAND

Dawn
Subject: Peace Activism
Published by: Dawn Editorial Collective, 168 Rathgar
Road., Dublin 6
First Issue: 1974
Frequency: 10-12/year
Circulation: 900

ISRAEL

International Problems
Subject: International Relations
Published by: Israel Institute of International Affairs,
POB 17027, Tel Aviv 61170
First Issue: 1963
Frequency: 2-4/year
Circulation: 5,000
Text in English, French, and Hebrew

The Other Israel: Newsletter of the Israeli Council for Israeli-Palestinian Peace
Subject: Political Science
Published by: The Other Israel PO Box 2542, Holon
58125 Israel
First Issue: No. 1 (July 1983)
Added/Corp: Israeli Council for Israeli-Palestinian
Peace
Editor(s): Adam Keller
ISSN: 0792-4615
Telephone: 972 3 5565804
Fax: 972 3 5565804

ITALY

Azione Nonviolenta
Subject: Peace Activism
Published by: Via Filippini, 25/A, 37121 Verona
First Issue: 1964
Frequency: Monthly

Comunita Internazionale
Subject: International Relations
Published by: (Societa Italiana per L'Organizzazione
Internazionale) Casa Editrice Dott, Antonio Milani,
Via Japelli 5,35100 Padua
First Issue: 1946
Frequency: 4/year
Circulation: 3,000
Text in English, French, and Italian

Incontro
Subject: Peace Activism
Published by: Via Consolata N.11, 10122 Torino
First Issue: 1949
Frequency: Monthly
Circulation: 8,000

JAPAN

International Cooperation/Kokusai Kyoryoku
Subject: International Relations
Published by: Japan International Cooperation Agency,
Box 216, Mitsui Building, Shinjuku-ku, Tokyo 160
First Issue: 1953
Frequency: Monthly
Circulation: 9,000
Text in Japanese

Peace Research in Japan
Subject: Political Science—International Relations
Published by: Japan Peace Research Group University
of Tokyo, Faculty of Law, Tokyo, Japan
First Issue: 1967
Frequency: 1/year
Added/Corp: Nihon Heiwa Kenkyu Kondankai

The Japanese Annual of International Law
Subject: Law—International Law
Published by: Yushodo Booksellers Ltd 29 San El Cho
Shinjuku Ku, Tokyo 160 Japan
First Issue: No. 1 (1957)
Frequency: 1/year
Added/Corp: International Law Association. Japan
Branch

ISSN: 0448-8806
Telephone: 81 3 33571411

KOREA

Journal of International Affairs
Subject: International Relations
Published by: Kukje Munjesa, 95 Yeunji-Dong, Chongro-Ku, Seoul
First Issue: 1970
Frequency: Monthly
Text in Korean

Korea & World Affairs
Subject: Political Science—International Relations
Published by: Research Center of Peace and Unification of Korea CPO Box 6545, Seoul 100 Korea
First Issue: Vol. 1 (Spring 1977)
Frequency: 4/year
Added/Corp: Pyonghwa Tongil Yonguso (Korea)
ISSN: 0251-3072

Korea & World Politics
Subject: International Relations
Published by: Institute for Far Eastern Studies, Kyungnam University, 28-42 Samchung-dong, Chongro-ku, Seoul
Telephone: 82-2-3700-0700
Fax: 82-2-0700-0707

Korean Journal of National Unification
Subject:
Published by: Korea Institute for National Unification, CPO Box 8232 Seoul 100-682
Telephone: 82-2-234-9113
Fax: 82-2-238-3291

Korean Journal of Population and Development
Subject: Population and Development
Published by: The Center for Social Sciences, Seoul National University, San 56-1, Shinrim-dong, Kwanak-ku, Seoul 151-172
Frequency: Bi-annually
Telephone: 82-2-886-5476
Fax: 82-2-886-0976

Oughtopia
Subject: Reconstruction of Human Society
Published by: Center for the Reconstruction of Human Society, Kyung Hee University
First Issue: 1976
Telephone: 82-2-961-0205
Fax: 82-2-966-1804

Peace Forum
Subject: Peace
Published by: The Graduate Institute of Peace Studies, Kyung Hee University, Jinjob-up, Namyangju city Kyonggi-do 473-860
First Issue: 1985
Telephone: 82-346-528-7001/20
Fax: 82-346-528-7630

Peace Studies
Subject: Peace
Published by: Institute of International Peace Studies Kyung Hee University, 1, Hoegi-dong, Dongdaemoon-ku, Seoul 130-701
First Issue: 1981
Telephone: 82-2-961-0201
Fax: 82-2-966-1804

LEBANON

United Nations Resolutions on Palestine and Arab-Israeli Conflict
Subject: Political Science—International Relations
Published by: Institute for Palestine Studies PO Box 7164, Beirut, Lebanon
First Issue: 1975
Telephone: 01-814174, 01-312512

MONGOLIA

Buddhists for Peace
Subject: Religions and Theology—Buddhism
Published by: Asian Buddhist Conference for Peace Gangdanthekchenling Monaster, Ulan Bator-51 Mongolia
First Issue: Vol. 1, No. 1 (1979)
Frequency: 4/year
Editor(s): B. Wangchindorj
Telephone: 976 1 53538

NETHERLANDS

Arbitration International
Subject: Law—International Law
Published by: Kluwer Law International/Netherlands PO Box 85889, 2508 CN The Hague, Netherlands
First Issue: Vol. 1, No. 1 (April 1985)
Frequency: Quarterly (Jan., Apr., July, Oct.)
Added/Corp: Chartered Institute of Arbitrators (Great Britain) London Court of International Arbitration

Subs Addr: Kluwer Law International, PO Box 322, 3300 AH Dordrecht, The Netherlands. Telephone: 011 31 78 6392392
Editor(s): Jan Paulsson
ISSN: 0957-0411
Telephone: 31 70 3081555
E-mail: marissa.galatis@kli.wkap.nl
Fax: 31 70 3081560

Asian Yearbook of International Law
Subject: Law—International Law
Published by: Martinus Nijhoff Publishers Subsidiary of Kluwer Academic Publishers, PO Box 269, 2501 AZ The Hague Netherlands
First Issue: Vol. 1 (1991)
Frequency: 1/year
Added/Corp: Foundation for the Development of International Law in Asia
Subs Addr: Kluwer Academic Publishers/us Subscriptions, PO Box 253, Accord Station, Hingham, MA, 02018
Telephone: (617) 871-6600
ISSN: 0928-432X
Telephone: 31 79 684400
Fax: 31 79 615698

Co-Existence
Subject: Peace Activism
Published by: Martinus Nijhoff, P.O. Box 566, 2501 CN, The Hague
First Issue: 1963
Frequency: 4/year
Circulation: 700

Developments in International Law
Subject: Law—International Law
Published by: Kluwer Academic Publishers Postbus 322, 3300 ah Dordrecht The Netherlands
First Issue: Vol. 1 (1979)
Frequency: Irregular
Telephone: 31 78 6392392
E-mail: kluwer@wkap.com (North America) or services@wkap. nl
Internet: http://www.wkap.nl
Fax: 31 78 6546474

European Journal of International Law
Subject: Law—International Law
Published by: Kluwer Law International/Netherlands PO Box 85889, 2508 CN The Hague, Netherlands
First Issue: Vol. 1, No. 1/2 (1990)
Frequency: 4/year
Added/Corp: European University Institute

ISSN: 0938-5428
Telephone: 31 70 3081555
E-mail: marissa.galatis@kli.wkap.nl
Fax: 31 70 3081560

Hague Yearbook of International Law/ Annuaire De La Haye De Droit International
Subject: Law—International Law
Published by: Kluwer Academic Publishers Postbus 322, 3300 AH Dordrecht, The Netherlands
First Issue: Vol. 1 (1988)
Frequency: 1/year
Added/Corp: Hague Academy of International Law Association of Attenders and Alumni
Subs Addr: Kluwer Academic Publishers/us Subscriptions, PO Box 253, Accord Station, Hingham, MA, 02018. Telephone: (617)871-6600
Telephone: 31 78 6392392
E-mail: kluwer@wkap.com (North America) or services@wkap. nl
Internet: http://www.wkap.nl
Fax: 31 78 6546474

IFOR Report
Subject: Peace Activism
Published by: International Fellowship of Reconciliation, Hof van Sonoy 15-17, 1811 LD Alkmaar
First Issue: 1919
Frequency: 5/year
Circulation: 2,500

Journal of International Arbitration
Subject: Law—International Law
Published by: Kluwer Law International/Netherlands PO Box 85889, 2508 CN The Hague, Netherlands
First Issue: Vol. 1, No. 1 (Apr. 1984)
Frequency: 4/year
Subs Addr: Kluwer Law International, PO Box 322, 3300 AH Dordrecht Netherlands. Telephone: 011 31 78 6392392
Editor(s): Jacques Werner
ISSN: 0255-8106
Telephone: 31 70 3081555
E-mail: marissa. galatis@kli.wkap.nl
Fax: 31 70 3081560

Kerk en Vrede
Subject: Peace Activism
Published by: Kerk en Vrede, Utrectseweg 159, Amersfoort
First Issue: 1925
Frequency: Monthly
Circulation: 3,000

Leiden Journal of International Law

Subject: Law—International Law
Published by: Kluwer Law International/Netherlands
   PO Box 85889, 2508 CN The Hague, Netherlands
First Issue: Vol. 1, No. 1 (May 1988)
Frequency: 3/year
Added/Corp: Leiden Journal of International Law
   Foundation. Rijksuniversiteit te Leiden. Faculteit
   der Rechtsgeleerdheid
Subs Addr: Kluwer Law International, PO Box 322,
   3300 AH Dordrecht Netherlands. Telephone: 011
   31 78 6392392
ISSN: 0922-1565
Telephone: 31 70 3081555
E-mail: marissa.galatis@kli.wkap.nl
Fax: 31 70 3081560

Militia Christi

Subject: Peace Activism
See: **Kerk en Vrede**

Netherlands Yearbook of International Law

Subject: Law—International Law
Published by: Martinus Nijhoff Publishers Subsidiary
   of Kluwer Academic Publishers, PO Box 269, 2501
   AZ The Hague, Netherlands
First Issue: Vol. 1 (1970)
Frequency: 1/year
Added/Corp: T.M.C. Asser Institute
ISSN: 0167-6768
Telephone: 31 79 684400
Fax: 31 79 615698

Nieuwe Literatuur Over Oorlog en Vrede

Subject: Peace Research
See: **Transaktie**

Nordic Journal of International Law
(ACTA Scandinavica Juris Gentium)

Subject: Law—International Law
Published by: Kluwer Law International/Netherlands
   PO Box 85889, 2508 CN The Hague, Netherlands
First Issue: Vol. 55, No. 1/2 (1986)
Frequency: 4/year
Editor(s): Frederik Danelius
ISSN: 0902-7351
Telephone: 31 70 3081555
E-mail: marissa.galatis@kli.wkap.nl
Fax: 31 70 3081560

Onze Wereld En Vrede

Subject: Peace Research
Published by: Netherlands Organization for Interna-
tional Development Cooperation, Editorial Room,
   Kloveniers Burgwal 23, 1011 JV Amsterdam
First Issue: 1957
Frequency: Monthly
Circulation: 37,000

The Palestine Yearbook of International Law

Subject: Law—International Law
Published by: Kluwer Law International/Netherlands
   PO Box 85889, 2508 CN The Hague Netherlands
First Issue: Vol. 1 (1984)
Added/Corp: Shaybani Society of International Law
Telephone: 31 70 3081555
E-mail: marissa.galatis@kli.wkap.nl
Fax: 31 70 3081560

Spanish Yearbook of International Law

Subject: Law—International Law
Published by: Martinus Nijhoff Publishers Subsidiary
   of Kluwer Academic Publishers, PO Box 269, 2501
   AZ The Hague, Netherlands
First Issue: Vol. 1 (1991)
Frequency: 1/year
Added/Corp: Consejo Superior de Investigaciones
   Cientificas (Spain) Asociacion Espanola de Profe-
   sores de Derecho Internacional y Relaciones Inter-
   nacionales
ISSN: 0928-0634
Telephone: 31 79 684400
Fax: 31 79 615698

T Kan Anders

Subject: Peace Activism
Published by: T Kan Anders, Werkgemeenschap voor
   Pacifisme, Ekologie en Socialisme, Vlamingstraat
   82, 2611 LA Delft
First Issue: Vol. 4, 1981
Frequency: 4/year
Circulation: 2,000

Transaktie

Subject: Peace Research
Published by: Polemologisch Instituut van de Rijksuni-
   versiteit, Heresingel 13, 9711 ER Groningen
First Issue: 1964
Frequency: Quarterly (until 1977, monthly)

Vredesopbouw

Subject: Peace Research
Published by: Stichting Vredesopbouw, Parkstraat 9,
   3581 PA Utrecht
First Issue: 1964
Frequency: Monthly
Circulation: 1,500

NEW ZEALAND

C.P.S. Bulletin
Subject: Peace Activism
Published by: New Zealand Christian Pacifist Society,
    396 Port Hills Road, Christchurch 2
First Issue: 1946
Frequency: 4/year
Circulation: 650

New Zealand Christian Pacifist
Subject: Peace Activism
See: **C.P.S. Bulletin**

Peace Bulletin
Subject: Peace Activism
See: **C.P.S. Bulletin**

World Affairs
Subject: International Relations
Published by: United Nations Association of New
    Zealand, Box 1011, Wellington
First Issue: 1945
Frequency: 4/year
Circulation: 2,200

NORWAY

Internasjonal Politikk
Subject: International Relations
Published by: Norwegian Institute of International
    Affairs, Bygdoey Alle 3, Postboks 8159 Dep Oslo 1
First Issue: 1938
Frequency: Bi-monthly
Circulation: 2,750
Text in Norwegian; summaries in English

PHILIPPINES

Justice & Peace Review
Subject: Political Science—Civil Rights
Published by: Ecumenical Movement for Justice and
    Peace Room 502 Estuar Bldg., 41 Timog Avenue,
    Quezon City, Philippines
First Issue: Vol. 1, No. 1 (1986)
Frequency: 4/year
Added/Corp: Kilusan para sa Katarungan at Kapaya-
    paan (Philippines)
ISSN: 0116-6360

The Philippine Yearbook of International Law
Subject: Law—International Law
Published by: Philippine Society of International Law
    UP Law Complex Bocobo Hall, Quezon City 1101
    Philippines
First Issue: Vol. 1 (1966/1968)
Frequency: Irregular
Added/Corp: Philippine Society of International Law.
    University of the Philippines. Legal Resources
    Center. University of the Philippines. Law Center
ISSN: 0115-8805
Telephone: 63 2 977137

POLAND

The Polish Yearbook of International Law
Subject: Law—International Law
First Issue: 1 (1966/1967)
Frequency: 1/year
Added/Corp: Polski Instytut Spraw Miqedzynaro-
    dowych. Instytut Nauk Prawnych (Polska
    Akademia Nauk) International Law Association.
    Polish Branch. Instytut Panstwa i Prawa (Polska
    Akademia Nauk)
Subs Addr: ARS Polona, PO Box 1001, 00068 Warsaw
    Poland. Telephone: 48 22 261201
ISSN: 0554-498X

RUSSIA

International Affairs
Subject: International Relations
Published by: Vsesoyuznoe Obshchestvo "Znanie,"
    Proezd Serova, 4 Moscow
First Issue: 1955
Frequency: Monthly
English, French, and Russian editions

International Peace and Disarmament Series/Scientific Research Council on Peace and Disarmament
Subject: Political Science—International Relations
Published by: Izdatelstvo Nauka/Akademiia Nauk (Pub-
    lishing House of the Russian Academy of Sciences),
    90 Profsoyuznaya UL, 117864 Moscow, Russia
First Issue: 19??
Frequency: Irregular
Added/Corp: Nauchnyi Sovet po Issledovaniiu Prob-
    lem Mira i Razoruzheniia (Akademiia Nauk SSSR)
Subs Addr: Victor Kamkin, 4950 56 Boiling Brook
    Parkway, Rockville, MD, 20852. Telephone:
    (301)881-5973
Telephone: 95 2340584

SOUTH AFRICA

Risk Afrique Executive Briefing
Subject: Political Science—International Relations
Published by: Peace and Conflict Studies PO Box 95824, 0154 Waterkloof South Africa
Frequency: 1/year
Telephone: 27 12 455476

Track Two
Subject: Political Science
Published by: University of Cape Town Centre for Conflict Resolution, Rondebosch 7700 South Africa
First Issue: 19??
Frequency: 4/year
Editor(s): Fiona Adams
ISSN: 1019-7435
Telephone: 27 21 222512
Fax: 011 27 21 222622

SRI LANKA

World Peace Journal
Subject: Peace Activism
Published by: World Government Movement, C/O Bandulp Sri Gunaardhana, Ed., 270 Park Road, Colombo 5
First Issue: 1974
Frequency: Bi-monthly
Circulation: 10,000
Text in English and Sinhala

SWEDEN

Cesic Studies in International Conflict
Subject: Political Science—International Relations
Published by: Lund University Press Box 141, S 22100 Lund, Sweden
First Issue: 1989
Frequency: Irregular
ISSN: 1100-4177
Telephone: 46 46 312000
E-mail: order@studli.se
Internet: http://www.studli.se/
Fax: 46 46 305338

Fred Och Frihet
Subject: Peace Activism
Published by: Women's International League for Peace and Freedom, Swedish Section, Hovslagar-gatan 2,

111 48 Stockholm
First Issue: 1928
Frequency: 4/year
Circulation: 3,000
Cumulative index every five years
Swedish text

Horn of Africa Bulletin
Subject: Political Science—International Relations
Published by: Life and Peace Institute PO Box 1520, S 75145 Uppsala, Sweden
First Issue: 1989
Frequency: 6/year
Editor(s): Susanne Thurfjell
Telephone: 46 18 169500
E-mail: lpi@algonet.se
Fax: 46 18 693059

International Studies in the Nordic Countries Newsletter
Subject: Political Science—International Relations
Published by: Nordic Cooperation Committee for International Politics Box 1253, S-111 82 Stockholm Sweden
First Issue: 1989
Added/Corp: Nordic Cooperation Committee for International Politics, including Peace and Conflict Research
Editor(s): Karin Lindgren
ISSN: 0345-4975
Telephone: 08/23 40 60

Internationella Studier
Subject: International Relations
Published by: Swedish Institute of International Affairs, Lilla Nygatan 23, 111 28 Stockholm
First Issue: 1968
Frequency: Bi-monthly
Circulation: 4,000

New Routes
Subject: Religions and Theology
Published by: Life and Peace Institute PO Box 1520, S 75145 Uppsala, Sweden
First Issue: 1997
Frequency: 4/year
Telephone: 46 18 169500
E-mail: lpi@algonet.se
Fax: 46 18 693059

Pax
Subject: Peace Activism
Published by: Svenska Fredsoch Skiljedomsfoerenin-

gen, Kungsgatan 55, 111 22 Stockholm
First Issue: 1972
Frequency: 10/year

States in Armed Conflict
Subject: History
Published by: Department of Peace and Conflict
  Research Ostra Agatan 53, S-753 22, Uppsala,
  Sweden
First Issue: 1988
Frequency: 1/year
Added/Corp: Uppsala Universitet. Institutionen fuer
  Freds-och Konfliktforskning
Telephone: 46 18 182500

Vietnam Bulletin
Subject: Peace Activism
Published by: United NFL Groups of Sweden, Fack 104
  32, Stockholm 19
First Issue: 1965
Frequency: 4/year
Circulation: 50,000

SWITZERLAND

Echoes: Justice, Peace & Creation News
Subject: Religions and Theology
Published by: World Council Of Churches 150 route
  de Ferney, CH 1211 Geneva, Switzerland
First Issue: 1992
Frequency: 2/year
Telephone: 41 22 7916111
E-mail: fcf@wcc.coe.org
Fax: 41 22 7910361

Pax et Libertas
Subject: Peace Activism
Published by: Women's International League for Peace
  and Freedom, 1 rue Varembe, 1211 Geneva 20
First Issue: 1925
Frequency: 4/year
Circulation: 500
Occasional articles in French and German
See also: **Peace and Freedom (UK); Peace and Free-
  dom (USA); Fred Och Frihet**

Review of International Cooperation
Subject: Peace Research
Published by: International Co-operative Alliance, 15
  Rte. des Morillons, CH-1218 Grand Saconnex/CH-
  1218 Geneva
First Issue: 1909

Frequency: 4/year
Circulation: 4,500
English, French, and Spanish editions

World Trade and Arbitration Materials
Subject: Business and Economics—International Eco-
  nomic Relations
Published by: Kluwer Law International/Netherlands
  PO Box 85889, 2508 CN The Hague, Netherlands
First Issue: Vol. 6, No. 1 (Jan. 1994)
Frequency: 6/year (Jan., Mar., May, July, Sept., Nov.)
Editor(s): Jacques Werner
ISSN: 1022-6583
Telephone: 31 70 3081555
E-mail: marissa.galatis@kli.wkap.nl
Fax: 31 70 3081560

THAILAND

Seeds of Peace
Subject: Political Science—Civil Rights
Published by: Thai Inter-Religious Commission for
  Development GPO Box 1960, Bangkok 10501,
  Thailand
First Issue: Vol. 1, No. 1 (Apr. 1985)
Frequency: 2/year
Added/Corp: Thai Inter-Religious Commission for
  Development

UNITED KINGDOM

ADIU Report
Subject: Peace Research
Published by: Armament and Disarmament Informa-
  tion Unit, Science Policy Research Unit, University
  of Sussex, Brighton, Sussex BN1 9RH
First Issue: 1979
Frequency: Bi-monthly
Circulation: 2,450

Anglican Pacifist
Subject: Peace Activism
See: **Challenge (UK)**

Arms Control
Subject: International Relations
Published by: Frank Cass & Co Ltd., Gainsborough
  House, 11 Gainsborough Rd, London E11 IRS
First Issue: 1980
Frequency: 3/year
See also: **Journal of Strategic Studies**

Background
Subject: International Relations
See: **International Studies Quarterly**

Bulletin of Arms Control
Subject: Military and Defense
Published by: Council of Arms Control/Center of Defense Studies Kings College University of London, Strand, London WC2R 2LS United Kingdom
First Issue: No. 1 (Feb. 1991)
Frequency: 4/year
ISSN: 0962-2047
Telephone: 44 171 8732065
Fax: 44 171 8732748

Bulletin on Peace Proposals
Subject: Political Science
Published by: Sage Publications Ltd. 6 Bonhill Street, London EC2A 4PU United Kingdom
First Issue: Vol. 1, No. 1 (1970)-(Sept. 1992)
Added/Corp: International Peace Research Association. International Peace Research Institute
Editor(s): Magne Barth
ISSN: 0007-5035
Telephone: 44 181 3740645
E-mail: market@sageltd.co.uk
Fax: 44 181 3748741

CAAT Newsletter
Subject: Peace Activism
Published by: Campaign Against the Arms Trade, 5 Caledonian Road, London N1 9DX
First Issue: 1974
Frequency: Bi-monthly
Circulation: 3,500

Call to Women
Subject: Peace Activism
Published by: Liaison Committee for Women's Peace Groups, 18 Oatlands Drive, Weybridge, Surrey KT13 9JL
First Issue: 1973
Frequency: Bi-monthly

Challenge
Subject: Peace Activism
Published by: Anglican Pacifist Fellowship, St. Mary's Vicarage, Bayswater Road, Headington, Oxford OX3 9EY
First Issue: 1961
Frequency: Bi-monthly
Circulation: 1,900

Chronicle
Subject: Peace Research
Published by: Dag Hammarskjöld Information Centre on the Study of Violence and Peace, 110 Eton Place, Eton College Road, London NW3 2DS
First Issue: 1979
Frequency: 4/year
Circulation: 2,000

Common Futures
Subject: Peace Research
Published by: Future Studies Centre, c/o Birmingham Settlement, 318 Summer Lane, Birmingham B19 3RL
First Issue: 1974
Frequency: 4/year
Circulation: 500

Common Life
Subject: Peace Activism
Published by: Vedanta Movement, Batheaston Villa, Batheaston, Bath
First Issue: 1951
Frequency: 4/year
Circulation: Issued free

Conflict Studies
Subject: International Relations
Published by: Institute for the Study of Conflict, 12-12A Golden Square, London W1R 3AF
First Issue: 1969
Frequency: Monthly

Conflict Studies
Subject: Political Science—International Relations
Published by: Research Institute for the Study of Conflict and Terrorism 136 Baker Street, London W1M 1FH United Kingdom
First Issue: No. 1 (Dec. 1969)
Frequency: 10/year
Added/Corp: Institute for the Study of Conflict. Current Affairs Research Services Centre (London, England) Centre for Security and Conflict Studies. Research Institute for the Study of Conflict and Terrorism
Editor(s): Joan Bates
ISSN: 0069-8792
Telephone: 44 171 2242659
Fax: 44 171 4863064

Cooperation and Conflict
Subject: Political Science
Published by: Sage Publications Ltd. 6 Bonhill Street, London EC2A 4PU United Kingdom

First Issue: Vol. 1 (1965)
Frequency: Quarterly (March, June, Sept., Dec.)
Added/Corp: Nordic Committee for the Study of
International Politics
Editor(s): Christian Thune
ISSN: 0010-8367
Telephone: 44 181 3740645
E-mail: market@sageltd.co.uk
Fax: 44 181 3748741

Defence and Peace Economics
Subject: Business and Economics—International Economic Relations
Published by: Harwood Academic Publishers PO Box
90, Reading RG1 8JL United Kingdom
First Issue: Vol. 5, No. 1 (1994)
Frequency: Irregular (4 issues per volume)
Editor(s): Profs. Keith Hartley and William Rogerson
ISSN: 1024-2694
Telephone: 44 1734 560080
Fax: 44 1734 568211

East-West Digest
Subject: International Relations
Published by: Foreign Affairs Publishing Co., 139
Petersham, Nr. Richmond, Surrey
First Issue: 1965
Frequency: Fortnightly
Circulation: 5,000

End Papers
Subject: Political Science
Published by: Bertrand Russell Peace Foundation Ltd
Bertrand Russell House, 45 Gamble Street, Nottingham NG7 4ET United Kingdom
First Issue: (Winter 1981/1982)-(1993)
Added/Corp: Bertrand Russell Peace Foundation
Editor(s): Ken Coates
ISSN: 0262-7922
Telephone: 44 1602 708318
Fax: 44 1602 420433

European Journal of International Relations
Subject: Political Science—International Relations
Published by: Sage Publications Ltd. 6 Bonhill Street,
London EC2A 4PU United Kingdom
First Issue: Vol. 1, No. 1 (March 1995)
Frequency: 4/year
Editor(s): Walter Carlsnaes
ISSN: 1354-0661
Telephone: 44 181 3740645
E-mail: market@sageltd.co.uk
Fax: 44 181 3748741

Fortnight
Subject: Peace Activism
Published by: Fortnight Publications Ltd., 7 Lower
Crescent, Belfast 7
First Issue: 1970
Frequency: Bi-monthly

The Friend
Subject: Peace Activism
Published by: Friend Publications Ltd., Drayton
House, Gordon Street, London WC1
First Issue: 1843
Frequency: Weekly
Circulation: 6,350
Quaker publication

**Global Society: Journal of Interdisciplinary
International Relations**
Subject: Political Science—International Relations
Published by: Carfax Publishing Company po Box 25,
Abingdon, Oxfordshire OX14 3UE United Kingdom
First Issue: 1996
Frequency: 3/year
ISSN: 1360-0826
Telephone: 44 1235 401000
E-mail: enquiries@carfax.co.uk
Fax: 44 1235 401550

International Affairs
Subject: International Relations
Published by: (Royal Institute of International Affairs)
Oxford University Press, Walton Street, Oxford
OX2 6DP
First Issue: 1922
Frequency: 4/year
Circulation: 7,750

Intelligence and National Security
Subject: Political Science—International Relations
Published by: Frank Cass & Company Ltd. Newbury
House, 890-900 Eastern Avenue, Ilford Essex IG2
7HH United Kingdom
First Issue: Vol. 1, No. 1 (Jan. 1986)
Frequency: 4/year
Editor(s): Christopher Andrew and Michael Handel
ISSN: 0268-4527
Telephone: 44 181 5998866
E-mail: 100067.1576@compuserve.com
Fax: 44 181 5990984

International Development Abstracts
Subject: Business and Economics

Published by: Elsevier Geo Abstracts An Imprint of Elsevier Science Ltd., The Boulevard, Langford Lane, Kidlington, Oxford OX5 1GB United Kingdom
First Issue: Vol. 1 (1982)
Frequency: 6/year
Added/Corp: University College of Swansea. Centre for Development Studies
Subs Addr: Elsevier Science Ltd./Oxford Fulfillment Centre, po Box 800, Kidlington OX5 1DX United Kingdom. Telephone: 011 44 865 843355
Editor(s): Marion Amos
ISSN: 0262-0855
Telephone: 44 1865 843000, 44 1865 843699
Fax: 44 1865 843010

International Interactions
Subject: International Relations
Published by: Gordon and Breach Science Publishers Ltd, 42 William IV Street, London WC2N 4DE
First Issue: 1974
Frequency: 2/year (4 Nos. Per Vol.)
Illustrated index; cumulative index

International Law Reports
Subject: Law—International Law
Published by: Grotius Publications Ltd po Box 115, Cambridge CB3 9BP United Kingdom
First Issue: 1950
Frequency: Irregular
ISSN: 0309-0671
Telephone: 44 1223 323410

International Relations Research Directory
Subject: Political Science—International Relations
Published by: Europa Publications Ltd. 18 Bedford Square, London WC1B 3JN United Kingdom
Telephone: 44 171 5808236
Fax: 44 171 6361664

International Studies Quarterly
Subject: International Relations
Published by: (International Studies Association) Butterworth Scientific Ltd., Journals Division, Box 63 Westbury House Bury Street, Guildford, Surrey GU2 5BH
First Issue: 1957
Frequency: 4/year
Circulation: Background

Journal of Peace Research
Subject: Political Science—International Relations
Published by: Sage Publications Ltd. 6 Bonhill Street,

London EC2A 4PU United Kingdom
First Issue: Vol. 1 (1964)
Frequency: Quarterly (Feb., May, Aug., Nov.)
Added/Corp: International Peace Research Institute
Editor(s): Nils Petter Gleditsch
ISSN: 0022-3433
Telephone: 44 181 3740645
E-mail: market@sageltd.co.uk
Fax: 44 181 3748741

Journal of Strategic Studies
Subject: International Relations
Published by: Frank Cass & Co. Ltd., Gainsborough House, 11 Gainsborough Road, London E11 1RS
First Issue: 1978
Frequency: 4/year
See also: **Arms Control**

Just Peace
Subject: Peace Activism
Published by: Pax Christic Centre, Blackfriars Hall, Southampton Road, London NW5
First Issue: 1936
Frequency: 10/year
Circulation: 3,000

Low Intensity Conflict & Law Enforcement
Subject: Law—Law Enforcement and Criminology
Published by: Frank Cass & Company Ltd. Newbury House, 890-900 Eastern Avenue, Ilford Essex IG2 7HH United Kingdom
First Issue: Vol. 1, No. 1 (Summer 1992)
Frequency: 3/year
ISSN: 0966-2847
Telephone: 44 181 5998866
E-mail: 100067.1576@compuserve.com
Fax: 44 181 5990984

Medicine and War
Subject: Peace Research
Published by: (Medical Association for the Prevention of War), John Wiley and Sons UK and Australia
First Issue: 1985
Frequency: Semi-annually
Circulation: 2,000

Medicine, Conflict, and Survival
Subject: Political Science—International Relations
Published by: Frank Cass & Company Ltd. Newbury House, 890-900 Eastern Avenue, Ilford Essex IG2 7HH United Kingdom
First Issue: Vol. 12, No. 1 (Jan.-Mar. 1996)
Frequency: 4/year

ISSN: 1362-3699
Telephone: 44 181 5998866
E-mail: 100067.1576@compuserve.com
Fax: 44 181 5990984

Military Balance

Subject: International Relations
Published by: International Institute for Strategic Studies, 23 Tavistock Street, London WC2E 7NQ
First Issue: 1959
Frequency: Annually
Circulation: 19,500

Millennium: Journal of International Studies

Subject: International Relations
Published by: London School of Economics and Political Science, Houghton Street, London WC2A 2AE
First Issue: 1971
Frequency: 3/year
Circulation: 900

Molesworth Bulletin

Subject: Peace Activism
Published by: The Old School House, Clopton, Kettering, Northants NN14 3DZ
First Issue: 1984
Frequency: Monthly

New Internationalist

Subject: International Relations
Published by: New Internationalist Publications Ltd., 42 Hythe Bridge Street, Oxford OX1 2EP
First Issue: 1973
Frequency: Monthly
Circulation: 35,000

Newspeace

Subject: Peace Activism
Published by: Fellowship of Reconciliation, 9 Coombe Rd., New Malden, Surrey KT3 4QA
First Issue: 1971
Frequency: Monthly
Circulation: 1,100

New World

Subject: Peace Research
Published by: United Nations Association of Great Britain & Northern Ireland, 3 Whitehall Court, London SW1A 2EL
First Issue: 1958
Frequency: Bi-monthly
Circulation: 12,000

Ocean Development and International Law

Subject: Law—Maritime Law
Published by: Taylor & Francis Ltd./uk Rankine Road, Basingstoke RG24 8PR United Kingdom
First Issue: Vol. 1, No. 3 (Fall 1973)
Frequency: 4/year
Subs Addr: Taylor & Francis Inc., 1900 Frost Road, Suite 101, Bristol, PA, 19007-1598. Telephone: (215) 785-5800, (800) 821-8312. Fax: (215) 785-5515
ISSN: 0090-8320
Editor(s): Jon L. Jacobson
Telephone: 44 1256 840366
E-mail: info@tandf.co.uk
Fax: 44 1256 479438

Pacifist

Subject: Peace Activism
Published by: Peace Pledge Union, 6 Endsleigh Street, London WC1
First Issue: 1961
Frequency: Monthly
Circulation: 900

Peace Action Newsletter

Subject: Peace Activism
See: **Quaker Peace & Service**

Peace and Freedom

Subject: Peace Activism
Published by: Women's International League for Peace and Freedom, 17 Victoria Park Sq., London E2 9PB
First Issue: 1952
Frequency: 4/year
Circulation: 500

Peace and Truth

Subject: Religions and Theology
Published by: Sovereign Grace Union 5 Rosier Crescent Swanwick, Derbys DE55 1RS United Kingdom
First Issue: 1914
Frequency: 4/year (Jan., Apr., July, Oct.)
Added/Corp: Sovereign Grace Union
Editor(s): John M. Brentnall
Telephone: 44 1773 608431

Peace by Peace

Subject: Peace Activism
Published by: Fredheim, 224 Lisburn Rd., Belfast, BT9 6GE
First Issue: 1976
Frequency: Monthly

Peace News
Subject: Peace Activism
Published by: Peace News Ltd., 8 Elm Avenue, Nottingham
First Issue: 1936
Frequency: Fortnightly
Circulation: 6,000

Peace News for Nonviolent Revolution
Subject: Political Science
Published by: Peace News Ltd. 5 Caledonian Road, London N1 9DX United Kingdom
First Issue: No. 2336 (Dec. 1990)
Frequency: Monthly
Editor(s): Ken Simons
Telephone: 44 171 2783344
Internet: peacenews@gn.apc.org
Fax: 44 171 2780444

Peace Press
Subject: Peace Activism
Published by: International Confederation for Disarmament and Peace, 6 Endsleigh Street, London WC1
First Issue: 1965
Frequency: Monthly
Circulation: 600
See also: **Pacifist**

Peace Review
Subject: Political Science—International Relations
Published by: Carfax Publishing Company PO Box 25, Abingdon, Oxfordshire OX14 3UE United Kingdom
First Issue: Vol. 1, No. 1 (Winter 1989)
Frequency: 4/year (Feb., May, Aug., Nov.)
Editor(s): John L. Harris and Robert Elias
ISSN: 1040-2659
Telephone: 44 1235 401000
E-mail: enquiries@carfax.co.uk
Fax: 44 1235 401550

Quaker Peace & Service
Subject: Peace Activism
Published by: Quaker Peace and Service, Friends House, Euston Road, London NW1 2BJ
First Issue: 1968
Frequency: 4/year; issued free

Reconciliation Quarterly
Subject: Peace Activism
Published by: Fellowship of Reconciliation, 9 Coombe Road, New Malden, Surrey KT3 4QA
First Issue: 1924

Frequency: 4/year
Circulation: 1,750
See also: **IFOR Report; Paz y Justicia; Newspeace**

Sanity
Subject: Peace Activism
Published by: Campaign for Nuclear Disarmament, 11 Goodwin Street, London N4 3HQ
First Issue: 1961
Frequency: Monthly
Circulation: 35,000

Science & Global Security: The Technical Basis for Arms Control and Environmental Policy Initiatives
Subject: Political Science—International Relations
Published by: Gordon & Breach Science Publishers PO Box 90, Reading Berkshire RG1 8JL United Kingdom
First Issue: Vol. 1, Nos. 1/2 (1989)
Frequency: Irregular (3 issues per volume)
Editor(s): Harold A. Feiveson
ISSN: 0892-9882
Telephone: 44 1734 560080
E-mail: info@gbhap.com
Fax: 44 1734 568211

Security Dialogue
Subject: Political Science
Published by: Sage Publications Ltd. 6 Bonhill Street, London EC2A 4PU United Kingdom
First Issue: Vol. 23, No. 3 (Sept. 1992)
Frequency: 4/year (March, June, Sept., Dec.)
Added/Corp: International Peace Research Institute
ISSN: 0967-0106
Telephone: 44 181 3740645
E-mail: market@sageltd.co.uk
Fax: 44 181 3748741

Sipri Yearbook
Subject: Political Science—International Relations
Published by: Oxford University Press/UK Walton Street, Oxford OX2 6DP United Kingdom
First Issue: 1987
Frequency: 1/year
Subs Addr: Oxford University Press/USA, Journals Marketing Department, Oxford University Press, 2001 Evans Road, Cary, NC, 27513
Telephone: (800) 451-7556, (919) 677-0977
Fax: (919) 677-1714
ISSN: 0953-0282
Telephone: 44 1865 556767
E-mail: jnlorders@oup.co.uk

Internet: http://www.oup.co.uk
Fax: 44 1865 267773

Spokesman
Subject: Peace Activism
See: **End Papers**

Studies in Conflict and Terrorism
Subject: Sociology
Published by: Taylor & Francis Ltd./uk Rankine Road,
    Basingstoke RG24 8PR United Kingdom
First Issue: Vol. 15, No. 1 (Jan./Mar. 1992)
Frequency: 4/year
Subs Addr: Taylor & Francis Inc., 1900 Frost Road,
    Suite 101, Bristol, pa, 19007-1598
Telephone: (215) 785-5800, (800) 821-8312
Fax: (215) 785-5515
Editor(s): George K. Tanham
ISSN: 1057-610X
Telephone: 44 1256 840366
E-mail: info@tandf.co.uk
Fax: 44 1256 479438

Survival
Subject: International Relations
Published by: International Institute for Strategic Stud-
    ies, 23 Tavistock Street, London WC2E 7NQ
First Issue: 1959
Circulation: 7,300

Teachers for Peace Newsletter
Subject: Peace Activism
Published by: Teachers for Peace, 22-24 Underwood
    St., London N1 7JG
First Issue: 1981
Frequency: 4/year

The Arbitration and Dispute Resolution Law Journal
Subject: Law—International Law
Published by: LLP Ltd. 69 77 Paul Street, London
    EC2A 4LQ United Kingdom
First Issue: 1992
Frequency: 4/year
Subs Addr: Lloyd's of London Press Inc./North Ameri-
    ca, 611 Broadway, Suite 308, New York, NY,
    10012. Telephone: (212)529-9500
Editor(s): Andrew Burr
ISSN: 0965-7053
Telephone: 44 171 5531000
Fax: 44 171 5531100

The British Yearbook of International Law
Subject: Law—International Law

Published by: Oxford University Press/uk Walton
    Street, Oxford OX2 6DP United Kingdom
First Issue: Vol. 1 (1921)
Frequency: 1/year
Added/Corp: Royal Institute of International Affairs.
    British Institute of International Affairs
Subs Addr: Oxford University Press/usa, Journals
    Marketing Department, Oxford University Press,
    2001 Evans Road, Cary, NC, 27513
Telephone: (800) 451-7556, (919) 677-0977
Fax: (919) 677-1714
Editor(s): Ian Brownlie and D.W. Bowett
ISSN: 0068-2691
Telephone: 44 1865 556767
E-mail: jnlorders@oup.co.uk
Internet: http://www.oup.co. uk
Fax: 44 1865 267773

The Spokesman
Subject: Political Science
Published by: Bertrand Russell Peace Foundation Ltd
    Bertrand Russell House, 45 Gamble Street, Not-
    tingham NG7 4ET United Kingdom
First Issue: 1995
Frequency: 1/year
Added/Corp: Bertrand Russell Peace Foundation
Editor(s): Ken Coates
Telephone: 44 1602 708318
Fax: 44 1602 420433

War/Peace Report
Subject: International Relations
See: **International Interactions**

World Arbitration & Mediation Report
Subject: Law—International Law
Published by: Transnational Juris Publishers 1 Bridge
    Street/Candy Dubenski Irvington, NY 10533
First Issue: Vol. 1, No. 1 (May 1990)
Frequency: 4/year
Added/Corp: BNA International Inc
Editor(s): Joel Kolko
ISSN: 0960-0949
Telephone: (914) 591-4288
Fax: (914) 591-2688

World Today
Subject: International Relations
Published by: (Royal Institute of International Affairs)
    Oxford University Press, Walton Street, Oxford
    OX2 6DP
First Issue: 1945
Frequency: Monthly
Circulation: 5,000

WRI Newsletter
Subject: Peace Activism
Published by: War Resisters' International, 55 Dawes Street, London SE17
Frequency: Bi-monthly
Circulation: 950

UNITED NATIONS

Disarmament
Subject: International Relations
Published by: United Nations Publications, Sales Section, Room A-3315, New York, NY 10017
First Issue: 1978
Frequency: 3/year

Disarmament Newsletter
Subject: International Relations
Published by: United Nations, Department of Disarmament Affairs, United Nations Plaza, New York, NY 10017
First Issue: 1983
Frequency: 4/year
Circulation: Issued free

U.N. Chronicle
Subject: International Relations
Published by: United Nations Publications, Room A-3315, New York, NY 10017 (Or: Distribution and Sales Section, Palais des Nations, CH-1211 Geneva 10, Switzerland)
First Issue: 1964
Frequency: Monthly
Circulation: 12,000
English, French, and Spanish editions

UNESCO Chronicle
Subject: Peace Research
Published by: UNESCO, 7-9 Place de Fontenoy, 75700 Paris
First Issue: 1955
Frequency: 11/year
Text in Arabic English, French, and Spanish
Published at same address: UNESCO **Courier;** UNESCO **Features**

UNITED STATES OF AMERICA

AD Rem: The Magazine of the International Law Students Association
Subject: Law—International Law

Published by: International Law Students Association/ ilsa 2223 Massachusetts Avenue, Northwest, Washington, DC 20008
First Issue: Vol. 1, Issue 1 (1992)
Frequency: 4/year
Added/Corp: International Law Students Association
Editor(s): David S. Anderson
ISSN: 1074-0961
Telephone: (202) 939-6030
Fax: (205) 265-0386

Alternatives: A Journal of World Policy
Subject: International Relations
Published by: Transaction Periodicals Consortium, Rutgers University, New Brunswick, NJ 08903 (Also available from: Allied Publishers Private Ltd., 15 Graham Road, Ballard Estate, Bombay 400038, India)
First Issue: 1974
Frequency: 4/year
Circulation: 1,000

Armed Forces and Society
Subject: International Relations
Published by: (Inter-University Seminar on Armed Forces & Society) Seven Locks Press, 7425 MacArthur Blvd., Box 37, Cabin John, MD 20818 (Or: British Inter-University Seminar, University of Hull, 195 Cottingham Rd., Hull HU5 2EQ, UK)
First Issue: 1974
Frequency: 4/year
Circulation: 2,000

Arms Control and Disarmament Agreements
Subject: Military and Defense
Published by: Superintendent of Documents US Government Printing Office, 732 North Capital Street Northwest US GPO Washington, DC 20402
First Issue: 1972
Frequency: Irregular
Added/Corp: United States. Arms Control and Disarmament Agency
Telephone: (202) 275-3328
Internet: http://www. census.gov
Fax: (202) 786-2377

Arms Control Today: A Publication of the Arms Control Association
Subject: Law—International Law
Published by: Arms Control Association 1726 M Street, Suite 201 Washington, DC 20036
First Issue: 1974
Frequency: 10/year

Added/Corp: Arms Control Association (Washington, D.C.)
Editor(s): Tom Pfeiffer
ISSN: 0196-125X
Telephone: (202) 463-8270
Fax: (202) 463-8273

Asian Survey

Subject: International Relations
Published by: Institute of International Studies, University of California Press, 2223 Fulton Street, Berkeley, CA 94720
First Issue: 1961
Frequency: Monthly
Circulation: 3,600

Ballast

Subject: Peace Activism
Published by: Live Without Trident, Box 12007, Seattle, WA 98102
First Issue: 1978
Frequency: Monthly
Circulation: 1,500

Baptist Peacemaker

Subject: Religions and Theology—Protestantism
Published by: Baptist Peace Fellowship 499 Patterson Street Memphis, TN 38111
First Issue: Vol. 1, No. 1 (Dec. 1980)
Frequency: 4/year (Jan., Apr., July, Oct.)
Added/Corp: Deer Park Baptist Church (Louisville, Ky.) Baptist Peace Fellowship of North America
Editor(s): Glen Hinson and Carman Sharp
ISSN: 0735-5815
Telephone: (901) 324-7675

Boston University International Law Journal

Subject: Law—International Law
Published by: Boston University School of Law 765 Commonwealth Avenue, Boston, MA 02215
First Issue: Vol. 1, Issue 1 (Spring 1982)
Frequency: 2/year
Added/Corp: Boston University, School of Law
Editor(s): Chris Meier
ISSN: 0737-8947
Telephone: (617) 353-3157

Brooklyn Journal of International Law

Subject: Law—International Law
Published by: Brooklyn Law School 250 Joralemon Street Brooklyn, NY 11201
First Issue: Vol. 1 (Spring 1975)
Frequency: 3/year

Added/Corp: Brooklyn Law School
Editor(s): Brian Ross, Heather Cooper
ISSN: 0740-4824
Telephone: (718) 780-7588
Fax: (718) 780-0368

Bulletin of Concerned Asian Scholars

Subject: International Relations
Published by: Box R, Berthoud, CO 80513
First Issue: 1968
Frequency: 4/year
Circulation: 2,500

Bulletin of Regional Cooperation in the Middle East

Subject: Political Science—International Relations
Published by: Search for Common Ground 1601 Connecticut Avenue, Northwest, Suite 200, Washington, DC 20009
First Issue: Vol. 2 (March 1, 1993)
Frequency: 4/year
Added/Corp: Search for Common Ground (Organization). Initiative for Peace and Cooperation in the Middle East
ISSN: 1082-3646
Telephone: (202) 265-4300
E-mail: bulletin@sfcg.org
Fax: (202) 232-6718

Bulletin of the Atomic Scientists

Subject: Peace Research
Published by: Educational Foundation for Nuclear Science, 5801 Kenwood, Chicago, IL 60637
First Issue: 1945
Frequency: Monthly
Circulation: 25,000

Bulletin/Search for Common Ground, Initiative for Peace and Cooperation in the Middle East

Subject: Political Science—International Relations
Published by: Search for Common Ground 1601 Connecticut Avenue Northwest, Suite 200 Washington, DC 20009
First Issue: Vol. 1, No. 1 (March 1, 1992)-Vol. 1, No. 4 (Dec. 1, 1992)
Added/Corp: Search for Common Ground (Organization). Initiative for Peace and Cooperation in the Middle East
ISSN: 1065-0237
Telephone: (202) 265-4300
E-mail: bulletin@sfcg.org
Fax: (202) 232-6718

California Western International Law Journal
Subject: Law—International Law
Published by: California Western School of Law 225 Cedar Street San Diego, CA 92101
First Issue: Vol. 1 (Fall 1970)
Frequency: 2/year
Added/Corp: California Western School of Law
Editor(s): Dale E. Hawley
ISSN: 0886-3210
Telephone: (619) 525-1477, (800) 255-4252
E-mail: lawreview@cwsl.edu
Fax: (619)231-6774

Case Western Reserve Journal of International Law
Subject: Law—International Law
Published by: Case Western Reserve University/School of Law 11075 East Boulevard Cleveland, OH 44106
First Issue: Vol. 1, No. 1 (Fall 1968)
Frequency: 3/year
Added/Corp: Franklin Thomas Backus School of Law
Editor(s): James P. Merriman and John G. Beck
ISSN: 0008-7254
Telephone: (216) 368-3304, (216) 368-3312
Fax: (216) 368-3310

Catholic Peace Voice
Subject: Religions and Theology
Published by: Pax Christi USA 348 East 10th Street Erie, PA 16503
First Issue: 1994
Frequency: 4/year
ISSN: 1083-1223
Telephone: (814) 453-4955
E-mail: paxchrist@igc.apc.org
Fax: (814) 452-4784

Catholic Worker
Subject: Peace Activism
Published by: Catholic Worker Movement, 36 E 1st Street, New York, NY 10003
First Issue: 1933
Frequency: Monthly
Circulation: 100,000

CCAS Newsletter
Subject: International Relations
See: **Bulletin of Concerned Asian Scholars**

Center Peace
Subject: Peace Activism
Published by: Center on Law & Pacifism, Box 1584, Colorado Springs, CO 80901
Frequency: Bi-monthly

Center for Peace and Conflict Studies/Detroit Council for World Affairs, Newsletter
Subject: Peace Research
Published by: Wayne State University, Center for Peace and Conflict Studies, 5229 Cass Ave., Room 101, Detroit, MI 48202
First Issue: 1965
Frequency: 4/year
Circulation: 1,000

Chinese Yearbook of International Law and Affairs
Subject: Law—International Law
Published by: Chinese Yearbook International Law Affairs 500 West Baltimore Street Baltimore, MD 21201
First Issue: Vol. 1 (1981)
Frequency: 1/year (Oct. or Nov.)
Added/Corp: Chung-kuo kuo Chi fa Hsueh hui. Occasional Papers/Reprints Series in Contemporary Asian Studies
Editor(s): Hungdah Chiu and Chih-yu Wu
ISSN: 0731-0854
Telephone: (410) 328-3870

Columbia Journal of Transnational Law
Subject: Law—International Law
Published by: Columbia University School of Law 435 West 116th Street New York, NY 10027
First Issue: Vol. 3 (Fall 1964)
Frequency: 3/year
Added/Corp: Columbia Journal of Transnational Law Association. Columbia Society of International Law
Editor(s): Douglas Doetsch
ISSN: 0010-1931
Telephone: (212) 854-2693
Fax: (212) 222-4256

Commonwealth International Law Cases
Subject: Law—International Law
Published by: Oceana Publications, Inc. 75 Main Street Dobbs Ferry, NY 10522
First Issue: 1974
Frequency: Irregular
ISSN: 1075-5845
Telephone: (914) 693-1320, (800) 831-0758
E-mail: custserv@oceanalaw.com
Internet: http://www.oceanlaw.com
Fax: (914) 693-0402

Conflict
Subject: International Relations
Published by: Crane Russak and Company, Inc., 3 E

44th Street New York, NY 10017
First Issue: 1978
Frequency: 4/year

Conflict and Consciousness
Subject: Sociology
Published by: Peter Lang Publishing 275 7th Avenue 28th Floor New York, NY 10001
First Issue: 19??
Frequency: 1/year
ISSN: 0899-9910
Telephone: (212) 647-7706, (800) 770-5264
Fax: (212) 647-7707

Conflict Management and Peace Science
Subject: Political Science—International Relations
Published by: Peace Science Society International SUNY Department of Political Science, PO Box 6000 Binghamton, NY 13902-6000
First Issue: Vol. 5, No. 1 (Fall 1980)
Frequency: 2/year
Added/Corp: World Research Center (Cambridge, Mass.). World University Division. World University. Cornell University. Field of Peace Studies and Peace Science. Peace Science Society (International)
ISSN: 0738-8942
Telephone: (607) 777-2562
Fax: (607) 777-2675

Conflict Resolution
Subject: Peace Research
See: **Journal of Conflict Resolution**

Connecticut Journal of International Law
Subject: Law—International Law
Published by: University of Connecticut/School of Law 65 Elizabeth Street Hartford, CT 06105-2290
First Issue: Vol. 1 (1985/86)
Frequency: Irregular
Added/Corp: Connecticut Journal of International Law Association. University of Connecticut. School of Law
Editor(s): Mary Margaret Scharf
ISSN: 0897-1218
Telephone: (860) 570-5331
Fax: (860) 570-5332

Copred Peace Chronicle
Subject: Political Science—Civil Rights
Published by: Consortium on Peace Research Education and Development/COPRED 4400 University Drive, Mason University Fairfax, VA 22030
Telephone: (703)273-4485

Cornell International Law Journal
Subject: Law—International Law
Published by: Cornell International Law Cornell University Ithaca, NY 14853
First Issue: Vol. 1 (Spring 1968)
Frequency: 3/year
Added/Corp: Cornell Society of International Law
Editor(s): Paul D. Callister
ISSN: 0010-8812
Telephone: (607) 255-9666

Cosmopolitan Contact
Subject: International Relations
Published by: (Planetary Legion for Peace-PLP) Pantheon Press-General Enterprises, Box 1566, Fontana, CA 92335
First Issue: 1962
Frequency: Semi-annually
Circulation: 2,000

Crossroads
Subject: International Relations
Published by: Youth Institute for Peace in the Middle East, 275 7th Avenue, 25th Floor, New York, NY 10001
First Issue: 1970
Frequency: Monthly
Circulation: 10,000

CW/PS Special Studies
Subject: Peace Research
Published by: Center for War-Peace Studies, 218 E 18th St., New York, NY 10003
First Issue: 1977
Frequency: Irregular
See also: Global Report

Denver Journal of International Law and Policy
Subject: Law—International Law
Published by: University of Denver Law School 7039 East 18th Avenue Denver, CO 80220
First Issue: Vol. 1 (Fall 1971)
Frequency: 3/year
ISSN: 0196-2035
Telephone: (303) 871-6166

Determinations of the National Mediation Board
Subject: Law—Labor Laws and Legislation
Published by: National Mediation Board 1425 K Street Northwest Washington, DC 20572
First Issue: Vol. 6 (July 1, 1976-June 30, 1979)
Frequency: 1/year
Main/Corp: United States. National Mediation Board

ISSN: 0270-4196
Telephone: (202) 523-5335

Dickinson Journal of International Law
Subject: Law—International Law
Published by: Dickinson School of Law 150 South
   College Street Carlisle, PA 17013
First Issue: Vol. 2, No. 2 (Spring 1984)
Frequency: 3/year
Added/Corp: Dickinson School of Law
ISSN: 0887-283X
Telephone: (717) 243-4611, (717) 243-7883
Fax: (717) 243-4443

Disarmament
Subject: Political Science—International Relations
Published by: United Nations Publications 2 United
   Nations Plaza, Room DC2 0853, Department 007C
   New York, NY 10017
First Issue: Vol. 1 (May 1978)
Frequency: 4/year
Added/Corp: United Nations. United Nations. Dept. for
   Disarmament Affairs
ISSN: 0251-9518
Telephone: (212) 963-8303, (800) 253-9646
E-mail: UN

Disarmament News & International Views
Subject: Political Science—International Relations
Published by: Council on Religion and International
   Affairs 170 East 64th Street New York, NY 10021
Frequency: Monthly
ISSN: 0363-3721

Disarmament Study Series
Subject: Military and Defense
Published by: United Nations Publications 2 United
   Nations Plaza, Room DC2 0853, Department 007C
   New York, NY 10017
First Issue: Vol. 1 (1981)
Frequency: Irregular
Added/Corp: United Nations Centre for Disarmament
Telephone: (212) 963-8303, (800) 253-9646
E-mail: UN

Disarmament Times
Subject: Military and Defense
Published by: Disarmament Times 777 United Nations
   Plaza, Room 3B New York, NY 10017
First Issue: No. 1 (Mar. 1, 1978)
Frequency: 6/year (Jan., Apr., June, Oct., Nov., Dec.)
Added/Corp: NGO Committee on Disarmament
Editor(s): Jim Wurst

ISSN: 0259-3629
Telephone: (212) 687-5340
E-mail: disarmtimes@igc.apc.org
Fax: (212) 687-1643

Documents on Disarmament
Subject: Military and Defense
Published by: Superintendent of Documents US Gov-
   ernment Printing Office, 732 North Capital Street
   Northwest US GPO Washington, DC 20402
First Issue: 1959
Frequency: 1/year
Added/Corp: United States. Arms Control and Disar-
   mament Agency. United States. Dept. of State. His-
   torical Office
Subs Addr: US Government Bookstore, O'Neil Build-
   ing, 2023 3rd Avenue North, Birmingham, AL,
   35203
ISSN: 0082-8785
Telephone: (202) 275-3328
Internet: http://www. census.gov
Fax: (202) 786-2377

Duke Journal of Comparative & International Law
Subject: Law—International Law
Published by: Duke University School of Law Publica-
   tions Office, Box 90364 Durham, NC 27708
First Issue: Vol. 1991, No. 1 (1991)
Frequency: 2/year (June & Dec.)
Added/Corp: Duke University, School of Law
Editor(s): John J. Hoffman
ISSN: 1053-6736
Telephone: (919) 684-5966
Fax: (919) 613-7231

Emory International Law Review
Subject: Law—International Law
Published by: Emory University School of Law 1804
   North Decatur Road, 3rd Floor Atlanta, GA 30322
First Issue: Vol. 4, No. 1 (Spring 1990)
Frequency: 2/year
Added/Corp: Emory University, School of Law
ISSN: 1052-2840
Telephone: (404) 727-6830
Fax: (404) 727-6820

Fellowship
Subject: Political Science—International Relations
Published by: Fellowship of Reconciliation/Nyack Box
   271 Nyack, NY 10960
First Issue: Vol. 1 (March 1935)
Frequency: 6/year
Added/Corp: Fellowship of Reconciliation (U.S.)

Women's International League for Peace and Freedom
ISSN: 0014-9810
Telephone: (914) 358-4601
Fax: (914) 358-4924

Financial Report-Carnegie Endowment for International Peace

Subject: Political Science—International Relations
Published by: Carnegie Endowment for International Peace 345 East 46 Street New York, NY 10017
First Issue: 19??
Frequency: 1/year
Main/Corp: Carnegie Endowment for International Peace
ISSN: 0094-3029

Fordham International Law Journal

Subject: Law—International Law
Published by: Fordham University School of Law 140 West 62nd Street, Room 015 New York, NY 10023
First Issue: Vol. 4 No. 1 (1980)
Frequency: 5/year
Added/Corp: Fordham University, School of Law
Editor(s): Jody Ganz
ISSN: 0747-9395
Telephone: (212) 636-6931
Fax: (212) 636-6932

Foreign Affairs

Subject: International Relations
Published by: Council on Foreign Relations, Inc., 58 E 68th Street, New York, NY 10021
First Issue: 1922
Frequency: 5/year
Circulation: 85,000

Foreign Policy

Subject: Political Science—International Relations
Published by: Foreign Policy 2400 N Street Northwest, Suite 700 Washington, DC 20037
First Issue: No. 1 (Winter 1971)
Frequency: 4/year
Added/Corp: Carnegie Endowment for International Peace. National Affairs, Inc
Editor(s): Charles William Maynes
ISSN: 0015-7228
Telephone: (202) 862-7937
Fax: (202) 463-7914

Four Lights

Subject: Peace Activism
See: **Peace and Freedom** (USA)

Georgetown International Review

Subject: Law—International Law
Published by: Center for Strategic and International Studies 1800 K Street Northwest Suite 520 Washington, DC 20006
First Issue: Vol. 1 (1975)
Frequency: 4/year (Winter, Spring, Summer, Autumn)
Subs Addr: MIT Press Books, 55 Hayward Street, Cambridge, MA, 02142
Editor(s): Stanton Burnett, Walter Laqueur and Brad Roberts
ISSN: 0360-6082
Telephone: (202) 887-0200 ext. 306

Global Perspectives

Subject: International Relations
Published by: Transnational Studies Association, Box 361, Orlando, FL 32802
First Issue: 1983
Frequency: Semi-annually
Circulation: 1,500

Global Report

Subject: Political Science—International Relations
Published by: Center for War/Peace Studies 218 East 18th Street New York, NY 10003
First Issue: 197?
Frequency: 4/year
ISSN: 0730-9112
Telephone: (212)475-1077
Fax: (212)475-0715

Guardian

Subject: Peace Activism
Published by: Institute for Independent Social Journalism, 33 W 17th Street, New York, NY 10011
First Issue: 1948
Frequency: Weekly
Circulation: 65,000

Gulf War Claims Reporter

Subject: Law—International Law
Published by: Dixon & Dixon International Law Institute, 615 New Hampshire Avenue NW Washington, DC 20009
First Issue: 1992
Frequency: 4/year
Added/Corp: International Law Institute (Washington, D.C.)
ISSN: 1061-7345

Harvard International Law Journal

Subject: Law—International Law

Published by: Harvard Law School Publications Center 1541 Massachusetts Avenue Cambridge, MA 02138
First Issue: Vol. 8 (Winter 1967)
Frequency: 2/year (Feb. & June)
ISSN: 0017-8063
Editor(s): John Barquin
Telephone: (617) 495-3694, (617) 495-7984
Fax: (617) 496-2148

Harvard International Review

Subject: Political Science
Published by: Harvard International Review PO Box 401 Cambridge, MA 02138
First Issue: Vol. 1, No. 1 (Feb. 1979)
Frequency: 4/year (Jan., Apr., July, Nov.)
Subs Addr: Harvard International Review, PO Box 3000, Subscription Service Department, Denville, NJ, 07834
Editor(s): Jay Stewart
ISSN: 0739-1854
Telephone: (617) 495-9607
Fax: (617) 496-4472

Hoover Essays

Subject: Political Science
Published by: Hoover Institution Press Stanford University, hhmb Room 28 Stanford, CA 94305
Frequency: Irregular (4-6 issues)
Added/Corp: Hoover Institution on War, Revolution, and Peace
Editor(s): Alvin Rabushka
ISSN: 0748-4380
Telephone: (415) 723-3373
E-mail: larson@hoover.stanford.edu
Fax: (415) 723-1687

Houston Journal of International Law

Subject: Law—International Law
Published by: Houston Journal of International Law University of Houston, Law Center, BLB Suite 29 Houston, TX77204
First Issue: Vol. 1 (Spring 1978)
Frequency: 3/year
Editor(s): Bradley W Paulson
ISSN: 0194-1879
Telephone: (713) 743-2212

Human Rights Internet Reporter

Subject: Political Science—Civil Rights
Published by: Human Rights Internet 8 York Street, Second Floor, Ottawa Ontario K1N 5S6 Canada
First Issue: Vol. 6 No. 1 (Sept./Oct. 1980)
Frequency: Irregular (2 issues per volume with occa-

sional supplements)
Added/Corp: Human Rights Internet
ISSN: 0275-049X
Telephone: (613) 789-7407
Fax: (613) 789-7414

Inter Dependent

Subject: International Relations
Published by: United Nations Association of the USA, 300 E 42nd Street, New York, NY 10017
First Issue: 1974
Frequency: 8/year
Circulation: 30,000

Interfaith Impact

Subject: Political Science
Published by: Interfaith Impact Peace and Justice 110 Maryland Avenue Northeast, PO Box 63 Washington, DC 20002
Frequency: Irregular
Telephone: (202) 543-2800

International Arbitration Report

Subject: Law—International Law
Published by: Mealey Publications PO Box 446 Wayne, PA 19087-0446
First Issue: Vol. 1, Issue 1 (Jan. 1986)
Frequency: Monthly
Added/Corp: Mealey Publications
Editor(s): Michael P. Mealey and Pamela J. Craft
ISSN: 0886-0114
Telephone: (610) 688-6566
Internet: http://www.mealeys.com
Fax: (610) 688-7552

International Journal on World Peace

Subject: Political Science—International Relations
First Issue: Vol. 1, No. 1 (Autumn 1984)
Frequency: 4/year
Added/Corp: Professors World Peace Academy
Editor(s): Gordon L. Anderson
ISSN: 0742-3640

International Law Forum

Subject: Law—International Law
Published by: University of Detroit 651 East Jefferson Avenue Detroit, MI 48226
Frequency: 2/year
Added/Corp: University of Detroit Mercy, School of Law
Telephone: (313) 596-0200, (313) 596-0238

International Law Practicum

Subject: Law—International Law

Published by: New York State Bar Association One Elk Street Albany, NY 12207
First Issue: Vol. 1, No. 1 (Spring 1988)
Frequency: 2/year (Apr., & Oct.)
Added/Corp: New York State Bar Association, International Law and Practice Section
Editor(s): Ronald David Gleenberg
ISSN: 1041-3405
Telephone: (518) 463-3200

International Legal Materials
Subject: Law—International Law
Published by: American Society of International Law 2223 Massachusetts Avenue Northwest Washington, DC 20008-2864
First Issue: Vol. 1, No. 1 (Aug. 1962)
Frequency: 6/year (Jan., Mar., May, July, Sept., Nov.)
Added/Corp: American Society of International Law
Editor(s): Marilou M. Righini
ISSN: 0020-7829
Telephone: (202) 939-6000
Fax: (202) 797-7133

International Organization
Subject: Political Science—International Relations
Published by: Massachusetts Institute of Technology (MIT) Press 55 Hayward Street Cambridge, MA 02142
First Issue: Vol. 1 (Feb. 1947)
Frequency: 4/year
Added/Corp: World Peace Foundation. University of Wisconsin—Madison
Editor(s): John S. Odell
ISSN: 0020-8183
Telephone: (617) 253-2889, (617) 625-8481
E-mail: journals-orders@mit.edu
Fax: (617) 577-1545

International Peace Research Newsletter
Subject: Peace Research
Published by: International Peace Research Association, Mershon Center, The Ohio State University, Columbus, OH 43201
First Issue: 1963
Frequency: 4/year
Circulation: 1,350

International Peace Studies Newsletter
Subject: Peace Research
Published by: Center for Peace Studies, University of Akron, Akron, OH 44325
First Issue: pre-1974
Frequency: 4/year

International Political Science Review
Subject: International Relations
Published by: (International Political Science Association) Sage Publications, Inc., 275 S Beverly Drive, Beverly Hills, CA 90212
First Issue: 1980
Frequency: 4/year

International Security
Subject: International Relations
Published by: (Harvard University, Center for Science and International Affairs) MIT Press, 28 Carleton Street, Cambridge, MA 02142
First Issue: 1976
Frequency: 4/year
Circulation: 5,000

ILSA Journal of International & Comparative Law
Subject: Law—International Law
Published by: Nova Southeastern University 3305 College Avenue Ft. Lauderdale, FL 33314
First Issue: Vol. 1, No. 1 (Spring 1995)
Frequency: 2/year (Mar., Nov.)
Added/Corp: International Law Students Association
Editor(s): J. Craig Garrett
ISSN: 1082-944X
Telephone: (954) 423-5325
E-mail: garrettj@alpha.acast.nova.edu
Fax: (954) 423-5327

Journal of Defense & Diplomacy Annual Country Reports
Subject: Military and Defense
Published by: Journal of Defense & Diplomacy 6849 Old Dominion Drive/Suite 200 McLean, VA 22101
First Issue: Vol. 1 (1986)-(1991)
Added/Corp: Defense and Diplomacy Inc
ISSN: 0886-5485

Journal of International Law and Policy
Subject: Law—International Law
Published by: University of Davis School of Law Davis, CA 95616
Frequency: 2/year
Subs Addr: William S. Hein & Company, 1285 Main Street, Buffalo, NY, 14209. Telephone: (800) 828-7571, (716) 882-2600
Telephone: (916) 752-6717

Journal of Interamerican Studies and World Affairs
Subject: International Relations
Published by: Sage Publications Inc., 275 S. Beverly

Dr, Beverly Hills, CA 90212 (U.K. Address: 28 Banner St., London EC1Y 8QE)
First Issue: 1959
Frequency: 4/year

Journal of International Affairs
Subject: International Relations
Published by: Columbia University, School of International Affairs, 420 W 118th Street, New York, NY 10027
First Issue: 1947
Frequency: Semi-annually
Circulation: 2,100
Index every five years

Journal of International Law and Practice
Subject: Law
Published by: Detroit College of Law/Michigan State University 130 East Elizabeth Street Detroit, MI 48201
First Issue: 199?
Frequency: 3/year
Editor(s): Tommie Tishler
ISSN: 1085-4940
Telephone: (313) 226-0151
Fax: (313) 965-5097

Journal of Peace Science
Subject: Peace Research
See: **Conflict Management and Peace Science**

Journal of Peace Studies
Subject: Peace Research
Published by: The Peace Studies Institute, Manhattan College, Riverdale, New York
First Issue: 1975

Just Peace
Subject: Political Science
Published by: Women for Meaningful Summits 1819 H Street NW, Suite 640 Washington, DC 20006
First Issue: No. 1 (Winter 1991)
Frequency: 4/year
Added/Corp: Women for Meaningful Summits
ISSN: 1062-6255

Linguistics and Language Behavior Abstracts: LLBA
Subject: Linguistics—Abstracting, Bibliographies and Statistics
Published by: Sociological Abstracts PO Box 22206 San Diego, CA 92192-0206
First Issue: Vol. 19, No. 1 (April 1985)

Frequency: 5/year
ISSN: 0888-8027
Editor(s): Lynette Hunter
Telephone: (619) 695-8803
Fax: (619) 695-0416

Macroscope
Subject: Peace Activism
See: **World Policy Forum**

Michigan Yearbook of International Legal Studies
Subject: Law—International Law
Published by: University of Michigan Law School/ Hutchins Hall 625 South State Street Ann Arbor, MI 48109
First Issue: Vol. 1 (1979)-Vol. 9 (1988)
ISSN: 8756-0615
Telephone: (313) 763-9548

Monograph Series in World Affairs
Subject: Political Science—International Relations
Published by: Lynne Rienner Publishers 1800 30th Street, Suite 314 Boulder, CO 80301
First Issue: 1963/64
Frequency: Irregular
Editor(s): Karen A. Feste
ISSN: 0077-0582
Telephone: (303) 444-6684, Fax: (303) 444-0824

National Guardian
Subject: Peace Activism
See: **Guardian**

National Security Management Programs. Administrative Procedures
Subject: Military and Defense
Published by: US Department of the Defense National Defense University 4th & P Streets SW, Fort McNair Building 62 Washington, DC 20319
Main/Corp: National Defense University
Telephone: (202) 475-1966
Fax: (202) 287-9388

National Security Studies Quarterly: A Publication of the National Security Studies Program, Graduate School of Arts and Sciences, Georgetown University
Published by: Georgetown University Box 571029 Washington, DC 20057
First Issue: 1995
Frequency: 4/year
Editor(s): James Ludes
ISSN: 1082-5444
Telephone: (202) 687-1639

E-mail: nssq@gunet.georgetown.edu
Fax: (202) 687-5175

New York International Law Review
Subject: Law—International Law
Published by: New York State Bar Association One
   Elk Street Albany, NY 12207
First Issue: Vol. 1, No. 1 (Winter 1987/1988)
Frequency: 2/year (Jan., July)
Added/Corp: New York State Bar Association, Interna-
   tional Law and Practice Section
Editor(s): Ronald David Greenberg
ISSN: 1050-9453
Telephone: (518) 463-3200

**New York University Journal of International Law
& Politics**
Subject: Political Science
Published by: New York University School of Law
   110 West Third Street New York, NY 10012
First Issue: Vol. 1 (April 1968)
Frequency: 4/year
Added/Corp: New York University, School of Law.
   New York University, International Law Society,
   Journal of International Law & Politics
Main/Corp: New York University International Law
   Society
Editor(s): Arunas Gudaitis
ISSN: 0028-7873
Telephone: (212) 998-6540, (212) 998-6560
Fax: (212) 995-4032

Nuclear Times
Subject: Peace Activism
Published by: Nuclear Times, Inc., 298 Fifth Avenue,
   Room 512, New York, NY 10001
First Issue: 1982
Frequency: Monthly
Circulation: 25,000

Objector
Subject: Peace Activism
Published by: Central Committee for Conscientious
   Objectors, Western Region, 1251 Second Avenue,
   San Francisco, CA 94122
First Issue: 1979
Frequency: Every six weeks
Circulation: 3,000

Orbis (Philadelphia)
Subject: International Relations
Published by: Foreign Policy Research Institute, 3508
   Market Street, Suite 350, Philadelpia, PA 19104

First Issue: 1957
Frequency: 4/year
Circulation: 3,500

Parenting for Peace and Justice Network: [Newsletter]
Subject: Sociology—Social Services and Welfare
Published by: Institute for Peace and Justice 4144 Lin-
   dell Boulevard, Suite 221 St Louis, MO 63108
Frequency: 6/year
Added/Corp: Parenting for Peace and Justice Network
   Institute for Peace and Justice (U.S.)
ISSN: 0890-3859
Telephone: (314) 533-4445

Pax
Subject: Sociology
Published by: Center for Peace Through Culture 217
   Pershing Avenue, San Antonio, TX 78209
First Issue: 1983
Frequency: 3/year

Pax Christi
Subject: Peace Activism
Published by: International Catholic Movement for
   Peace, 3000 N Mango Avenue, Chicago, IL 60634
Frequency: Monthly

Peace Action
Subject: Political Science
Published by: Peace Action 1819 H Street Northwest,
   Suite 420 Washington, DC 20006
First Issue: 1993
Frequency: 4/year
Telephone: (202) 862-9740
Fax: (202) 862-9762

Peace and Change
Subject: Political Science—International Relations
Published by: Blackwell Publishers 238 Main Street
   Cambridge, MA 02142
First Issue: Vol. 1, No. 1 (Fall 1972)
Frequency: 4/year (Jan., Apr., July, Oct.)
Added/Corp: Conference on Peace Research in Histo-
   ry. Consortium on Peace Research, Education, and
   Development (U.S.) Council on Peace Research in
   History. Kent State University. Center for Peaceful
   Change
Editor(s): Scott L. Bills and Sudarshan Kapoor
ISSN: 0149-0508
Telephone: (617) 547-7110, (800) 835-6770
Fax: (617) 547-0789

Peace and Conflict: Journal of Peace Psychology
Subject: Psychology

Published by: Lawrence Erlbaum Associates, Inc. 10
  Industrial Avenue, Mahwah, NJ 07430
First Issue: 1995
Frequency: 4/year
Editor(s): Milton Schwebel
ISSN: 1078-1919
Telephone: (201) 236-9500, (800) 926-6579
Fax: (201) 636-0072

Peace & Democracy

Subject: Political Science—International Relations
Published by: Campaign for Peace and Democracy PO
  Box 1640 Cathedral Station, New York, NY 10025
First Issue: Vol. 8, No. 1 (Summer 1994)
Frequency: 2/year
Added/Corp: Campaign for Peace and Democracy
Telephone: (212)666-5924

Peace & Democracy News: The Bulletin of the Campaign for Peace and Democracy/East and West

Subject: Political Science—International Relations
Published by: Campaign for Peace and Democracy PO
  Box 1640 Cathedral Station New York, NY 10025
First Issue: Vol. 1, No. 1 (Spring 1984)-Vol. 7, No. 2
  (Winter 1993/4)
Added/Corp: Campaign for Peace and Democracy/East
  and West, Campaign for Peace and Democracy
Editor(s): Gail Daneker
ISSN: 0749-5900
Telephone: (212) 666-5924

Peace and Freedom

Subject: Political Science
Published by: Women's International League for Peace
  and Freedom 1213 Race Street Philadelphia, PA
  19107-1691
First Issue: 1941
Frequency: 6/year (Jan., Mar., May, July, Sept., Nov.)
Added/Corp: Women's International League for Peace
  and Freedom, United States Section
Editor(s): Wendy Rosenfield
ISSN: 0015-9093
Telephone: (215) 563-7110
Fax: (215) 864-2022

Peace & Justice News

Subject: Peace Activism
Published by: Peace & Justice Associates, 3940 Poplar
  Level Road, Louisville, KY 401123
Frequency: Bi-monthly

Peace Corps Times

Subject: Business and Economics—Economic Assis-
tance and Development
Published by: Peace Corps Washington, DC 20525
First Issue: Vol. 1, No. 1 (March 1978)
Frequency: 4/year
ISSN: 0884-9196
Telephone: (202) 606-3010
Fax: (202) 606-3110

Peace Currents

Subject: Peace Activism
Published by: Sacramento Peace Center, 1917a 16
  Street, Sacramento, CA 95814
Frequency: Bi-monthly

Peace Education Center Newsletter

Subject: Peace Activism
Published by: Peace Education Center, 1118 S Harri-
  son, East Lansing, MI 48823
Frequency: Bi-monthly

Peace Gazette

Subject: Peace Activism
Published by: Mount Diablo Peace Centre, 65 Eckley
  Lane, Walnut Creek, CA 94598
Frequency: Monthly

Peacelines

Subject: Peace Activism
Published by: Women Strike for Peace, 145 S 13th
  Street, Philadelphia, PA 19107
First Issue: 1983
Frequency: Bi-monthly
Circulation: 2,000

Peacemaker

Subject: Peace Activism
Published by: Peacemaker Movement, Box 627, Gar-
  berville, CA 95440
First Issue: 1948
Frequency: Monthly
Circulation: 1,200

Peace Newsletter

Subject: Political Science—International Relations
Published by: Syracuse Peace Council 924 Burnet
  Avenue Syracuse, NY 13203
Frequency: Monthly
Added/Corp: Syracuse Peace Council
Editor(s): Bill Mazza
ISSN: 0735-4134
Telephone: (315) 472-5478

Peace Research Abstracts Journal

Subject: Political Science—International Relations

Published by: SAGE Periodicals Press 2455 Teller Road Thousand Oaks, CA 91320
First Issue: Vol. 1 (June 1964)
Frequency: 6/year (Feb., Apr., June, Aug., Oct., Dec.)
Added/Corp: Canadian Peace Research Institute International Peace Research Association
ISSN: 0031-3599
Telephone: (805) 499-0721
E-mail: info@sagepub.com
Internet: http://www.sagepub.com
Fax: (805) 499-0871

Peace Watch
Subject: Political Science—International Relations
Published by: United States Institute of Peace 1550 M Street Northwest, Suite 700 Washington, DC 20005
First Issue: Vol. 1, No. 1 (Dec. 1994)
Frequency: 12/year
Added/Corp: United States Institute of Peace
ISSN: 1080-9864
Telephone: (202) 457-1700

Peace Work
Subject: Political Science
Published by: American Friends Service Committee/ Massachusetts 2161 Massachusetts Avenue Cambridge, MA 02140
First Issue: No. 6 (Jan. 1973)
Frequency: Eleven times a year
Added/Corp: American Friends Service Committee
Editor(s): Pat Farren
ISSN: 0748-0725
Telephone: (617) 661-6130
Fax: (617) 354-2832

Planet Earth
Subject: Peace Activism
Published by: Planetary Citizens, Box 1715, New Rochelle, NY 10802
Frequency: Semi-annually

Plowshare News
Subject: Peace Activism
Published by: Plowshare Peace Center, Box 1623, Roanoke, VA 24008
Frequency: Monthly

Program & Legislative Action Bulletin
Subject: Political Science
Published by: Women's International League for Peace and Freedom 1213 Race Street Philadelphia, PA 19107-1691
Frequency: Monthly

Editor(s): Maren Gaughan
Telephone: (215) 563-7110
Fax: (215) 864-2022

Progressive
Subject: Peace Activism
Published by: Progressive, Inc., 409 E Main, Madison, WI 53703
First Issue: 1909
Frequency: Monthly
Circulation: 50,000

Quaker Service Bulletin
Subject: Peace Activism
Published by: American Friends Service Committee, 1501 Cherry Street, Philadelphia, PA 19102
First Issue: 1919
Frequency: 3/year
Circulation: 85,000

Reporter for Conscience' Sake
Subject: Peace Activism
Published by: National Inter-religious Service Board for Conscientious Objectors, 550 Washington Bldg., 15th Street & New York Avenue, NW, Washington, DC 20005
First Issue: 1940
Frequency: Monthly
Circulation: 6,000

Report of the ... Strategy for Peace, US Foreign Policy Conference
Subject: Political Science—International Relations
Published by: Stanley Foundation 216 Sycamore Street, Suit 500 Muscatine, IA 52761-3838
First Issue: 35th (Oct. 27-29, 1994)
Added/Corp: Stanley Foundation
ISSN: 0748-9641
Telephone: (319) 264-1500
Fax: (319) 264-0864

Research in Social Movements, Conflicts and Change
Subject: Sociology
Published by: JAI Press Inc. 55 Old Post Road, Suite 2, PO Box 1678 Greenwich, CT 06836-1678
First Issue: Vol. 1 (1978)
Frequency: Irregular
Editor(s): Louis Kreisberg
ISSN: 0163-786X
Telephone: (203) 661-7602
Fax: (203) 661-0792

Resource Center for Non-Violence Newsletter
Subject: Peace Activism

Published by: Resource Center for Non-Violence, Box 2324, Santa Cruz, CA 95063
Frequency: 4/year

Sane World
Subject: Peace Activism
Published by: Sane, Inc., 711 G Street, S.E., Washington, DC 20003
First Issue: 1961
Frequency: Monthly
Circulation: 28,000

Satygraha
Subject: Peace Activism
Published by: Chicago Clergy and Laity Concerned, 220 S State Street, Chicago, IL 60604
First Issue: 1969
Frequency: Monthly
Circulation: 3,900

Science and Public Affairs Bulletin of the Atomic Scientists
Subject: Peace Research
See: **Bulletin of the Atomic Scientists**

Security Affairs/JINSA
Subject: Political Science—International Relations
Published by: Jewish Inst Natl Sec Affairs 1717 K Street NW, Suite 300 Washington, DC 20006
First Issue: 198?
Frequency: 6/year
Added/Corp: Jewish Institute for National Security Affairs (Washington, D.C.)
ISSN: 0889-4876
Telephone: (202) 833-0020
Fax: (202) 331-7702

Shalom
Subject: Peace Activism
Published by: Jewish Peace Fellowship, Box 271, Nyack, NY 10960
First Issue: 1941
Frequency: 4/year
Circulation: 5,000

Social Justice: A Journal of Crime, Conflict & World Order
Subject: Law—Law Enforcement and Criminology
Published by: Social Justice PO Box 40601 San Francisco, CA 94140
First Issue: Vol. 15, No. 1 (Spring 1988)
Frequency: 4/year
Editor(s): Tony Platt, Paul Takagi and Gregory Shank

ISSN: 1043-1578
Telephone: (415) 550-1703, (415) 647-4472

Stanford Journal of International Law
Subject: Law—International Law
Published by: Stanford University School of Law Crown Quadrangle 42 Stanford, CA 94305
First Issue: Vol. 16 (Summer 1980)
Frequency: 2/year
Added/Corp: Stanford University. School of Law
Subs Addr: Stanford Law School, Crown Quadrangle 14, Stanford, CA, 84305
Telephone: (415) 723-1375
Editor(s): Susan Williams
ISSN: 0731-5082
Telephone: (415) 723-4421
Fax: (415) 725-0253

Texas International Law Journal
Subject: Law—International Law
Published by: University of Texas School of Law Publications 727 East 26th Street, Suite 2101 Austin, TX 78705
First Issue: Vol. 7, No. 1 (Summer 1971)
Frequency: 3/year
Added/Corp: University of Texas at Austin, School of Law
Editor(s): Laura Ferguson and Cindy Degitz
ISSN: 0163-7479
Telephone: (512) 471-1106

The American Journal of International Law
Subject: Law—International Law
Published by: American Society of International Law 2223 Massachusetts Avenue Northwest Washington, DC 20008-2864
First Issue: Vol. 1 (Jan. 1907)
Frequency: 4/year (Jan., Apr., July, Oct.)
Editor(s): Theodor Meron and Detlev F. Vogts
Added/Corp: American Society of International Law
ISSN: 0002-9300
Telephone: (202) 939-6000
Fax: (202) 797-7133

The American University Journal of International Law and Policy
Subject: Law—International Law
Published by: American University Law Review 4801 Massachusetts Avenue Northwest, Suite 621 Washington, DC 20016
First Issue: Vol. 1 (Summer 1986)
Frequency: 6/year
Editor(s): Shannon Keniry

ISSN: 0888-630X
Telephone: (202) 274-4433
E-mail: amulrev@american.edu
Fax: (202) 274-0773

The Arms Control Reporter
Subject: Political Science—International Relations
Published by: Institute for Defense and Disarmament Studies 675 Massachusetts Avenue, 8th Floor Cambridge, MA 02139
First Issue: No. 1 (Jan. 1982)
Frequency: 11/year
Added/Corp: Institute for Defense and Disarmament Studies (U.S.)
Editor(s): Chalmers Hardenbegh
ISSN: 0886-3490
Telephone: (617) 354-4337
E-mail: acr@idds.org
Fax: (617) 354-1450

The Buffalo Journal of International Law
Subject: Law—International Law
Published by: William S. Hein & Company Inc. 1285 Main Street Buffalo, NY 14209
First Issue: Vol. 1, Issue 1 (Spring 1994)
Frequency: 4/year
Added/Corp: University of Buffalo. School of Law
ISSN: 1074-4835
Telephone: (716) 882-2600, (800) 828-7571
E-mail: wsheinco@class.org
Fax: (716) 883-8100

The International Journal of World Studies
Subject: Political Science—International Relations
Published by: International Center for Democracy 7676 New Hampshire Avenue/Suite 304 Langley Park, MD 20783
First Issue: Vol. 1, No. 1 (Winter 1984)
Frequency: 4/year
ISSN: 0742-4698

The International Law News
Subject: Law—International Law
Published by: American Bar Association 750 North Lake Shore Drive Chicago, IL 60611
First Issue: Vol. 1 (Jan. 1972)
Frequency: 4/year
Added/Corp: American Bar Association, Section of International Law, American Bar Association, Section of International and Comparative Law
Editor(s): Gerold W. Libby
ISSN: 0047-0813
Telephone: (312) 988-5500, (312) 988-5241
Fax: (312) 988-6014

The Journal of Conflict Resolution
Subject: Political Science—International Relations
Published by: SAGE Periodicals Press 2455 Teller Road Thousand Oaks, CA 91320
First Issue: Vol. 1, No. 4 (Dec. 1957)
Frequency: 6/year (Feb., Apr. Jun., Aug., Oct., Dec.)
Added/Corp: University of Michigan. Center for Research on Conflict Resolution. University of Michigan. Dept. of Journalism. University of Michigan. Peace Science Society (International)
Editor(s): Bruce M. Russett
ISSN: 0022-0027
Telephone: (805) 499-0721
E-mail: info@sagepub.com
Internet: http://www.sagepub.com
Fax: (805) 499-0871

The Journal of International Law and Economics
Subject: Law—International Law
Published by: National Law Center George Washington University, 2008 G Street Northwest Washington, DC 20052
First Issue: Vol. 5, No. 2 (1971)-Vol. 15, No. 3 (1981)
Added/Corp: George Washington University, National Law Center
ISSN: 0022-2003
Telephone: (202) 676-3847

The International Journal of Humanities and Peace
Subject: Humanities
Published by: International Journal of Humanities and Peace 1436 North Evergreen Drive Flagstaff, AZ 86001
First Issue: Vol. 6, No. 7 (Spring 1989)
Frequency: Irregular (approximately 2 volumes per year)
Editor(s): Vasant V. Merchant
ISSN: 1042-4032
Telephone: (520) 774-4793

The National Security Affairs Forum
Subject: Military and Defense
Published by: National War College Fort Lesley Washington, DC 20319
Frequency: 3/year
Added/Corp: National War College (U.S.)
ISSN: 0146-244X

The New Haven Studies in International Law and World Public Order
Subject: Law—International Law
Published by: Kluwer Academic Publishers/ Massachusetts PO Box 358, Accord Station Hingham, MA

02018
First Issue: 1986
Frequency: Irregular
ISSN: 0738-2812
Telephone: (617) 871-6600

The Peace Gardener
Subject: Gardening and Horticulture
Published by: Peace Gardener 204 15th Avenue NE Jamestown, ND 58401
First Issue: 196?
Frequency: 4/year
Added/Corp: Federated Garden Clubs of North Dakota
ISSN: 0744-0472

The Risk Report:
Tracking Weapons of Mass Destruction
Subject: Military and Defense
Published by: Wisconsin Project of Nuclear Arms Control 1701 K Street, Suite 805 Washington, DC 20006
First Issue: Vol. 1, No. 1 (Jan.-Feb. 1995)
Frequency: 10/year
Added/Corp: Wisconsin Project of Nuclear Arms Control
Subs Addr: Risk Report, PO Box 970, Oxon Hill, MD, 20750
ISSN: 1080-2916
Telephone: (800) 410-7475

The United Nations Disarmament Yearbook
Subject: Political Science—International Relations
Published by: United Nations Publications 2 United Nations Plaza, Room DC2 0853, Department 007C New York, NY 10017
First Issue: Vol. 1 (1976)
Frequency: 1/year
Added/Corp: United Nations Centre for Disarmament
Telephone: (212) 963-8303, (800) 253-9646
E-mail: UN

The World Jurist
Subject: LAW
Published by: World Peace Through Law Center 1000 Connecticut Avenue NW, Suite 202 Washington, DC 20036
First Issue: Vol. 7 No. 7/8 (July/Aug. 1970)
Frequency: 6/year
Added/Corp: World Peace Through Law Center
Editor(s): Timothy Handy
ISSN: 0043-8618
Telephone: (202) 466-5428
Fax: (202) 452-8540

The Yale Journal of International Law
Subject: Law—International Law
Published by: Yale Law School PO Box 208215 New Haven, CT 06520
First Issue: Vol. 10, No. 1 (Fall 1984)
Frequency: 2/year
Added/Corp: Yale Law School
ISSN: 0889-7743
Editor(s): Laura Chalk
Telephone: (203) 432-7652
Fax: (203) 432-2592

Tulsa Journal of Comparative and International Law
Subject: Law—International Law
Published by: University of Tulsa/College of Law 3120 East 4th Place Tulsa, OK 74104
First Issue: 1993
Frequency: 2/year
ISSN: 1073-192X
Telephone: (918) 631-3190
Fax: (918) 631-3556

UCLA Journal of International Law and Foreign Affairs
Subject: Law—International Law
Published by: UCLA School of Law PO Box 951476 Los Angeles, CA 90095
First Issue: 1996
Frequency: 2/year
ISSN: 1089-2605

U.S. Arms Control and Disarmament Agency Annual Report
Subject: Military and Defense
Published by: Arms Control and Disarmament Agency 320 21st Street Northwest, Public Affairs, Washington, DC 20451
First Issue: 1961
Frequency: 1/year
Main/Corp: United States. Arms Control and Disarmament Agency
Telephone: (202) 647-8677

Virginia Journal of International
Subject: Law—International Law
Published by: Virginia Journal of International Law University of Virginia School of Law Charlottesville, VA 22901
First Issue: Vol. 3 (1963)
Frequency: 4/year
Added/Corp: John Bassett Moore Society of International Law

Editor(s): Brian Paul Menard
ISSN: 0042-6571
Telephone: (804) 924-3415

Vista
Subject: International Relations
See: **Inter Dependent**

War Resister
Subject: Peace Activism
Published by: War Resisters' League-West, 85 Carl Street, San Francisco, CA 94117
Frequency: Bi-monthly

Washington Peace Letter
Subject: Political Science
Published by: Washington Peace Center 2111 Florida Avenue Northwest Washington, DC 20008
First Issue: 1986
Frequency: 11/year
ISSN: 1050-2823
Telephone: (202) 234-2000
Fax: (202) 265-5233

Washington Quarterly: A Review of Strategic and International Issues
Subject: International Relations
Published by: (Georgetown University, Center for Strategic and International Studies) Transaction Periodicals Consortium, Rutgers University, New Brunswick, NJ 08903
First Issue: 1978
Frequency: 4/year
Circulation: 2,500

West International Law Bulletin
Subject: Law—International Law
Published by: International Law Bulletin West Publishing Company, 170 Old Country Road Mineola, NY 11501
First Issue: Vol. 2, Issue 1 (Winter 1984)
ISSN: 0748-9056

Who's Who in the Peace Corps
Subject: Biographies
Published by: Reference Press International PO Box 4126 Greenwich, CT 06830
First Issue: 1993
ISSN: 1065-8459

Willamette Journal of International Law and Policy
Subject: Law—International Law
Published by: Willamette University College of Law, 245 Winter Street Southeast Salem, OR 97301

Frequency: 1/year
Telephone: (503) 370-6380
Fax: (503) 370-6186

W.I.N. (Workshop In Non-Violence)
Subject: Peace Activism
Published by: (War Resisters' League) Workshop In Nonviolence Institute, 326 Livingston Street, 3rd Floor, Brooklyn, NY 11217
First Issue: 1965
Frequency: Weekly
Circulation: 10,000
See also: **WRL News; Nonviolence et Société**

Wisconsin International Law Journal
Subject: Law—International Law
Published by: University of Wisconsin Law School 975 Bascom Mall Madison, WI 53706
First Issue: Vol. 1 (1982)
Frequency: 2/year
Added/Corp: University of Wisconsin—Madison, Law School. Wisconsin International Law Society
Editor(s): Russ Klingaman
ISSN: 0743-7951
Telephone: (608) 262-8294, (608) 262-5815

Witness for Peace Newsletter
Subject: Philosophy
Published by: Witness for Peace 2201 P Street Northwest, Room 109 Washington, DC 20037
Frequency: 4/year
Added/Corp: Witness for Peace (Organization)
Telephone: (202) 797-1160

Woman Strike for Peace
Subject: Peace Activism
Published by: 799 Broadway, New York, NY 10003
First Issue: 1962
Frequency: 4/year
Circulation: 3,000
Published at same address: **N.Y. Peaceletter** (Quarterly)

World Affairs
Subject: Political Science—International Relations
Published by: Heldref Publications 1319 Eighteenth Street Northwest Washington, DC 20036
First Issue: Vol. 1 (June 1837)
Frequency: 4/year
Editor(s): Evron M. Kirkpatrick
ISSN: 0043-8200
Telephone: (202) 296-6267, (800) 365-9753
Fax: (202) 296-5149

World Goodwill Commentary
Subject: Peace Activism
Published by: Lucis Trust, 866 United Nations Plaza, Suite 566-7 New York, NY 10017 (Or: 1 Rue do Varembe (3e), C.P.31, 1211 Geneva 20, Switzerland; Or: 3 Whitehall Court, Suite 54, London SW1A 2EF, UK)
First Issue: 1968
Frequency: 4/year
Circulation: 12,000

World Military Expenditures and Arms Transfers/ U.S. Arms Control and Disarmament Agency
Subject: Military and Defense
Published by: Superintendent of Documents US Government Printing Office, 732 North Capital Street Northwest US GPO Washington, DC 20402
First Issue: 1965-1974
Frequency: 1/year
Added/Corp: United States Arms Control and Disarmament Agency
ISSN: 0897-4667
Telephone: (202) 275-3328
Internet: http://www.census.gov
Fax: (202) 786-2377

World Peacemakers
Subject: Peace Activism
Published by: 2852 Ontario Road, NW, Washington, DC 20009
Frequency: 4/year

World Peace News
Subject: Political Science—International Relations
Published by: World Peace News 777 United Nations PL, 11th Floor New York, NY 10017
First Issue: Nov. 1970
Frequency: 6/year
Added/Corp: American Movement for World Government
Editor(s): Thomas Liggett
ISSN: 0049-8130
Telephone: (212) 686-1069

World Policy Forum
Subject: Peace Activism
Published by: World Policy Institute, 777 United Nations Plaza, New York, NY 10017
First Issue: 1979
Frequency: Semi-annually
Circulation: 20,000
Formerly: Macroscope
See also: **World Policy Journal**

World Policy Journal
Subject: International Relations
Published by: World Policy Institute, 777 United Nations Plaza, New York, NY 10017
First Issue: 1983
Frequency: 4/year
Circulation: 10,000
See also: **World Policy Forum**

World Politics
Subject: International Relations
Published by: (Princeton University, Center of International Studies) Princeton University Press, Princeton, NJ 08540
First Issue: 1948
Frequency: 4/year
Circulation: 4,000

WRL News
Subject: Peace Activism
Published by: War Resisters' League, 339 Lafayette Street, New York, NY 10012 (Affiliated to: War Resisters' International)
First Issue: 1945
Frequency: Bi-monthly
Circulation: 10,000
See also: **Nonviolence et Société; W.I.N**

Yearbook of the International Law Commission
Subject: Law—International Law
Published by: United Nations Publications 2 United Nations Plaza, Room DC2 0853, Department 007C New York, NY 10017
First Issue: 1949
Frequency: 1/year
Main/Corp: United Nations. International Law Commission
ISSN: 0082-8289
Telephone: (212) 963-8303, (800) 253-9646
E-mail: UN

YUGOSLAVIA

Review of International Affairs
Subject: International Relations
Published by: (Savez Udruzenja Pranika Jugoslavie) Medjunarodna Politika, Nemanjina 34, 1000 Belgrade
First Issue: 1950
Frequency: Fortnightly
Circulation: 18,000
Text in English

LIST OF CONTRIBUTORS

Contributors are listed in alphabetical order together with their affiliations. Titles of articles which they have authored follow in alphabetical order. Where articles are co-authored, this has been indicated by citing the name of the co-writer.

List of Contributors

Abrams, Irwin M. (Antioch University, Yellow Springs, Ohio, USA)
Bertha von Suttner **VII:** 47-50
Die Waffen nieder! **II:** 43-44
Nobel Peace Prizes **III:** 412-417

Aguirre, Mariano (Center for Peace Research, Madrid, Spain)
Peace Movement in the Iberian Peninsula (Co-Writer: Lemkow, Luis) **IV:** 233-235

Aida, Shuhei (University of Electro-Communications, Chofu-City, Tokyo, Japan)
Eco-technology **II:** 100-103

Akoun, Andre (Sorbonne University, Paris, France)
Perverse Effects of Modern Individualism **IV:** 330-333

Albertoni, Ettore A. (Milan, Italy)
Ernesto Teodoro Moneta **VII:** 52-54

Alger, Chadwick F. (Ohio State University, Columbus, Ohio, USA)
Emerging Tool Chest for Peacebuilders **II:** 129-145
International Peace Research Association (IPRA) (Co-Writer: Møller, Bjørn) **III:** 98-99

Al-Khazendar, Sami (The Academic Centre for Political Studies, Amman, Jordan)
League of Arab States **III:** 169-176

Arnett, Eric (Stockholm International Peace Research Institute, Solna, Sweden)
Comprehensive Nuclear Test Ban Treaty (CTBT) **I:** 268-271
Non-Proliferation Treaty (NPT) (Co-Writer: Grasa, Rafael) **III:** 444-446

Artigiani, Robert (United States Naval Academy, Annapolis, Maryland, USA)
Revolution **IV:** 440-448

Ashford, Oliver M. (Didecot, UK)
Richardson, Lewis Fry **IV:** 448-451

Aspeslagh, Robert (Netherlands Institute of International Relations "Clingendael," The Hague, Netherlands)
Peace Education **IV:** 182-192

Avenhaus, Rudolf (Universität der Bundeswehr Müchen, Neubiberg, Germany)
Arms Control, Modeling of **I:** 81-87

Badham, Paul (University of Wales, Cardiff, UK)
Theology of Liberation (Co-Writer: Bernaldez, Pedro B.) **V:** 167-172

Balducci, Ernesto (Centro Studi Badia Fiesolona, Florence, Italy)
Peace Movement in Italy **IV:** 222-226

Banks, Michael (University of London, London, UK)
Mediation **III:** 244-248

Barash, David P. (University of Washington, Seattle, Washington, USA)
Peace, Historical Views of **IV:** 200-206
Track II Diplomacy **V:** 211-212

Baratta, Joseph P. (World Association of World Federalists, New York, USA)
Clark, Grenville **I:** 227-230
Federalism, World **II:** 201-213

Barney, Gerald O. (Barney and Associates Inc., Arlington, Virginia, USA)
Global 2000 Reports **II:** 305-308

Bartlett, Christopher J. (University of Dundee, Dundee, UK)
Naval Limitation Treaties between the World Wars. **III:** 358-365

Beer, Francis A. (University of Colorado, Boulder, Colorado, USA)
Just War **III:** 130-133
Words of Peace and War **V:** 360-363

Bernaldez, Pedro B. (Kyung Hee University, Seoul, Republic of Korea)
Arms Conversion (Co-Writer: Southwood, Peter) **I**: 87-93
Caribean Basin Initiative (CBI) (Co-Writer: Rhenan-Segura, Jorge) **I**: 170-173
Council of Europe (Co-Writer: Hartland, John) **I**: 385-390
Disarmament and Development (Co-Writer: Graham, Mac; Smith, Chris) **II**: 45-49
Economic Intergration (Co-Writer: Gomba, Boris) **II**: 78-82
Nonintervention and Noninterference (Co-Writer: Palmer, Norman D.) **III**: 434-437
Nordic Political Cooperation (Co-Writer: Wendt, Frantz) **III**: 458-464
Organization of American States (Co-Writer: Blanksten, George I.) **IV**: 91-94
Pax Christi International (Co-Writer: Vandeweyer, Luc) **IV**: 132-136
Peace Corps (Co-Writer: Ruppe, Loret Miller) **IV**: 180-182
Peace Pledge Union (PPU) (Co-Writer: Hetherington, William) **IV**: 257-262
Religion and Peace **IV**: 425-433
Resolution for Permanent World Peace Settlement Through Pax UN **IV**: 433-434
Security Regimes: Focusing on Asia-Pacific **V**: 32-37
Theology of Liberation (Co-Writer: Badham, Paul) **V**: 167-172
World Peace Games (Co-Writer: Carazo, Rodrigo A.) **V**: 398-399
Year of Peace (1986): Initiation, Promulgation and Commemoration **V**: 419-421

Carlos Felipe Ximenes Belo **VII**: 262-263
Dalai Lama **VII**: 223-227
David Trimble **VII**: 269-270
Eile Wiesel **VII**: 211-213
Frederik Willem de Klerk **VII**: 240-243
International Campaign to Ban Landmines (ICBL) **VII**: 265-269
John Hume **VII**: 270-272
Jose Ramos-Horta **VII**: 259-261
Joseph Roblat (Co-Writer: Suh, Mark Byung-Moon) **VII**: 257-259
Jody Williams **VII**: 263-265
Mikhail Sergeuevich Gorbachev **VII**: 228-231
Nelson Mandela **VII**: 236-240
Oscar Arias Sanchez **VII**: 213-217
Pugwash Conferences on Sicence and World Affairs **VII**: 254-257
Rigoberta Menchu Tum **VII**: 234-236
Shimon Peres **VII**: 243-247
United Nations Peacekeeping Forces **VII**: 217-222

Yasser Arafat **VII**: 251-254
Yitzhak Rabin **VII**: 247-251

Bertini, Catherine (World Food Programme, Rome, Italy)
Food Insecurity and the Role of Targeted Food Aid **II**: 238-244

Bess, Michael (Charleston, Illinois, USA)
Transnationalism: The European Case (Co-Writer: Bernaldez, Pedro B.) **V**: 218-226

Bhattarai, Niranjan (Royal Nepalese Embassy, Islamabad, Pakistan)
Zone of Peace: Proposal of Nepal **V**: 426-427

Blanksten, George I. (Northwestern University, Evanston, Illinois, USA)
Organization of American States (OAS) (Co-Writer: Bernaldez, Pedro B.) **IV**: 91-94

Bolanos, Gerado (University for Peace, San Jose, Costa Rica)
University for Peace (Co-Writer: Bernaldez Pedro B.) **V**: 319-322

Booth, Ken (University of Wales, Aberystwyth, UK)
Conscription (Co-Writer: McInnes, Colin) **I**: 345-349
Containment (Co-Writer: Cox, Michael) **I**: 364-370
Critical Security Studies (Co-Writer: Richard Wyn Jones) **I**: 400-404
East-West Conflict (Co-Writer: Davies, Simon) **II**: 63-71
Helsinki Process **II**: 429-435
Military-Industrial Complex (Co-Writer: Pauline, Ewan) **III**: 284-288
Nuclear Weapons, No First Use of (Co-Writer: Davies, Simon) **IV**: 56-64
Organization of African Unity (OAU) (Co-Writer: Thomas, Jaye) **IV**: 88-91

Borawski, John (North Atlantic Assembly, Paris, France)
Treaty on Conventional Armed Forces in Europe (Co-Writer: Bouvard, Loïc) **V**: 230-231

Boulding, Kenneth E. (University of Colorado, Colorado, USA) *Deceased
Evolutionary Movement Toward Peace (Co-Writer: Bernaldez, Pedro B.) **II**: 192-195

Boutros-Ghali, Boutros (Former Secretary-General of UN, Egypt)
Democratization, An Agenda for **II**: 13-35

Boutwell, Jeffrey (Pugwash Conferences, Cambridge,

Massachusetts, USA)
Pugwash Conferences on Science and World Affairs
   (Co-Writer: Suh, Mark Byung-Moon) **IV:** 383-386

Bouvard, Loïc (National Assembly of France, Paris,
France)
Treaty on Conventional Armed Forces in Europe
   (Co-Writer: Borawski, John) **V:** 230-231

Brock-Utne, Birgit (University of Oslo, Oslo, Norway)
Feminism and Peace **II:** 216-219

Brosman, Catharine Savage (Tulane University of
Louisiana, New Orleans, Louisiana, USA)
Camus, Albert **I:** 167-170
Gide, André **II:** 296-298
Malraux, André **III:** 219-223
Sartre, Jean-Paul **V:** 9-12

Brown, Seyom (Brandeis University, Waltham,
Massachusetts, USA)
Global Peace and Global Accountability **II:** 353-358

Bukarambe, Bukar (Nigerian Institute of International
Affairs, Lagos, Nigeria)
*Indian Ocean: The Duality of Zone of Peace Concept and
   Politics of Security Revisited* **III:** 20-32

Burton, John W. (Jaeger Circt Burce, Australia)
Conflict Resolution, History of **I:** 316-321

Buzan, Barry (University of Westminster, London, UK)
Comprehensive Security **I:** 271-279

Bykov, Oleg N. (Institute of World Economy and
International Relations, Moscow, Russian Federation)
Lenin, Vladimir Ilyich **III:** 182-184

Carazo, Rodrigo Alberto (University for Peace, San
Jose, Costa Rica)
Manifest Destiny **III:** 230-231
Monroe Doctrine **III:** 290-294
Pan-Americanism (Co-Writer: Bernaldez, Pedro B.)
   IV: 119-122
World Peace Day Association **V:** 397-398
World Peace Games (Co-Writer: Bernaldez, Pedro B.)
   V: 398-399

Carrithers, Gale H. (Louisiana State University, Baton
Rouge, Lousiana, USA)
Donne, John **II:** 50-53

Carter, April (University of Queensland, Queensland,
Australia)
Campaign for Nuclear Disarmament (CND) **I:** 163-167
Unilateralism **V:** 240-243

Castro, Loreta N. (Miriam College, Diliman, Quezon
City, Philippines)
Peace and Peace Education: A Holistic View **IV:** 164-171

Ceruti, Mauro (Université de Genève, Geneva,
Switzerland)
International Conflicts and Equilibria **III:** 66-70

Chamberlin, Waldo (Hanover, New Hampshire, USA)
*Deceased
Commission to Study the Organization of Peace
   I: 255-256

Chander, B. K. Jagdish (Brahma Kumar World Spiritual
University, India)
Restoration of Morality, Tolerance and Humanity
   IV: 438-440

Chatfield, Charles (Wittengerg University, Springfield,
Ohio, USA)
Pacifism **IV:** 114-116
Peace Movement in the United States **IV:** 235-240

Cheng, Chung-Ying (University of Hawaii at Manoa,
Honolulu, Hawaii, USA)
Confucianism and Neo-Confucianism **I:** 328-330

Chittister, Joan (Benedictine Sisters, Erie, Pennsylvania,
USA)
St. Benedict **V:** 3-5

Choi, Woonsang (Tokyo International University, Tokyo,
Japan)
Arbitration, International (Co-Writer: White, Robin C. A.)
   I: 66-71

Choo, Seong-Wan (Kyung Hee University, Seoul,
Republic of Korea) *Deceased
Pan-Africanism **IV:** 117-119

Choue, Chung Won (Kyung Hee University, Seoul,
Republic of Korea)
*Constructing a Cooperative Security Structure in Asia:
   A Korean Perspective* (Co-Writer: Lee, Ki-Jong)
   I: 349-356

Choue, Dong-Young (Kyung Hee University, Seoul,
Republic of Korea)

Movement for Reunion of Separated Families in Korea
   (Co-Writer: Kim, Jong-Hoi) **III**: 300-303

Choue, Young Seek (Kyung Hee University, Seoul,
Republic of Korea)
Magna Carta of Global Common Society **III**: 201-210
*Oughtopian Peace Model: A Design for Permanent World
   Peace* **IV**: 102-105
Pax United Nations **IV**: 139-145

Christie, Kenneth (University of Natal, Durban, South
Africa)
*Regionalism, Economic Security and Peace:
   The Asia-Pacific* **IV**: 407-412

Chung, Byung Jo (Dongguk University, Seoul, Republic
of Korea)
Buddhism as a Principle of Peace and Tolerance
   I: 154-158

Cooper, Sandi E. (City University of New York, New
York, USA)
Peace Movements of the Nineteenth Century **IV**: 241-245

Cox, Michael (University of Wales, Aberystwyth, UK)
Containment (Co-Writer: Booth, Ken) **I**: 364-370

Cuéllar, Javier Pérez De (Former Secretary-General of
the UN, Peru)
United Nations: Achievements and Agenda **V**: 243-247

Curle, Adam (Etton College, London, UK)
Mediation: A Tool for Peace Oriented Transformation
   III: 248-250
Peace and Social Development **IV**: 174-176

Daase, Christopher (Freie Universität Berlin, Berlin,
Germany)
Human Nature Theories of War **II**: 441-445

Daffern, Thomas C. (International Institute of Peace
Studies and Global Philosophy, London, UK)
Education for Global Citizenship **II**: 104-117

Dai, David (National Taiwan Normal University, Taipei,
China (Taiwan))
Lao Tzu **III**: 168-169

Dajani-Shakeel, Hadia (University of Toronto, Toronto,
Ontario, Canada)
Islam **III**: 109-112

Dalmolen, Albert (Elmira, New York, USA)
Muste, Abraham Johannes **III**: 319-322

Danesh, Hossain B. (Landegg Academy, Wienacht,
Switzerland)
Bahá'í Peace Program **I**: 117-122

Davies, Simon (University of Wales, Aberystwyth, UK)
East-West Conflict (Co-Writer: Booth, Ken) **II**: 63-71
Nuclear Weapons, No First Use of (Co-Writer: Booth,
   Ken) **IV**: 56-64

Detter Delupis, Ingrid (University of London, London, UK)
Treaties of the Modern Era **V**: 226-230

Dilloway, James (International Humanist and Ethical
Union, Geneva, Switzerland)
Geneva, Spirit of **II**: 279-286
Human Rights and Peace **II**: 451-455
International Bill of Human Rights **III**: 58-63
League of Nations **III**: 177-181
Peace with Freedom **IV**: 283-288

Duncan, Wood J. (Arnside, Cumbria, UK)
Penn, William **IV**: 312-315
Quakerism **IV**: 391-394

Dunn, David (Staffordshire University, Stroke on Treut,
UK),
Peace Studies (Co-Writer: Bernaldez, Pedro B.)
   IV: 266-271

Dunn, John (King's College, University of Cambridge,
Cambridge, UK)
*Construction of the Principle of Toleration and its
   Implications for Contemporary Democratic States*
   I: 357-364

Dwivedi, O. P. (University of Guelph, Guelph, Ontario,
Canada)
*Human Rights and Environmental Rights: Their
   Sustainable Development Compatibility* **II**: 445-451

Easwaran, Eknath (Petaluma, California, USA)
Gandhi, Mohandas Karamchand **II**: 265-270
Khan, Abdul Ghaffar **III**: 149-152

Eckhardt, William (Lentz Peace Research Laboratory,
Dunedin, Florida, USA)
Technology of Peace **V**: 159-160

Eckstein, Susanna (Stockholm International Peace Research Institute, Solna, Sweden)
Chemical Disarmament (Co-Writer: Zanders, Jean Pascal)
  I: 186-192

Eguren, Luis E. (The Academic Centre for Political Studies, Amman, Jordan)
Peace Brigades/Peace Teams (Co-Writer: Mahony, Liam)
  IV: 176-180

Eisler, Riane (Center for Partnership Studies, Pacific Grove, California, USA)
Feminist Thought and Peace (Co-Writer: Loye, David)
  II: 224-228
Population Pressure, Women's Roles, and Peace
  IV: 340-343
Sexual Equality and Peace (Co-Writer: Loye, David)
  V: 43-45

Elsenhans, Harmut (Universität Leipzig, Leipzig, Germany)
World Economy, Social Change and Peace **V:** 368-373

Evan, William M. (University of Pennsylvania, Philadelphia, Pennsylvania, USA)
Global Ethics, Human Rights Laws and Democratic Governance **II:** 330-338
Perpetual Peace **IV:** 317-319
United Nations Governance **V:** 276-282

Ewan, Pauline (University of Wales, Aberystwyth, UK)
Military-Industrial Complex (Co-Writer: Booth, Ken)
  III: 284-288

Examen O. P., Sister Teresa (Sienna College, Quezon City, Philippines)
Problems of Ethnicity and Religion in the Philippines
  IV: 354-364

Ferdowsi, Mir A. (Ludwig-Maximilians-Universität-München, Munich, Germany)
Bandung Conference **I:** 129-132
Brezhnev Doctrine **I:** 146-148
New International Economic Order (NIEO) **III:** 386-389
North-South Conflict **IV:** 18-22
Organization of the Islamic Conference (OIC) **IV:** 94-96
Self-reliance **V:** 40-42
Truman Doctrine **V:** 231-232
World Trade Organization (WTO) **V:** 407-413

Ferguson, John (Selly Oak Colleges, Birmingham, UK)

Religion and Peace **IV:** 425-433

Fernando, Jude L. (University of Pennsylvania, Philadelphia, USA)
Civil Society and Non-Governmental Organizations
  I: 201-208

Fischer, John Irwin (Louisiana State University, Baton Rouge, Louisiana, USA)
Swift, Jonathan **V:** 150-152

Fisher, David (International Atomic Energy Agency (IAEA), Vienna, Austria)
Proliferation of Nuclear Weapons, Ending the
  IV: 364-370

Fournier, Francine (UNESCO, Paris, France)
UNESCO Prize for Peace Education **V:** 233-240

Freedman, Lawrence (King's College London, London, UK)
Nuclear Strategy **IV:** 30-35

Frei, Daniel (Universität Zürich, Zürich, Switzerland)
*Deceased
Neutrality (Co-Writer: Bernaldez, Pedro B.) **III:** 372-380

Frizzell, Lawrence (Seton Hall University, South Orange, New Jersey, USA)
Hebrew Bible and Peace **II:** 420-424
Peace According to the New Testament **IV:** 145-149
St. Francis of Assisi **V:** 5-7
War in the Hebrew Bible **V:** 335-339

Fuiman, Jason (The George Washington University, Washington, DC, USA)
Arab-Israeli Conflict: Peace Plans and Proposals
  (Co-Writer: Reich, Bernard; Hollis, Rosemary) **I:** 35-62

Galtung, Johan (University of Hawaii, Honolulu, Hawaii, USA)
Peace Theory: An Introduction **IV:** 274-283
Positive Versus Negative Peace **IV:** 343-346

Gann, L. H. (Hoover Institute on War, Revolution and Peace, Stanford, California, USA)
Orwell, George **IV:** 96-97
World Council of Churches (WCC) **V:** 367-368

Gareau, Frederick H. (Florida State University, Tallahassee, Florida, USA)

Diplomatic Recognition **II:** 44-45
Functionalism **II:** 254-256
Intervention **III:** 107-109
Negotiation, Direct **III:** 365-366
Supranationalism **V:** 143-145

Hamerton-Kelly, Robert (Stanford University, Stanford, California, USA)
Human Value and Materialistic Civilization **II:** 458-464

Hamilton, Keith (University College of Wales, Aberystwyth, UK)
Congress of Vienna **I:** 332-335
International City **III:** 63-66
National Socialism **III:** 341-345

Hampe, Peter (Akademie für Politische Bildung, Buchensee, Germany)
Imperialism **III:** 8-17

Hanning, Hugh (London, UK)
United Nations Peacekeeping Operations (Co-Writer: Bernaldez, Pedro B.) **V:** 292-298

Harbottle, Michael (London Centre for International Peacebuilding, London, UK)
Confidence Building in International Diplomacy **I:** 284-287

Hartley, Keith (University of York, York, UK)
Economics of Disarmament and Conversion **II:** 82-91

Harwood-Jones, John (Scarborough, Ontario, Canada)
Christianity **I:** 195-198

Hassan, Ihab (University of Wisconsin, Milwaukee, Wisconsin, USA)
War Novel in the United States (1945-85) **V:** 349-352

Heartland, John (Council of Europe, Strasbourg Cedex, France)
Council of Europe (Co-Writer: Bernaldez, Pedro B.) **I:** 385-390

Hetherington, William (Peace Pledge Union, London, UK)
Peace Pledge Union (PPU) (Co-Writer: Bernaldez, Pedro B.) **IV:** 257-262

Heywood, Stanley J. (Montana State University, Bozeman, Montana, USA)
Peace Education for Youth **IV:** 196-200

Hinchcliff, John (Aukland Institute of Technology, Aukland, New Zealand)

Just War Theory **III:** 133-140
New Zealand's Contribution to Nuclear Disarmament **III:** 402-407

Ho, Kenneth P. H. (University of Hong-Kong, Pokfulam Road, Hong Kong)
Confucius **I:** 330-332
Mencius **III:** 251-252
Tao Yuan-ming **V:** 153-154

Hollis, Rosemary (George Washington University, Washington, DC, USA)
Arab-Israeli Conflict: Peace Plans and Proposals (Co-Writer: Reich, Bernard; Fuiman Jason) **I:** 35-62
Camp David Accords (Co-Writer: Reich, Bernard) **I:** 159-163

Holsti, K. J. (University of British Columbia, Vancouver, Canada)
Autarky **I:** 111-113
Balance of Power **I:** 122-126
Détente **II:** 35-38

Holsti, Ole R. (Duke University, Durham, North Carolina, USA)
Crisis **I:** 393-396
Crisis Management **I:** 396-400
Dulles, John Foster **II:** 54-55

Hong, Ki-Jun (Kyung Hee University, Seoul, Republic of Korea)
Arms Control, Evolution of (Co-Writer: Péricles Gasparini Alves) **I:** 74-80
Multilateralism (Co-Writer: Greene, Owen) **III:** 306-318

Hopwood, Keith (University of Wales, Lampeter, UK)
Peace in the Ancient World **IV:** 206-217

Hubers, Paul (American University, Washington, DC, USA)
Jung, Carl Gustav (Co-Writer: Said, Abdul Aziz) **III:** 129-130
Madariaga, Salvador de (Co-Writer: Said, Abdul Aziz) **III:** 199-201
Thorsson, Inga (Co-Writer: Said, Abdul Aziz) **V:** 183

Hurst, John (University of California, Berkeley, California, USA)
Pedagogy for Peace **IV:** 307-312

Hutchinson, John (University of California at Los Angeles, Los Angeles, California, USA)
Trade Unionism **V:** 212-214

Hyun, Jong-Min (Kyung Hee University, Seoul, Republic of Korea)
International Day of Peace and International Year of Peace **III:** 89-90

Hyun, Theresa M. (Kyung Hee University, Seoul, Republic of Korea)
Montaigne **III:** 294-295

Iisaka, Yoshiaki (Seigakuin University, Saitama-ken, Japan)
Emergence of Global Community and the Establishment of New Global Ehics **II:** 126-129
Ethics in the Post-industrialized and Informationalized Society **II:** 164-169

Ionno J., Sandra (Syntony Quest, San Francisco, USA)
Student/Young Pugwash Organization (Co-Writer: Laszlo, Alexander R.) **V:** 141-143

Irmak, Kenan H. (Universität Bielefeld, Bielefeld, Germany)
German Peace Movement [Friedensbewegung] (Co-Writer: Pritchard, Colin) **II:** 290-296

Itow, Shigeyuki (Kyushu University, Fukuoka, Japan)
Japan: Debates on Peace (1950s-1980s) **III:** 120-122

Jasani, Bhupendra (Stockholm International Peace Research Instutute (SIPRI), Solna, Sweden)
Outer Space, Militarization in the Cold War **IV:** 105-110

Jaye, Thomas (University of Wales, Aberystwyth, UK)
Organization of African Unity (OAU) (Co-Writer: Booth, Ken) **IV:** 88-91

Jeong, Ho-Won (George Mason University, Virginia, USA)
Epistemological Foundations for Peace Research **II:** 151-156
Theoretical Traditions of Peace and Conflict Studies **V:** 172-179

Jones, Richard Wyn (University of Wales, Aberystwyth, UK)
Critical Security Studies (Co-Writer: Booth, Ken) **I:** 400-404

Jones, Robert A. (Sheffield Hallam University, Sheffield, UK)
European Union **II:** 184-192

Käkönen, Jyrki (University of Tampere, Tampere, Finland)
Green Security **II:** 392-402

Karas, J. H. W. (Climatic Research Unit, University of East Anglia, Norwich, UK)
Nuclear Winter (Co-Writer: Kelly, P. M.) **IV:** 64-67

Kavanagh, J. P. (UN Information Center, Tokyo, Japan)
Status and Role of the United Nations **V:** 100-108

Kaya, Seiji (Small Kindness Movement, Tokyo, Japan)
Small Kindness Movement **V:** 52-54

Kegley, Geoffrey G. (University of South Carolina, Columbia, South Carolina, USA)
Global Environment and Peace (Co-Writer: Kegley, Jr. Charles W.) **II:** 319-324

Kegley, Jr., Charles W. (University of South Carolina, Columbia, South Carolina, USA)
Global Environment and Peace (Co-Writer: Kegley, Geoffrey G.) **II:** 319-324

Kelly, P. M. (University of East Anglia, Norwich, UK)
Nuclear Winter (Co-Writer: Karas, J. H.) **IV:** 64-67

Kende, István (Budapest, Hungary) *Deceased
Local Wars Since 1945 **III:** 187-191

Kennard, Jean E. (University of New Hampshire, Durham, New Hampshire, USA)
Feminist Literature and Pacifism in the First World War **II:** 219-224

Keukeleire, Stephan (Katholieke Universiteit, Leuven, Belgium)
Common Foreign and Security Policy (CFSP) of the European Union **I:** 256-263

Kim, C. I. Eugene (Western Michigan University, Michigan, USA) *Deceased
Korean Armistice Agreement **III:** 152-154
Neocolonialism **III:** 370-372

Kim, Jong-Hoi (Kyung Hee University, Seoul, Republic of Korea)
Movement for Reunion of Separated Families in Korea (Co-Writer: Choue, Dong-Young) **III:** 300-303

Kim, Ki Sung (Stanford University, Stanford, California, USA)
Ethnic-Religious Conflict, Nationalism and Tolerance **II:** 173-177

Kim, Kwan-Bong (Kyung Hee University, Seoul, Republic of Korea)
Baruch Plan **I:** 132-133
North Korea's Nuclear Activities and the US-North Korea Accord of 1994 **IV:** 12-18

Kivikari, Urpo (Turku School of Economics and Business Administration, Turku, Finland)
East-West Trade: Finland's Changing Role **II:** 71-76

Kostecki, Wojciech (Institute for Political Studies, Warsaw, Poland)
Eastern Europe, Transformation of **II:** 59-63

Kraut, Bruce H. (Princeton University, Princeton, New Jersey, USA)
Aristophanes **I:** 71-74

Krieger, David (Nuclear Age Peace Foundation, Santa Barbara, USA)
Nuclear Weapons Abolition **IV:** 49-56
Nuremberg in the Nuclear Age **IV:** 67-68
Oceans: The Common Heritage **IV:** 77-80

Kriesberg, Louis (Syracuse University, Syracuse, New York, USA)
International Conflicts, De-escalation of **III:** 70-81
Social Conflicts and Peace **V:** 54-61

Kuçuradi, Ioanna (Hacettepe Üniversitesi, Ankara, Turkey)
Universal Norms and Tasks of Global Common Society **V:** 314-319

Küng, Hans (Universität Tübingen, Tübingen, Germany)
Global Ethic **II:** 324-330

Kwon, Gi Heon (Kyung Hee University, Seoul, Republic of Korea)
Humancenterism **II:** 464-466

Lamot, Marc (Katholieke Universiteit Leuven, Leuven, Belgium)
Peace Movement in Belgium **IV:** 220-222

Landes, Richard (Connecticut College, Connecticut, USA)
Pax Dei (Co-Writer: Paxton, Frederick S.) **IV:** 136-139

Langer, Ingrid (Ludwig-Maximilians-Universität München, Munich, Germany)
Caudillismo **I:** 173-174

Larue, Gerald A. (University of Southern California, Los Angeles, California, USA)
Humanistic Values for the 21st Century **II:** 466-475

Laszlo, Alexander R. (Syntony Quest, San Francisco, USA)
Student/Young Pugwash Organization (Co-Writer: Ionno J., Sandra) **V:** 141-143

Lebow, Richard Ned (Ohio State University, Columbus, Ohio, USA)
Deterrence **II:** 39-41

Lee, Ki-Jong (Kyung Hee University, Seoul, Republic of Korea)
Constructing a Cooperative Security Structure in Asia: A Korean Perspective (Co-Writer: Choue, Chung Won) **I:** 349-356

Lee, Won-Sul (International Association of University Presidents, Seoul, Republic of Korea)
New Ethics in the Industrialized and Informationalized Society **III:** 383-386
Restoration of Humanity **IV:** 434-438

Lemkow, Luis (Universitat Aut noma de Barcelona, Barcelona, Spain)
Peace Movement in the Iberian Peninsula (Co-Writer: Aguirre, Mariano) **IV:** 233-235
War: Environmental and Biological Theories **V:** 332-335

Lentner, Howard H. (City University of New York, New York, USA)
Cold War **I:** 231-236
Democracy and Foreign Policy **II:** 10-13
State, Theory of the **V:** 97-100

Leurdijk, Dick A. (Netherlands Institute of International Relations "Clingendael," The Hague, Netherlands)
United Nations and NATO in Former Yugoslavia **V:** 247-256

Lewer, Nick (University of Bradford, West Yorkshire, UK)
Weapons, Non-Lethal **V:** 357-360

Liberska, Barbara (Academy of Social Sciences, Warsaw, Poland)
Globalization and Regional Challenges: The Case of Central Europe **II:** 375-380

Lider, Julian (Swedish Institute of International Affairs, Stockholm, Sweden)

Pal, Leslei A. (Carleton University, Ottawa, Canada)
Non-Governmental Organizations (NGOs) **III:** 431-434

Palmer, Norman D. (University of Pennsylvannia, Philadelphia, Pennsylvannia, USA) * Deceased
Collective Security and Collective Self-defence **I:** 236-239
Colombo Plan **I:** 239-241
Nonintervention and Noninterference (Co-Writer: Bernaldez, Pedro B.) **III:** 434-437
Open Door Policy **IV:** 80-81

Park, Jong-Chul (Kyung Hee University, Seoul, Republic of Korea)
Second Renaissance **V:** 17-20
Third Democratic Revolution **V:** 179-182

Park, Soo-Heon (Kyung Hee University, Seoul, Republic of Korea)
Regional Common Society **IV:** 401-407

Park, Yong Shin (Yonsei University, Seoul, Rebublic of Korea)
New Morality for the Global Community **III:** 389-396

Paskins, Barrie (University of London, London, UK)
Nuremberg Principles (Co-Writer: Bernaldez, Pedro B.) **IV:** 69-75

Paul, Jan-Peter (European Commission DG VII, Bruxelles, Belgium)
Economic Blockade **II:** 76-78

Paul, T. V. (McGill University, Montréal, Canada)
Enduring Regional Conflicts and Nuclear Proliferation **II:** 146-151

Paxton, Frederick S. (Connecticut College, New London, Connecticut, USA)
Pax Dei (Co-Writer: Landes, Richard) **IV:** 136-139

Perry, Glenn E. (Indiana State University, Indiana, USA)
Arab-Israeli Wars **I:** 62-66
Pan-Arabism **IV:** 122-126

Peterson, M. J. (University of Massachusetts at Amherst, Amherst, Masschusetts, USA)
Commission of Investigation and Conciliation **I:** 244-245
Commission of Mediation, Conciliation, and Arbitration **I:** 245-246
Permanent Mandates Commission **IV:** 315-317

Pierard, Richard V. (Indiana State University, Terre Haute, Indiana, USA)
Graham, Billy **II:** 389-392

Pöllinger, Sigrid (Universität Zentrum für Friedensforchung, Wien, Austria)
Christian-Marxist Dialogue for Peace **I:** 192-195

Porter, Brian E. (University of Kent at Canterbury, Kent, UK)
Conciliar Movement **I:** 279-282
Congress System **I:** 335-340
Davies, David **II:** 6-8
Gladstone, William Ewart **II:** 298-302
Hague Conferences **II:** 415-417
Tolstoy, Leo **V:** 188-190

Pradhan, Ram C. (M. P. Sharma Memorial Institute, Centre for Peace Education and Conflict Resolution, Delhi, India)
India: Historical Concepts and Institutions of Peace **III:** 17-20
Peace Education and Human Rights: A Third World Critique (Co-Writer: Bernaldez, Pedro B.) **IV:** 192-195

Pritchard, Colin (University of Southampton, Southampton, UK)
European Peace Movements: Rise and Falls 1958-65, 1978-85 and 1990-98 **II:** 177-181
German Peace Movement [Friedensbewegung] (Co-Writer: Irmak, Kenan H.) **II:** 290-296

Puchala, Donald J. (University of South Carolina, South Carolina, USA)
Human Security **II:** 456-458
United Nations and the Myth of the Unity of Mankind **V:** 256-264

Puckett, Robert H. (Indiana State University, Terre Haute, Indiana, USA)
Natural Rights **III:** 357-358

Ra, Jong-Yil (Kyung Hee University, Seoul, Republic of Korea)
Chauvinism **I:** 186-186
Fascism **II:** 197-199
Jingoism **III:** 122-123
Machiavelli, Niccolò **III:** 195-196
Machiavellianism **III:** 196-199
Utopianism **V:** 323-326
World Citizenship **V:** 364-366

Radest, Howard B. (University of South Carolina, Columbia, South Carolina, USA)
Toward a New Global Ethic **V:** 200-211

Constant de Rebecque **VII:** 61-63
Philip J. Noel-Baker **VII:** 154-156
Quakers **VII:** 130-132
Ralph Bunche **VII:** 135-138
René Cassin **VII:** 171-173
Sean MacBride **VII:** 182-185
Sir Norman Angell **VII:** 108-111
Sir William Randal Cremer **VII:** 43-45
Theodore Roosevelt **VII:** 50-52
Thomas Woodrow Wilson **VII:** 74-76
Tobias Michael Carel Asser **VII:** 65-67
United Nations Children's Fund (UNICEF) **VII:** 168-170
United Nations High Commissioner for Refugees (UNHCR)
 VII: 147-149
Willy Brandt **VII:** 177-179

Rhenán-Segura, Jorge (Geneva, Switzerland)
Caribbean Basin Initiative (CBI) (Co-Writer: Bernaldez,
 Pedro B.) **I:** 170-173
Costa Rica: Neutrality **I:** 384-385

Riordan, Jim (University of Bradford, West Yorkshire, UK)
Sport and Peace **V:** 84-87

Rochester, J. Martin (University of Missouri, St. Louis,
Missouri, USA)
*United Nations Reform: Historical and Contemporary
 Perspectives* **V:** 298-305

Ross, Jeffrey Ian (Washington, DC, USA)
Contemporary International Terrorism, Nautre of
 I: 370-382
Guevara, Ernesto (Che) (Co-Writer: Gurr, Ted Robert)
 II: 403-405
Gulf Conflict: Domestic Protest and Political Terrorism
 II: 405-413
Internal War (Co-Writer: Gurr, Ted Robert) **III:** 49-50
*Psychological Causes of Oppositional Political
 Terrorism: A Model* **IV:** 373-380
*Structural Causes of Oppositional Political Terrorism:
 Towards a Causal Model* **V:** 121-131

Rotblat, Joseph (Pugwash Conferences, London, UK)
Einstein, Albert **II:** 118-126
Pugawash Movement (Co-Writer: Suh, Mark
 Byung-Moon) **IV:** 386-390

Ruiz, Lester Edwin J. (New York Theology Seminary,
New York, USA)
*Myth, Identity, and the Politics of Conviction:
 Participation in the Struggle for a Just World Order*
 (Co-Writer: Mendlovitz, Saul H.) **III:** 325-338

Rupp, Hans Karl (Marburg, Germany)
Heinemann, Gustav **II:** 428-429
Niemöler, Martin **III:** 411-412

Ruppe, Loret Miller (Bethesda, USA)
Peace Corps (Co-Writer: Bernaldez, Pedro B.)
 IV: 180-182

Russett, Bruce M. (Yale University, New Haven,
Connecticut, USA)
Peace and Democracy **IV:** 152-158

Ryan, Stephen (University of Ulster, Londonderry,
Northern Ireland, UK)
Ethnic Conflict and International Relations **II:** 169-173

Sági, Mária (Research Institute for Culture, Budapest,
Hungary)
Community and Autonomy **I:** 266-268
Cultural Identity **I:** 420-423

Said, Abdul Aziz (American University, Washington, DC,
USA)
Jung, Carl Gustav (Co-Writer: Hubers, Paul) **III:** 129-130
Madariaga, Salvador de (Co-Writer: Hubers, Paul)
 III: 199-201
Thorsson, Inga (Co-Writer: Hubers, Paul) **V:** 183

Samway, Patrick (New York, USA)
Faulkner, William **II:** 199-201

Scalapino, Robert A. (University of California, Berkeley,
California, USA)
Association of Southeast Asian Nations (ASEAN) **I:** 108-110

Schäffner, Christina (Aston University, Birmingham, UK)
Language and Peace **III:** 161-167

Schalbroeck, Ivo (Brussels, Belgium)
Bouthoul, Gaston **I:** 143-146
Peace in the Middle Ages **IV:** 217-220
Polemology **IV:** 334-338
Sorokin, Pitirim **V:** 83-84
Wright, Quincy **V:** 416-418

Schmid, Josef (Otto-Friedrich-Universität Bamberg,
Bamberg, Germany)
Malthusian Doctrine, Critique of **III:** 224-230

Schmidt, James W. (Boston University, Boston,
Massachusetts, USA)

Weatherbee, Donald E. (University of South Carolina, Columbia, South Carolina, USA)
ASEAN Regional Forum **I:** 98-102
Asia Pacific Economic Cooperation (APEC) **I:** 103-108

Webb, Keith (University of Kent of Canterbury, Canterbury, UK)
Conflict: Inherent and Contingent Theories **I:** 311-316
Structural Violence and the Definition of Conflict
　V: 137-141

Wendt, Frantz (Hellerup, Denmark)
Nordic Council (Co-Writer: Bernaldez, Pedro B.)
　III: 456-458
Nordic Political Cooperation (Co-Writer: Bernaldez, Pedro B.) **III:** 458-464
Nordic Security Problems (Co-Writer: Bernaldez, Pedro B.) **III:** 465-471

Wesel, Reinhard (Ludwig-Maximilians-University of München, Munich, Germany)
Agricultural Trade Development and Assistance Act of 1954 (United States) **I:** 11-13
Colonialism **I:** 241-244
Food Weapon **II:** 244-246
Myrdal, Gunnar **III:** 322-325
Universal Declaration on the Eradication of Hunger and Malnutrition **V:** 306-308
World Food Conference **V:** 374-376

White, Robin C. A. (University of Leicester, Leicester, UK)
Arbitration, International (Co-Writer: Choi, Woonsang)
　I: 66-71

Wiener, Jarrod (University of Kent of Canterbury, Canterbury, UK)
General Agreement on Tariffs and Trade (GATT)
　II: 274-279

Wilkinson, Paul (University of St Andrews, Scotland, UK)
Terrorism (Co-Writer: Bernaldez, Pedro B.) **V:** 160-167

Williams, Alan V. (University of Manchester, Manchester, UK)
Zoroastrianism **V:** 427-432

Williams, Howard (University of Wales, Wales, UK)
Idea of a Liberal Democratic Peace **III:** 1-8

Woodhouse, Tom (University of Bradford, West Yorkshire, UK)
Peacebuilding From Below **IV:** 293-296

Woodward, Beverly (Brandeis University, Massachusetts, USA)
Training for Nonviolent Action, International Seminars on
　V: 214-216

Yoo, Jong Youl (Kyung Hee University, Seoul, Republic of Korea)
Global Familism **II:** 338-341
Strategic Weapons in the Cold War Era **V:** 117-121

Young, Nigel (Colgate University, Hamilton, New York, USA)
Conscientious Objection **I:** 340-345
Transnationalism **V:** 216-217

Yun, Hyong-Sik (Kyung Hee University, Seoul, Republic of Korea)
Civilizational View of History **I:** 225-227
Social Peace **V:** 61-64

Yuzhong, Feng (Liaoning University, Shenyang, The People's Republic of China)
Roles of Morality in the Next Century **IV:** 452-454

Zanders, Jean Pascal (Stockholm International Peace Research Institute (SIPRI), Solna, Sweden)
Chemical Disarmament (Co-Writer: Eckstein, Susanna)
　I: 186-192

Zhao, Suisheng (Colby College, Waterville, Maine, USA)
Regionalism in Asia-Pacific, Organizational Forms of
　IV: 412-423

Zuelzer, Wolf (Wayne State University, Detroit, Michigan, USA)
Nicolai, Georg Friedrich **III:** 407-411

Zvada, Ján (Commission of the Presidium of the Czech Academy of Sciences for Research on Peace and Disarmament Problems, Prague, Czech Republic)
Peace Research in the Former Czechoslovakia
　IV: 263-266

NAME INDEX

The Name Index has been compiled so that readers may proceed directly to the page where the work of an individual is cited. For each entry the volume number, which appears in bold type, is followed by the relevant page number(s).

Readers are advised that the accuracy of spelling of names has been affected by the variable use of initials and occasionally by the transliteration process.

Name Index

A

Aaron, **III:** 126
Aarvik E, **VII:** 217
Abdullah, **IV:** 4
Abdullah A, **IV:** 123
Abraham, **II:** 174; **V:** 335
Abrahams I, **III:** 128
Acheson D, **I:** 1; **II:** 209; **III:** 423, 425
Achilles, **IV:** 206
Acimovic L, **III:** 98
Acton J E E D, **I:** 2
Acton L, **I:** 358; **III:** 196; **IV:** 441
Adams J, **III:** 112
Adams J Q, **III:** 291; **IV:** 444
Addams J, **I:** li; **II:** 220, 221, 222, 224; **III:** 414, 416; **VII:** 49, 103, 104, 105, 125
Adenauer C, **II:** 429
Adenauer K, **II:** 428; **IV:** 98
Adolphus G, **IV:** 205
Ador G, **II:** 282
Afheldt H, **III:** 439
Agag, **V:** 335
Agnon S Y, **VII:** 294
Aguiya-Ironsi J, **II:** 216
Aharoni A, **III:** 99
Ahidjo A, **I:** 42
Akehurst, **III:** 436
Akers, **IV:** 376
al-Assad H, **I:** 52
al-Nasir J A, **IV:** 123
al-Qadhdhafi M, **IV:** 123
al-Sadat A, **VII:** 195
al-Said M N, **IV:** 123
al-Shafi H, **I:** 57
al-Sharaa F, **I:** 57
Alatas A, **VII:** 260
Albright M, **I:** 79
Alcock N, **V:** 138
Alder K, **VII:** 283
Aldridge R, **III:** 407
Alexander, **II:** 105; **III:** 86

Alexander C, **I:** 336
Alexander I, **I:** 332
Alexander V, **I:** 280
Alexandre T, **II:** 55
Alfaro R J, **V:** 268
Alfred K, **IV:** 218
Alfrink (Cardinal), **IV:** 133
Alfvén H, **VII:** 289
Alger C, **III:** 99; **V:** 385
Ali M, **IV:** 297
Allais M, **VII:** 281
Allen R, **III:** 53
Allende S, **II:** 11; **III:** 316, 420
Allison G T, **V:** 382
Allue M J C, **III:** 54
Altman S, **VII:** 285
Alvarez LW, **VII:** 289
Amador M, **VII:** 200
Amalek, **V:** 335, 337
Amin I, **IV:** 67
Amin S, **III:** 328
Amir Y, **VII:** 247
Amos, **II:** 252
Anam K, **VII:** 31
Anderson C D, **VII:** 287
Anderson P W, **VII:** 290
Andre P, **II:** 247
Andreae J V, **V:** 322
Andreski S, **I:** 9; **V:** 160
Andrews C, **II:** 268
Andrews C F, **V:** 49
Andrews R C, **II:** 269
Andric I, **VII:** 294
Anfinsen C B, **VII:** 284
Angell N, **I:** xxvi; **VII:** 67, 108, 109, 110
Angell R C, **V:** 216
Angelloz Y, **V:** 398
Annam Y, **III:** 220
Antoinette M, **I:** 126; **II:** 57
Antony M, **I:** 111

B

C

Cadava E, **III:** 326
Cadbury H J, **I:** xxxv; **III:** 139; **VII:** 130
Caesar J, **I:** 111, 200; **II:** 105, 280
Cain M, **I:** 23
Caldera R, **V:** 320
Caldicott H, **II:** 218, 224, 225; **III:** 404; **V:** 43
Calixtus II, **I:** 282; **II:** 284
Calley W, **III:** 133
Callowhill H, **IV:** 313
Calogero F, **VII:** 255
Calvin J, **II:** 280, 281
Calvin M, **VII:** 284
Calvo C, **VII:** 46
Camara D, **IV:** 116; **V:** 170
Camera H, **IV:** 116; **V:** 168, 170
Camp M D, **II:** 235
Campanella T, **I:** 226; **V:** 322
Camus A, **I:** 167, 168, 169, 170; **VII:** 293
Canetti E, **VII:** 294
Capet H, **IV:** 136
Capitini A, **IV:** 224
Caradon L, **V:** 298
Carazo Odio R, **III:** 89; **V:** 320
Carducci G, **VII:** 291
Carlson I, **I:** 247; **II:** 127; **V:** 103
Carnegie A, **I:** xxviii; **II:** 417; **IV:** 121, 244, 246, 247; **VII:** 44, 62, 100, 106
Carr E H, **I:** 272; **II:** 7; **III:** 200; **V:** 172, 381
Carrel A, **VII:** 275
Carrera R, **I:** 174
Carrol B A, **I:** xl
Carson R, **II:** 218
Cartagena R, **III:** 54
Carter J, **I:** 45, 46, 47, 48, 55, 159, 160, 161, 234, 306; **II:** 305, 306, 432; **III:** 78, 114, 115, 309; **IV:** 16, 368; **V:** 212, 306
Cartwright E, **II:** 164
Carver M, **IV:** 52
Casey-Hayford J, **IV:** 118
Caspersen S, **III:** 55
Cassin R S, **III:** 416; **VII:** 171, 172
Cassirer E, **I:** 225; **III:** 198, 198
Cassola C, **IV:** 224
Castillo Armas C, **II:** 403
Castlereagh L, **I:** 332, 336; **II:** 300
Castro F, **I:** 367; **II:** 403, 404; **III:** 424; **V:** 168
Catherine, **III:** 298
Ceasaire A, **IV:** 118
Ceausescu N, **II:** 69; **IV:** 10
Cech T R, **VII:** 285

Cecil L R, **II:** 281, 282, 283, 284, 436; **III:** 414; **VII:** 79, 119, 154
Cela C J, **VII:** 295
Celac M, **II:** 347
Cénacle P, **II:** 272
Cérésole P, **IV:** 115
Chāng Hao, **I:** 329
Chadwick H, **V:** 185
Chadwick J, **VII:** 287
Chailland, **II:** 405
Chain E B, **VII:** 276
Chamberlain A, **VII:** 86, 88, 90, 94, 95
Chamberlain H S, **III:** 343
Chamberlain J, **III:** 9
Chamberlain N, **I:** 34; **II:** 103, 470; **III:** 114
Chamberlain O, **VII:** 289
Chandeler R, **III:** 383
Chandrasekhar S, **VII:** 290
Chang Lu, **V:** 156
Chang T, **I:** 328, 329, 330
Chang Tao Ling, **V:** 156
Chang Tsai, **I:** 328
Channareth T, **VII:** 267
Channing W E, **I:** 181, 182
Charcot J M, **II:** 248
Charlemagne, **IV:** 218; **V:** 377
Charles II, **IV:** 391
Charles K I, **V:** 180
Charles L A, **VII:** 275
Charles VIII, **III:** 195
Charpak G, **VII:** 291
Chataway, **V:** 85
Chateaubriand, **II:** 438
Chatfield C, **I:** xli
Chauvin N, **I:** 186; **III:** 122
Chavel B, **III:** 127
Chazov E, **VII:** 209, 211
Chélan M, **V:** 109
Chelcācky P, **I:** xxxvi
Chen Duxiu, **III:** 232
Cherenkov P A, **VII:** 288
Chernenko K, **VII:** 228
Chevalier E, **II:** 235
Chevalier M, **IV:** 242
Chiang Kai-Shek, **I:** 1; **III:** 64, 220, 232, 419
Chickering R, **IV:** 126
Chilton, **III:** 164
Chirac J, **II:** 471; **III:** 391
Chou En-lai, **I:** 294; **VII:** 226
Choue Y S, **I:** xvii, 225; **II:** 309, 339, 387, 464, 465;

D

da Roque, **III:** 137, 405
Daalder H, **V:** 326
Dahrendorf R, **V:** 176, 401
Dalai Lama, **VII:** 223
Dale H H, **VII:** 276
Dalén N G, **VII:** 287
Dalindyebo J, **VII:** 239
Dalmas L, **IV:** 118
Dalton H, **I:** 34
Dam H C P, **VII:** 276
Dante A, **I:** 127; **II:** 1, 53, 201, 403; **V:** 380
Danzig R, **I:** 21
Dao De Jing, **IV:** 322
Darius, **V:** 3
Dārléans L P, **II:** 438
Darr W, **III:** 342
Daru P, **V:** 108
Darwin C, **II:** 461, 462; **III:** 224, 232; **V:** 333
Dasberg, **IV:** 183
Dāstournelles B, **II:** 416
Daubrun M, **I:** 134
Dausset J, **VII:** 278
David C, **V:** 212
David K, **V:** 3
David, **II:** 424; **IV:** 201; **V:** 335, 336
Davies D, **II:** 6, 7, 8
Davies P, **II:** 461, 462
Davignon, **II:** 182
Davis M, **I:** 383
Davis N, **III:** 113
Davisson C J, **VII:** 288
Davy A, **II:** 55
Dawes C G, **VII:** 88, 89, 90
Dazhao L, **III:** 232
de Abreu F E, **VII:** 277
de Balzac H, **I:** 126
de Barish E C, **III:** 89
de Beauséant C, **I:** 127
de Bèze T, **II:** 281
de Bloch J, **I:** xxvi, xxv, xxviii, xlv; **IV:** 243, 248
de Broglie P L-V, **VII:** 287
de Chantepie L, **II:** 235
de Chardin P T, **V:** 321
de Chardin T, **II:** 461
de Chasteller M, **V:** 110
de Chateaubriand F R, **I:** 182
De Conde A, **I:** lx
De Cuellar J P, **I:** lviii; **III:** 90; **V:** 295; **VII:** 217
de Duve C, **VII:** 278
De Gasperi M, **IV:** 223

de Gaulle C, **I:** 40; **III:** 289; **V:** 221; **VII:** 213
de Gennes P-G, **VII:** 291
de Gobineau A, **III:** 343
de Gortari C S, **II:** 81
de Hann M, **V:** 238
de Hevesy G, **VII:** 283
de Klerk, **VII:** 238
de Klerk F W, **III:** 24, 415; **VII:** 240
de la Boétie E, **III:** 454
de La Mole M, **V:** 109
de la Torre V R H, **III:** 410
de Laveleye E, **VII:** 46
de Ligt B, **I:** 15; **IV:** 251
de Madariaga S, **III:** 199
de Marcoartu A, **IV:** 243
de Mesquita B, **I:** 124
de Miossens D, **V:** 110
de Miranda A P, **IV:** 361
de Molinari G, **IV:** 242
de Nerval G, **II:** 271
de Paepe C, **IV:** 242
de Paula P N, **III:** 99
de Rabbi N A, **III:** 125
de Rosas J M, **I:** 174
de Rênal M, **V:** 109
de Saint-Pierre A, **II:** 201, 281, 452; **V:** 322
de Santa Anna A L, **I:** 174
de Sellon J J, **II:** 281
de Tocqueville A, **I:** 357; **II:** 12; **IV:** 130, 441
de Tourbey J, **II:** 235
de Traz R, **II:** 280
de Viau T, **II:** 272
De Vitoria, **III:** 130
De Vits M, **V:** 239
Debray R, **II:** 405
Debreu G, **VII:** 280
Dehmelt H G, **VII:** 290
Deisenhofer J, **VII:** 285
Delamare E, **II:** 236
Delaney M, **IV:** 117; **VII:** 235
Delbrück M, **VII:** 278
Deledda G, **VII:** 292
della Mirandola P, **II:** 465
Dellinger D, **IV:** 239
DeLupis I, **V:** 227, 228
Dembowski M, **V:** 108
Dencik L, **IV:** 336
Deng Xiaoping, **III:** 233, 421; **VII:** 226
Deonna L, **V:** 234, 236
Derrida J, **I:** 401; **III:** 327

E

Eagleton C, **I:** 255
Earl W S Jr, **VII:** 278
Easwaran E, **II:** 268
Eban A, **I:** 43, 284; **V:** 300
Ebert T, **IV:** 337
Eccles J C, **VII:** 277
Eckart D, **III:** 342
Eckhardt W, **V:** 138
Eckstein H, **I:** 311; **II:** 315; **III:** 49; **IV:** 442
Edelman G M, **VII:** 278
Eden A, **I:** 34, 37; **II:** 37, 103, 104, 282; **III:** 113; **IV:** 130
Edstrom, **V:** 87
Effendi S, **I:** 119
Ehrlich P R, **IV:** 65
Eichelberger C, **I:** 255; **IV:** 237
Eide A, **III:** 99
Eigen M, **VII:** 284
Eijkman C, **VII:** 276
Einstein A, **II:** 107, 118, 249, 443; **III:** 201, 407, 410; **IV:** 53, 223, 308, 386, 458; **V:** 141, 218, 261, 279; **VII:** 163, 204, 257, 259, 287
Einthoven W, **VII:** 276
Eirene, **IV:** 426
Eisenhower D D, **I:** 37, 96; **II:** 49, 55, 265; **III:** 137, 275, 284, 407, 418; **IV:** 74, 299, 366
Eisler R, **II:** 225, 227; **IV:** 341
Eizaguirre J E Y, **VII:** 291
Elbaum, **II:** 407
Eldredge, **II:** 225
Elias, **II:** 426
Elias N, **I:** 225
Elijah, **III:** 125

Elion G B, **VII:** 279
Eliot T S, **VII:** 293
Elizabeth I, **III:** 197
Elizabeth II, **II:** 214; **V:** 421
Elytis O, **VII:** 294
Emmanuel, **III:** 14
Enders J F, **VII:** 277
Engels F, **I:** 382; **II:** 226; **III:** 47, 226, 236, 352; **IV:** 246; **V:** 68, 78, 79
Enlai Z, **III:** 233; **IV:** 296, 297
Ennals M, **VII:** 191
Enriques M, **IV:** 361
Eppler E, **II:** 429
Erasmus D, **I:** xxi, 199, 201; **II:** 163; **V:** 380
Erikson E H, **V:** 14
Eriksson L, **IV:** 77
Erlander T, **III:** 466; **V:** 112
Erlanger J, **VII:** 276
Ernst R R, **VII:** 285
Eros, **II:** 443
Esaki L, **VII:** 289
Escalante R P, **III:** 89
Esquivel A P, **III:** 415; **IV:** 116; **V:** 236; **VII:** 199
Etzioni A, **III:** 36, 38; **IV:** 335
Eucken R, **VII:** 291
Eugenius IV, **I:** 281
Evan W M, **V:** 418
Evans G, **V:** 34
Evans H, **III:** 407
Evans L, **I:** 256; **II:** 178
Eyquem M, **III:** 294
Ezekiel, **II:** 422, 424

F

G

H

I

J

K

Kacowicz A, **IV:** 301
Kadhaffi C, **IV:** 67
Kafka, **IV:** 330
Kahler E, **V:** 323
Kahn H, **I:** 397; **V:** 121
Kaiser K, **II:** 417; **IV:** 57
Kaltenmark M, **V:** 154, 155, 156, 157
Kamenev L, **III:** 197, 410
Kamerlingh-Onnes H, **VII:** 287
Kanji K, **III:** 362
Kang Y, **III:** 231
Kanji K, **III:** 362
Kant I, **I:** xxix, 5, 144, 202; **II:** 2, 12, 106, 201; **III:** 1, 135, 143, 144, 146, 147, 207, 223, 295, 298, 409, 447; **IV:** 143, 152, 183, 290, 311, 317, 319; **V:** 218, 258, 322, 380; **VII:** 47, 98, 142
Kantor A, **IV:** 14
Kantorovich L V, **VII:** 280
Kapitsa P L, **VII:** 290
Karabel J, **IV:** 308
Karle J, **VII:** 285
Karlfeldt EA, **VII:** 292
Kastler A, **VII:** 289
Katary S L D, **IV:** 302
Kato S, **III:** 120
Katz B, **VII:** 278
Kaufmann W, **II:** 39
Kaunda K, **II:** 215
Kautilya, **I:** 122; **V:** 380
Kautsky, **V:** 74
Kawabata Y, **VII:** 294
Kaya S, **V:** 52
Kekkonen H, **V:** 234
Kekkonen U, **III:** 148, 469, 470
Kelleher C, **V:** 112
Kellogg F B, **III:** 414, 415; **VII:** 99, 100
Kelly P, **II:** 224; **V:** 43
Kemp A, **IV:** 300
Kendal H W, **VII:** 290
Kendall E C, **VII:** 277
Kende I, **V:** 355
Kendrew J C, **VII:** 284
Kennan G, **I:** 16
Kennan G F, **I:** 16, 232, 365; **III:** 418, 426, 441; **IV:** 57; **V:** 231
Kennedy J F, **I:** 114, 115, 234, 398; **II:** 398; **III:** 72, 79, 425; **IV:** 180, 239, 324, 365; **VII:** 167
Kennedy P, **I:** 272
Kennedy R F, **I:** 397; **II:** 359; **IV:** 131
Keohane R, **III:** 43, 48; **V:** 279, 382

Kerensky, **V:** 83, 181
Keresztesi M, **I:** xl
Kessler H C, **III:** 410
Key E, **II:** 218, 220, 221, 222; **III:** 410
Keynes M, **IV:** 429
Keys D, **II:** 340
Khan A G, **II:** 268, 269; **III:** 149, 151, 448; **IV:** 431
Khan B, **III:** 149
Khan G, **IV:** 217
Khan H, **IV:** 435
Khan W, **III:** 152
Khantawong C, **III:** 53
Khoman T, **III:** 53
Khomeini A, **V:** 260
Khorana H G, **VII:** 278
Khrushchev N S, **I:** 233, 294; **II:** 65, 103; **III:** 72, 79, 369, 425, 469; **IV:** 298, 299; **V:** 185; **VII:** 160
Kiesinger K, **VII:** 178
Kim D-J, **III:** 157, 303
Kim I S, **III:** 153, 157
Kim M B, **III:** 385
Kim S S, **V:** 391
Kim Y S, **IV:** 14, 229
Kimbangu S, **IV:** 425
King-Hall S, **I:** 15, 16, 219; **II:** 16, 219
King L Jr, **III:** 328
King M L, **I:** xxxvii, li, 287; **II:** 140, 268; **III:** 325, 328, 329, 416, 417, 446, 450, 453, 455; **IV:** 115, 131, 197, 255, 260, 261, 397; **VII:** 166, 167, 168, 209, 216, 271
Kingbury, **V:** 102
Kipling R, **VII:** 291
Kirk N, **III:** 404
Kirkpatrick J, **III:** 426
Kissinger H, **I:** 41, 42, 43, 65, 171, 339, 368; **II:** 36, 42, 36, 66; **III:** 48, 53, 138, 186, 415; **IV:** 99, 100; **V:** 306; **VII:** 180, 182, 193
Kissinger H A, **VII:** 248
Kiteuchi K, **IV:** 418
Klein L R, **VII:** 280
Kling H, **III:** 459
Kluckhohn, **V:** 262
Klug A, **VII:** 285
Knudsen G, **VII:** 51
Koch R, **VII:** 275
Kocher E T, **VII:** 275
Kodály Z, **I:** 422
Kodama K, **III:** 99
Koebner, **III:** 8
Kohl H, **III:** 333

L

La Fayette, **IV:** 117
La Fontaine H, **I:** xxviii; **IV:** 241, 247
La Pira G, **IV:** 223
La Rocque G, **III:** 259
La-bouisse H R, **V:** 272
Labayen J, **IV:** 363
Labayen J X, **IV:** 361
Ladd A, **IV:** 235
Lägerkvist P F, **VII:** 293
Lagerlöf S O L, **VII:** 292
Lahaye T, **III:** 384; **IV:** 435
Lakoff, **III:** 164
Lama D, **III:** 416; **VII:** 233
Lamartine, **II:** 438
Lamas C S, **VII:** 116
Lamb W E, **VII:** 288
Lambert L, **I:** 128
Landau L D, **VII:** 289
Landsteiner K, **VII:** 276
Lange C L, **I:** xxviii, xxx; **III:** 410, 414; **VII:** 80, 82
Lange D, **III:** 24, 405, 407
Lange H, **III:** 469
Lange-Schou, **I:** xxxii
Langmuir I, **VII:** 282
Lansbury G, **III:** 168; **IV:** 258
Lansing R, **II:** 54
Lao-Tsu, **II:** 161; **III:** 168, 169; **IV:** 290
Laqueur W, **II:** 404, 405
Lasky M, **IV:** 443
Lasky M D, **IV:** 443
Lasso J A, **V:** 269
Lasswell H D, **I:** 178; **II:** 249; **III:** 284
Laszlo E, **II:** 225; **IV:** 321
Latimer H, **V:** 186
Lattimore O, **I:** 255
Lau D C, **V:** 154
Laughlin R B, **VII:** 291
Laurence M, **II:** 221
Lawrence D H, **III:** 222; **V:** 350
Lawrence E O, **VII:** 288
Lawrence T E, **III:** 222
Laxness H K, **VII:** 293
Layne C, **III:** 1
Lazarsfeld P J, **I:** 267
Le Bon G, **II:** 197
Le Duc Tho, **III:** 415, 416; **VII:** 180
Leaky R, **II:** 444
Lean G, **V:** 388
Lebay C, **II:** 56
Leber G, **IV:** 57

Lebow N, **II:** 39
Lebow R N, **I:** 399
Lederach J P, **IV:** 294
Lederberg J, **VII:** 277
Lederman L M, **VII:** 290
Lee D M, **VII:** 291
Lee Kuan Yew, **II:** 215
Lee K W, **V:** 38
Lee W S, **III:** 53
Lee Y T, **VII:** 285
Lehn J-M, **VII:** 285
Leibniz G W, **I:** 405
Leif Eriksson, **IV:** 77
Leloir L F, **VII:** 284
Lemonnier C, **IV:** 242; **VII:** 96
Lenard P E A, **VII:** 286
Lenin V I, **I:** 272; **II:** 63; **III:** 9, 182, 320; **IV:** 114; **V:** 6, 74, 80
Lentz T F, **V:** 159
Leone S, **III:** 162
Leontief W, **V:** 385; **VII:** 280
Léopoldine, **II:** 440
Lerner M, **I:** 255
Lesgaft P F, **V:** 85
Lévesque R, **II:** 214
Levi-Montalcini R, **VII:** 279
Lévi-Strauss C, **V:** 10
Levine, **II:** 200
Levinson S O, **VII:** 99
Levy, **V:** 330
Levy J S, **II:** 366
Lewis A, **VII:** 280
Lewis E B, **VII:** 279
Lewis J L, **V:** 213
Lewis S, **VII:** 292
Li D, **III:** 232
Libby F, **IV:** 236
Libby W F, **VII:** 284
Liddell Hart B H, **I:** 219; **III:** 185, 441
Lie T, **VII:** 160
Lie T E, **II:** 352
Ligthart, **IV:** 183
Lin B, **V:** 232
Lincoln A, **I:** 228
Lindberg L N, **II:** 255
Lindbergh C, **III:** 114
Lindsay R, **III:** 114
Lindsey H, **I:** 197
Ling P H, **V:** 85
Linn J, **VII:** 105

M

MacArthur C T, **III:** 194
MacArthur D, **II:** 391; **III:** 137, 152, 193, 418;
   V: 266
Macaulays, **IV:** 117
MacBride S, **III:** 416; **VII:** 182, 184, 191
Macchi M, **IV:** 242
MacDonald R, **II:** 7; **III:** 168, 179, 361
Machiavelli N, **I:** 144, 202, 391; **II:** 197; **III:** 1, 142,
   195, 329; **IV:** 444; **V:** 325
MacKinnon C, **I:** 362
Maclean J D, **IV:** 251
Macleod J J R, **VII:** 276
MacLuhan M, **III:** 383
Macmillan H, **V:** 38, 299; **VII:** 158
MacNamara, **I:** 247
Madariaga S de, **III:** 199
Madison, **II:** 203, 211
Magdoff, **III:** 12
Magellan F, **IV:** 77
Magnifico L I, **III:** 195
Mahabir, **III:** 18
Mahāvīra, **III:** 117
Mahan, **II:** 417
Mahathir, **I:** 110; **IV:** 409; **V:** 35
Mahbubani K, **V:** 260
Mahfouz N, **VII:** 295
Mailer N, **V:** 350
Mainyu S, **V:** 431
Major J, **VII:** 270
Makarenko, **IV:** 183, 188
Malik J, **III:** 152
Mallin J, **II:** 404, 405
Malraux A, **II:** 298; **III:** 219; **V:** 160
Malthus T R, **III:** 223, 224, 226; **V:** 332
Manah V, **V:** 430
Manchukuo, **II:** 45
Mandela N, **I:** 254; **III:** 415, 429; **VII:** 236
Mandela R D, **VII:** 239
Mandès C, **II:** 272
Mann T, **VII:** 292
Mann-Heim K, **V:** 325
Mansfield H C Jr, **III:** 198
Manuel F, **V:** 324
Mao Zedong, **II:** 382; **III:** 112, 231, 272, 441;
   IV: 297; **V:** 122; **VII:** 226
Marcellinus, **V:** 2
Marconi G, **VII:** 286
Marcos, **III:** 328
Marcus J, **II:** 220
Marcus R A, **VII:** 285

Marcuse H, **I:** 3; **III:** 384; **IV:** 436, 437
Mardana, **V:** 46
Marighella C, **V:** 164
Markowitz H M, **VII:** 281
Marquez G G, **VII:** 294
Marriott J A, **I:** xxxiii
Mars, **IV:** 203
Marshall G C, **VII:** 144
Marshall T F, **I:** 20, 21, 22, 23, 232, 235, 365
Marti J, **V:** 321
Martin A J P, **VII:** 283
Martin du Gard R, **II:** 297, 298
Martin M, **V:** 167
Martin V, **I:** 281
Martineau H, **V:** 110
Martinson H, **VII:** 294
Maruyana M, **III:** 120
Marx K, **I:** 144, 202, 268, 382; **II:** 151, 226, 251,
   253, 298; **III:** 47, 226, 231, 320, 390, 408, 409;
   IV: 188, 330, 370, 371, 446; **V:** 9, 68, 78, 79, 81,
   323
Mase E, **VII:** 240
Mastrangelo, **I:** 371
Mathilde, **II:** 235
Matthew, **IV:** 145
Matthews W, **II:** 220
Mauriac F, **III:** 222; **VII:** 212, 293
Maurice C, **VII:** 292
Maurois A, **II:** 281, 282
Mayer E, **III:** 410
Mayer M G, **VII:** 289
Mayer P, **I:** xxxvii
Mayor F, **I:** lvi
Mazda A, **II:** 105; **V:** 428, 431
Mazen A, **I:** 58
Mazowiecki T, **II:** 59
Mazrui A, **V:** 384
Mazzini G, **II:** 341; **III:** 348; **IV:** 242, 371; **V:** 79
McCarthy E, **II:** 254
McClelland C, **I:** 394
McClintock B, **VII:** 279
McCloskey P, **III:** 404
McDougal M S, **I:** 178
McGhee R, **III:** 405
McGuire G A, **IV:** 118
Mckay C, **IV:** 118
McKenny M, **IV:** 302
McKeown C, **VII:** 189
McKinley W, **VII:** 69, 89
McKinnon D, **VII:** 260

N

O

P

Q

R

S

Saavedra D O, **VII:** 214
Sabatier P, **VII:** 282
Sachs N, **VII:** 294
Sadat A, **I:** 42, 43, 44, 45, 46, 47, 48, 49, 52, 159,
    160, 161, 162, 163; **II:** 159; **III:** 78; **IV:** 353;
    V: 212; **VII:** 244
Saheb H, **III:** 149
Sahib K, **III:** 150
Sahlins, **V:** 334
Saint-Just, **IV:** 445
Saint-Pierre, **IV:** 290
Saint-Simon H, **V:** 70, 322
Sainte-Beuve, **II:** 439
Sakamoto Y, **III:** 48, 99; **V:** 516, 393, 394
Sakharov A D, **II:** 211; **III:** 415; **VII:** 186
Sakmann B, **VII:** 279
Salam A, **VII:** 290
Salcedo-Bastardo, **I:** 174
Salgado P V, **IV:** 361
Salisbury, **II:** 300, 417
Sallust, **IV:** 214
Same A C, **IV:** 118
Sammartino P, **III:** 50
Sampson R, **V:** 260
Samuel, **V:** 336
Samuelson P A, **VII:** 280
Samuelsson B I, **VII:** 279
Sanchez L A, **III:** 410
Sanchez O A, **III:** 415; **VII:** 213
Sand G, **II:** 235
Sander F, **I:** 21; **VII:** 284, 285
Santayana G, **V:** 85,
Sarah, **II:** 174; **V:** 335
Saramago J, **VII:** 295
Sartre J-P, **I:** 168, 169, 170, 268; **IV:** 72, 332; **V:** 9,
    10, 11, 12; **VII:** 294
Sasidhorn N, **III:** 53, 54
Saso M, **V:** 154, 156
Sassoon S, **II:** 220; **IV:** 258
Sati al-Husri, **IV:** 122
Sato E, **III:** 416; **VII:** 185
Saul, **V:** 336
Saul K, **V:** 335
Savonarola, **III:** 195
Sawicki J, **III:** 98
Sayles M L, **IV:** 423
Scalapino R, **IV:** 412
Scargill A, **V:** 214
Schack A S, **VII:** 275
Schawlow A L, **VII:** 290

Scheel W, **IV:** 98, 99, 100
Scheingold S A, **II:** 255
Schell J, **II:** 210
Schelling T C, **II:** 39; **III:** 365; **V:** 241
Schiller H I, **III:** 422
Schmid A P, **I:** 373; **IV:** 337
Schmid H, **IV:** 336, 337, 373, 377; **V:** 123, 138, 331
Schmidt H, **II:** 292; **III:** 8
Schmitter P, **II:** 255
Schneider H, **III:** 446
Scholes M S, **VII:** 281
Schopenhauer, **III:** 409
Schott J J, **II:** 76, 77
Schram S R, **III:** 232
Schreiner O, **II:** 221
Schrieffer R J, **VII:** 289
Schubert J N, **II:** 256
Schultz T W, **VII:** 280
Schulze F J, **IV:** 57
Schumacher E F, **II:** 267
Schuman R, **I:** 387; **II:** 207; **III:** 290; **V:** 220
Schumpeter J A, **III:** 1, 11
Schuyler P, **V:** 67
Schwartz M, **VII:** 290
Schwarzhoff, **II:** 416
Schweitzer A, **III:** 414; **V:** 9 ; **VII:** 141
Schweitzers C, **V:** 9
Schwimmer R, **II:** 220, 221
Schwinger J, **VII:** 289
Schäffner, **III:** 164
Scott W, **II:** 57
Scruton R, **IV:** 269
Seaborg G T, **VII:** 283
Sedlak J, **IV:** 265
Sée H, **IV:** 441, 442
Seeger D, **I:** 344
Seferis G, **VII:** 294
Segr E G, **VII:** 289
Seidel A, **V:** 154, 156, 157
Seifert J, **VII:** 295
Seki H, **III:** 121
Selassie H, **IV:** 398
Sellon J J de, **II:** 280; **IV:** 241
Selten R, **VII:** 281
Semenov N N, **VII:** 284
Semple E, **V:** 332
Sen A, **VII:** 281
Seneca, **III:** 294
Senghaa D, **II:** 61
Senghaas, **IV:** 336

T

U

V

W

X

Ximenes Belo C F, **VII:** 259, 262   Xuan H, **V:** 153

Y

Z

SUBJECT INDEX

The Subject Index has been compiled as a guide to the reader who is interested in locating all the references to a particular subject area within the Encyclopedia. For each entry the volume number, which appears in bold type, is followed by the relevant page number(s). Every effort has been made to index as comprehensively as possible and to standardize the terms used in the index.

Subject Index

A

B

C

D

E

F

G

H

I

J

K

L

M

N

Nagaland Peace Mission **IV:** 176
Nagasaki **I:** 196; **II:** 146; **III:** 136, 310; **V:** 276
    peace memorials **IV:** 252
Namibia **I:** 251; **IV:** 156
Nansen International Office for Refugees **III:** 180
Nansen Office **VII:** 82-86, 94
Nansen Passport **VII:** 84
Napoleonic era **II:** 424
Narcissism-aggression **IV:** 375
Nation **III:** 348, 350
    definitions of **III:** 346, 248
    Father of **III:** 367
Nation-building **V:** 106
Nations-state
    and conflict/peace **IV:** 150
    and nationalism **III:** 345
Nation-state System **I:** 247
Nation-states **I:** 201; **II:** 342, 467; **III:** 100, 107
    and common interest **IV:** 220
    emergence of
        and conscientious objection **I:** 340, 341
    formation of **II:** 341, 342
    as moral agent **IV:** 318
    and national interest **III:** 339
    tendency towards hegemony **II:** 425
    and violence **III:** 321
    Beyond **II:** 255
    see also
        State
National Association for the Advancement of
    Colored People (NAACP) **IV:** 117
National collapse **II:** 325
National Committee for a Sane Nuclear Policy
    (SANE) **IV:** 115, 239
National Conference for Prevention of War (NCPW)
    IV: 236
National Consciousness **III:** 345
National Council of Korean Trade Unions (NCKTU)
    IV: 229
National Guardian **VIII:** 111
National Institute for Dispute Resolution (NIDR)
    VII: 449
National Interest **III:** 148, 339-341, 355; **V:** 382,
    384
    versus global interest **IV:** 338
    versus human interest **V:** 383
    Defense of **III:** 340
    egoistic **IV:** 403
National League for Democracy (NLD) **VII:** 234
National liberation

    wars of **V:** 347
    movements **II:** 67
    struggle **V:** 347
National Liberation Front **II:** 449
    in Algeria **III:** 72
National Peace Academy
    see United States Institute of Peace
National Peace Council (NPC) **IV:** 261; **VII:** 411-412
National Peace Foundation (NPF) **VII:** 449
National products **II:** 207
National security **I:** 272, 278; **II:** 456
    and national interest **III:** 339
National Security Affairs Forum **VIII:** 117
National Security Management Programs.
        Administrative Procedures **VIII:** 111
National Security Studies **I:** 400
National Security Studies Quarterly **VIII:** 111
National self-determination
    doctrine of **II:** 174
National service
    see Conscription
National socialism **III:** 341-345
    autarky **I:** 111
    and biological determinism **V:** 333
    and Pan-Germanism **IV:** 126
National Socialist German Workers Party **III:** 341
National Socialist Party **III:** 343
National Women's Welfare Center (NWWC) **VII:** 359
Nationalism **I:** 175, 186, 303, 383; **II:** 106, 174;
        III: 345-347, 348, 349, 351; **V:** 4, 143,
        201, 347
    and conflict **IV:** 103
    and democracy **III:** 346
    and fascism **II:** 197
    in Less Developed Countries **III:** 351
    and militarization **III:** 261
    and national socialism **III:** 342
    nineteenth century **I:** 335
    and revolution **IV:** 444
    and self-determination **V:** 37
    and separatism **III:** 349
    and socialism **V:** 76
    and sport **V:** 85
    Superpower-protected **V:** 223
    and war **I:** 2, 3, 339, 340; **VII:** 10
    African **IV:** 117
    exclusive **II:** 309
    tribal **III:** 350
    see also
        Nation-states

O

P

Q

R

S

T

U

V

W

X

Y

Z